TENNESSEE SECEDES

TENNESSEE SECEDES

A DOCUMENTARY HISTORY

DWIGHT T. PITCAITHLEY

THE UNIVERSITY OF TENNESSEE PRESS / KNOXVILLE

Library of Congress Cataloging-in-Publication Data

Names: Pitcaithley, Dwight T., author.
Title: Tennessee secedes : a documentary history / Dwight T. Pitcaithley.
Description: First edition. | Knoxville : The University of Tennessee
    Press, [2021] | Includes bibliographical references and index. |
    Summary: "Organized chronologically by source and speaker, this volume
    presents a selection of primary sources from December 1860 through the
    summer of 1861, inviting students to examine the arc of Tennessee's
    secession march. Dwight T. Pitcaithley introduces proclamations,
    declarations, addresses, resolutions, proposed constitutional amendments,
    and other materials from Tennessee legislators, members of Congress,
    and delegates to the East Tennessee Convention. These documents
    highlight the political divisions apparent in the Volunteer State during
    this season of unrest and the central role of the issue of slavery in
    those divisions. Complete with appendices featuring 1861 election
    returns, communications from the Tennessee Congressional Delegation of
    the Thirty-Sixth Congress, and a time line for Secession Winter—as well
    as questions for further discussion—*Tennessee Secedes* is an invaluable
    resource for students of the Civil War and Tennessee history, offering
    an insightful analysis of Tennessee's uncertain path to the Confederacy
    in the summer of 1861"—Provided by publisher.
Identifiers: LCCN 2021034998 (print) | LCCN 2021034999 (ebook) | ISBN
    9781621906827 (hardcover) | ISBN 9781621906889 (pdf)
Subjects: LCSH: Secession—Tennessee—Sources. | Tennessee—Politics and
    government—1861–1865—Sources.
Classification: LCC F436 .P59 2021 (print) | LCC F436 (ebook) | DDC
    976.8/04—dc23
LC record available at https://lccn.loc.gov/2021034998
LC ebook record available at https://lccn.loc.gov/2021034999

Designed and typeset
by Nathan W. Moehlmann,
Goosepen Studio & Press

For

ALEXANDER SYDENHAM PITCAITHLEY
CAROLYN TOWNSEND PITCAITHLEY
WILLIAM ALTON STEPHENS
CARRIEWOOD CLEVELAND STEPHENS

CONTENTS

INTRODUCTION

The secession of the Deep South following Abraham Lincoln's election in November 1860 set events in motion that led directly to civil war and the destruction of slavery. Lincoln and his Republican Party were perceived by white southerners as abolitionists, and his victory in the presidential election convinced influential Democrats that on inauguration day, March 4, 1861, the incoming administration would begin dismantling the South's peculiar institution. Persuaded by their certainty, seven states seceded from the United States between December 20 and February 23. Secessionists from South Carolina to Texas ignored the fact that the congressional election of 1860 had resulted in pro-slavery Democratic majorities in both the US House of Representatives and Senate. Keenly aware that Democrats would control federal budgets, cabinet and diplomatic appointments, and other actions of the executive branch for the next two years, Tennessee, on the other hand, paused and considered its options. Only after the bombardment of Fort Sumter and Lincoln's call for troops did the Volunteer State sever its relationship with the Union. Ultimately, fear of an overreaching federal government intent on abolishing slavery pushed the state into casting its lot with the nascent Confederate States of America. Tennessee's path to the Confederacy was neither straightforward nor inevitable. Initially rejected by the voters, secession was eventually achieved at the insistence of the governor and General Assembly.

〈〈 〉〉

The election of 1860 capped a turbulent decade during which the institution of slavery took center stage. From the Compromise of 1850 and the Kansas-Nebraska Act of 1854 to the *Dred Scott* decision in 1857, the expansion of slavery consumed much attention in Congress and legislative gatherings across the country. While the 1820 Missouri Compromise had settled the slavery question in the Louisiana Territory by prohibiting the institution north of the 36°30' latitude (excluding

Missouri), the acquisition of the Mexican Cession in 1848 brought the extension issue back to the forefront of politics. During the thirty years since the settlement of Missouri statehood, southern cotton production had tripled and the slave population had more than doubled from 1.5 million to 3.2 million. The annexation of Texas in 1845 created more opportunities for the expansion of cotton and slavery, but more was needed—or presumed by slaveowners to be needed.

During the 1850 debates over the disposition of the land acquired from Mexico, southerners demanded that they be allowed equal access to the new western territory. The eventual compromise divided the new acquisition into the New Mexico Territory to the south of the 36°30' line and the Utah Territory to the north, and provided that the settlers there (not Congress) would decide whether to allow or prohibit slavery. (California was admitted as a non-slave state.) Four years later, as pressure mounted for the organization of the Louisiana Territory west of Missouri, Congress adopted the 1850 "popular sovereignty" model and allowed the residents of the newly formed Kansas and Nebraska Territories to control the future of slavery there. This legislative reversal of the thirty-four-year prohibition of slavery north of the 36°30' parallel, considered sacred by many, angered northerners and led to the formation of the Republican Party whose core doctrine was opposition to the further extension of slavery.[1]

The issue of the expansion of slavery was further exacerbated by the Supreme Court in its *Dred Scott* decision. At stake was the freedom of Dred Scott, a slave who had been taken by his owner into the free state of Illinois and the free territory of Wisconsin for several years during the 1830s. Scott sued for his freedom on the basis of his extended residence in the two free jurisdictions. The case eventually made its way to the Supreme Court and the desk of Chief Justice Roger B. Taney. Two days after he had sworn in James Buchanan as the fifteenth president, Taney issued his decision that denied Scott his freedom because, as a black man and therefore (to Taney's reasoning) not a citizen, Scott could not sue in a federal court. Taney could have stopped there, but as a former slaveowner and a proslavery advocate, the chief justice continued, declaring the Missouri Compromise unconstitutional. The chief justice argued that Congress had no authority to prohibit slavery in the territories—although it had done so outside the Louisiana acquisition in the Northwest Territory in 1789, the Iowa Territory in 1838, the Oregon Territory in 1848, and the Minnesota Territory as recently as 1849. Southerners were delighted by the ruling while Republicans considered the territorial judgment an opinion rather than a ruling and ignored it.[2]

While slavery was protected locally by state constitutions and laws, the legal nature of slavery in the western territories—beyond state protection—was much less settled. As the decade progressed, southerners increasingly demanded that slavery be protected there by the federal government until settlers applied for statehood and drafted a state constitution. The newly formed Republican Party, while supporting slavery where it already existed in the states, also supported the right of Congress to prevent the extension of the institution into the territories. The "no extension" position of the party, however, was seen by an increasing number of southerners as cover for an abolitionist subtext.

Adding fuel to the fire was the issue of fugitive slaves and the growing unwillingness of northern states to accede to owners' claims. Personal liberty laws, primarily designed to prevent the kidnapping of northern free blacks, were sometimes invoked to prevent the return of escaped slaves. While some attempts to return slaves to below the Mason-Dixon Line resulted in violence and even death to the pursuant owners, the number of slaves escaping to the North was in reality quite small. The 1860 federal census reported only 803 fugitives that year throughout the fifteen slave states, including 29 from Tennessee. By comparison, almost four times that number of slaves were manumitted across the South—174 in Tennessee.[3] Nevertheless, the issue became a major rallying cry for secessionists.

On November 6, 1860, the country's white male voters elected the Republican, Abraham Lincoln, over the two Democratic candidates, Stephen A. Douglas and John C. Breckinridge, and Constitutional Union Party candidate and Tennessee native, John Bell. The official platforms of the four parties succinctly captured the issues of the day.

Northern Democrats had nominated Douglas on a platform that supported popular sovereignty allowing the settlers in the West to decide whether or not to allow slavery. While this approach to organizing the western territories had worked in 1850 and 1854, time had marched on and the South was no longer willing to accept the "nonintervention" tactic for determining slavery's future. Predictably, southern Democrats fled the party and nominated Buchanan's vice president, Breckinbridge, with a platform that demanded federal protection of slavery in the territories until the settlers therein applied for statehood. Breckinridge Democrats, still smarting from the failure of popular sovereignty to result in the establishment of slavery in the Kansas Territory, held that the federal government (meaning Congress) should take an active role in protecting slavery in western public lands during the territorial period, arguing that "citizens of the United States have an equal right to settle with their property in the territories." They assumed the *Dred Scott* decision had settled the question. While Douglas Democrats gave nominal support to Taney's 1857 decision, Douglas himself had pronounced that settlers could "abide by the decision of the Supreme Court" and still obstruct the introduction of slaves by simply failing to enact the required slave code. The Republican Party countered by holding that Congress could not give "legal existence to slavery in any territory of the United States." The platform made clear, however, that while the party opposed the extension of slavery to the west, it did not have any designs on slavery in the states: "The right of each state to order and control its own domestic institutions according to its own judgment exclusively, is essential to that balance of power on which the perfection and endurance of our political fabric depend." From the Republican perspective, slavery was preserved and maintained within states by local law, but was not generally protected in the territories—the Supreme Court's *Dred Scott* decision notwithstanding. John Bell's Constitutional Union Party platform avoided any reference to slavery and simply stated that no "political principles" should be recognized other than the "Constitution of the country, the Union of the states, and the enforcement of the laws." It was, of course, political disagreements over the nature and meaning of slavery in the Constitution that divided the parties.[4]

While the Deep South began marching toward secession in the weeks immediately following Lincoln's election, Tennessee, like her sister states of the Upper South, held back and considered the meaning of the first Republican elevated to the White House. Mindful of the gravity of the moment, Governor Isham G. Harris, directed the legislature to meet in special session on January 7, 1861. Between the time Harris summoned the general assembly on December 8 and the opening of the session, the political divisions of the state had already been staked out. Major speeches by Senator Andrew Johnson on December 19 and Senator Alfred O. P. Nicholson on Christmas Eve set the parameters of the secession debate—and they occupied near opposite ends of the political spectrum.

Johnson, speaking on the eve of South Carolina's withdrawal from the Union, argued forcefully that there was no right of secession in the Constitution, that the Union was designed to be perpetual. More to the point of southern discontent, he pointed out that the federal government had passed no law on slavery or any other subject that the South should find "unconstitutional and oppressive." Attempting to slow the rising emotions of his fellow southerners, Johnson asserted that if he were an abolitionist, "the first steps I would take would be to break the bonds of this Union, and dissolve this Government." Secession would end, he predicted, in the "overthrow of the institution of slavery." The "absurdity" of disunion in the wake of Lincoln's election was affirmed, he posited, in the fact that Democrats would control both houses of Congress for the next two years.[5]

Johnson's compelling logic was answered less than a week later by the junior senator from Tennessee. Nicholson complained that the South understood too well that the Republican Party believed slavery to be "a moral as well as social and political evil," that slaves were created equal to their owners, and that the end of slavery, under the incoming administration, was "inevitable." The Republican platform was, he believed, "a declaration of war against an institution which, in the South, is identified with all our interests, with all our happiness, with all our prosperity, socially, politically, and materially." Nicholson believed a convention of southern states should be called and should demand guarantees for the "constitutional recognition of our right to property in slaves in the Territories, and that this right of property shall never be disturbed by any future amendment of the Constitution."[6]

Within that context, Tennessee's general assembly gathered two weeks after South Carolina declared its separation from the United States and two days before Mississippi followed suit. As was the custom, the session began with a lengthy address by the governor. A native son of Tennessee and popular two-term governor who had campaigned vigorously for the southern Democratic candidate, John C. Breckinridge, during the presidential election of 1860, Isham G. Harris began by echoing President James Buchanan's remarks to Congress the month before: "The systematic, wanton, and long continued agitation of the slavery question . . . [has] produced a crisis in the affairs of the country." Harris wasted no time in presenting his reasons for calling the general assembly into session: "The attempt of the Northern people," to confine slavery "within the limits of the present Southern States," to appropriate the whole of the western territory to themselves, and to put slavery on the path of "ultimate extinction" was regarded by the "people of the Southern states as a gross and palpable violation of the spirit and obvious meaning of the compact of Union. . . ."

For Harris, the "crisis" had been brought on because the "Northern people" were ignoring the judgment of the Supreme Court in its 1857 *Dred Scott* ruling that the "Constitution distinctly recognizes property in *slaves*. . . ." (Italics in the original.) The court, Harris continued, had settled the question "beyond the possibility of doubt . . . ," yet the North had developed "the most violent and fanatical opposition" to the institution. The "anti-slavery cloud" which at first "was no larger than a man's hand," had now "grown to colossal proportions." After reading a long list of grievances caused by the "anti-slavery cloud," Harris announced that to evade the crisis would be "fatal to the institution of slavery forever." The time had arrived, he proclaimed, for the people of the South "either to abandon or to fortify and maintain it." Harris knew the choice was clear: "Abandon it, we cannot, interwoven as it is with our wealth, prosperity and domestic happiness."[7]

On the one hand, Harris believed the South and its domestic institutions would not achieve "permanent safety" until "Northern prejudice has been eradicated." On the other, he held that a remedy could be found in constitutional amendments: "constitutional amendments as will deprive the fanatical majorities of the North of the power to invade our rights or impair our security or value of our property." Specifically, the "evils" of northern interference with the institution of slavery could be "obviated to a great extent," through an amendment to the United States Constitution. Harris called for establishing a line through the territories in such a way as would divide them "equitably between North and South." Extended to the Pacific Ocean, this new line would define all territory north of it "forever free, and all South of it, *forever* slave." (Italics in the original.) And a revision of the fugitive slave clause would require a free state to pay "double the value of such slave" to the owner of a slave not delivered to his or her owner. Recalling the travails of Jonathan and Juliet Lemon in New York City (an eight-year-long dispute between Virginia and New York over the right of owners to travel with their slaves), Harris called for protection for owners and their slaves "while in transit, or temporarily sojourning in any of the States of the Confederacy."[8] A fourth article would "expressly prohibit Congress from abolishing slavery in the District of Columbia," or in any dock yard, navy yard, arsenal, or any other type of federal facility "within the limits of any slave State." Harris concluded with a proposal that the previous "provisions shall never be changed, except by the consent of all the slave States."[9]

The governor's suggestions for protecting slavery in the United States Constitution were similar to many others being offered during that period. Believing that the crisis could only be solved by amending the United States Constitution, elected officials proposed a total of sixty-eight constitutional amendments over Secession Winter. Beginning with James Buchanan's proposal on December 3, 1860, designed to protect slavery in the territories, strengthen the 1850 Fugitive Slave Act, and recognize the right of property in slaves; dozens of amendments originated from governors, congressmen, state legislatures, delegates to secession conventions, and the Washington Peace Conference.[10] The majority of the proposed amendments dealt with slavery in the territories, fugitive slaves, protecting slavery in the District of Columbia, and enabling slave owners to travel into and through non-slave states and territories. Ninety percent were specifically designed to move protections for slavery from the state level to the federal. Tennesseans accounted for nine proposed amendments, second only to Virginians who suggested sixteen.[11] Kentucky senator John J. Crittenden's six-part amendment became the most popular as it covered the major points of the slavery controversy, and became in many ways the standard against which all other amendments were judged.[12]

Tennessee's senior senator, Andrew Johnson, had recommended a set of "constitutional provisions" on December 13, 1860, even before Harris convened the special session. Johnson had had considerable experience in Tennessee politics having served the state in the United States House of Representatives for a decade during the 1840s, as governor for two terms, and then in the Senate beginning in 1857. Johnson opposed secession and has been described by one biographer as an "unconditional Unionist."[13] In an attempt to solve the problems of the day, Johnson offered his own set of suggestions to protect the institution of slavery. He proposed that the western territory be divided along an unspecified line: to the north slavery would be prohibited, but south of the line slavery would be "recognized and protected as property." States would be obligated to return fugitive slaves when "demanded by the proper authority, or pay double their cash value out of the treasury of the State." (Three weeks later, Governor Harris would include this same provision in his address to the Tennessee General Assembly.) Johnson included the usual requirements that slavery be protected in the District of Columbia and in federal installations located in slave states, and a stipulation that Congress could not amend the constitutional provision dealing with the "representation of three fifths of the slaves," nor affect the interstate slave trade. His final article, like the governor's, required that the preceding five amendments would be "unamendable" by future congresses.[14] Johnson was not the first to suggest that constitutional amendments protecting slavery be perpetually un-altered. That honor goes to US Representative Thomas C. Hindman of Arkansas who proposed that his proslavery amendments presented on December 12 "shall forever be irrepealable and unamendable."[15] Ultimately twenty-two suggestions for amending the Constitution to protect the institution of slavery carried this provision.

The only amendment to win the approval of Congress with broad appeal among both Democrats and Republicans was the so-called Seward/Adams/Corwin Amendment that prohibited Congress from interfering with or abolishing slavery in the states. It had been proposed in various forms by New York's William H. Seward, Georgia's Robert Toombs, Illinois's Stephen A. Douglas, Massachusetts's Charles Francis Adams, and Kentucky's John J. Crittenden among others. Tennessee US Representatives Emerson Etheridge and Thomas A. R. Nelson and state senator John W. Richardson all offered similar language. On January 22, 1861, Tennessee's general assembly passed its version which stated: "No amendment shall be made to the Constitution which, will authorize or give to Congress any power to abolish or interfere with slavery in any of the States by whose laws it is or may be allowed or permitted." Approved by the Senate during the early morning hours of March 4, 1861, the compromise came too late in the rush to seces-sion to make a difference. Only five states (Kentucky, Ohio, Rhode Island, Maryland, and Illinois) ratified the Corwin Amendment be-fore the country turned during the war from protecting slavery in the Constitution to abolishing it.[16]

The general assembly responded to Harris's address by seeking the opinion of Tennessee's voters. Scheduled for February 9, the ballot was divided into two parts: one would determine whether the state should establish a secession convention as many other southern states were doing; the other would elect delegates to such a statewide convention. In a further nod to popular democracy, the legislature stipulated that "no ordinance or resolution" for the purpose of changing Tennessee's relationship to the United States would be binding "until it is submit-ted to and ratified and adopted by a majority of the qualified voters in the State."[17] Tennessee would become only the third state (after

Texas and Virginia) to authorize a statewide referendum to ratify the secession verdict. Elected delegates to secession conventions in all of the other states that left the Union would make that fateful decision. In fact, conventions in Mississippi, Louisiana, Arkansas, and North Carolina specifically rejected resolutions that would have required voter endorsement of disunion.

Tennessee's voters soundly rebuffed the call for a special disunion gathering. On February 9, white men of Tennessee voted 55 to 45 percent against calling the convention. The vote for delegates for the suggested convention was even more emphatic. The state voted in favor of "Union" over "secession" delegates 78 to 21 percent![18] For the time being, the state had dramatically repudiated the secessionist movement.

As a result, unlike every other state that eventually joined the Confederacy, the debate over secession in Tennessee occurred in the house and senate of its general assembly, and the debate there reflected the divided nature of that Upper South state. Unlike the Deep South states, Tennessee had a large and vocal population that opposed secession. The day after Governor Harris offered his set of amendments as solutions to the South's problems, Representative William H. Wisener from Bedford County, located south of Nashville, offered a very different kind of resolution. Admitting that there were "difficulties and dangers" that threatened the government, Wisener emphatically announced that "secession is unconstitutional" and that "nullification is equally unconstitutional." Wisener pronounced "impeachment" and the "ballot-box" the "proper and constitutional remedies against unfaithful or incompetent public officers."[19] Wisener's Unionist remarks would not have surprised many of his neighbors. During the war, Bedford County supplied almost the same number of troops to the United States Army as it did to the Confederate Army, and Shelbyville, the county seat, assumed such a pro-Union position throughout the war than it became known as "Little Boston."[20] Wisener's fellow representative, John G. McCabe from Cannon County, in central Tennessee, also decried secession and proffered a similar resolution that stated, "We do not regard secession of [sic] disunion as an adequate remedy for existing evils."[21] Other legislators embraced secessionist rhetoric.

Joseph J. Beaty a confirmed secessionist, from northeast of Nashville, proposed a counter motion condemning Abraham Lincoln and Hannibal Hamlin as "Black Republicans," and their desire to prohibit the extension of slavery into the territories "as being utterly incompatible with the safety of the Southern States in the Union, without additional guarantees."[22] Senator James L. Thompson, representing Smith and Sumner Counties, assumed a similar position believing the election of a Republican president sufficient reason to "sever her connection with the Union. . . . Her honor, interest, and future welfare impels her to this course."[23]

In addition to the constitutional amendments proposed by Senator Johnson and Governor Harris, the legislature considered several other amendments that had been proposed by Tennesseans. United States Representative, Thomas Amos Rogers Nelson, had submitted a set of three articles dealing with the protection of slavery in the territories south of the 36°30' line of latitude and in the District of Columbia, the return of fugitive slaves, and an innovative and very problematic way of electing the president and vice president. Nelson proposed that the thirty-six-thirty line be used in national elections so that one of the executive branch members must "be an inhabitant" of the area north of the line and the other from the south of said line. Although one presumes that Nelson believed his scheme would bring sectional balance to the White House, he did not elaborate on his radical approach to solving the problem.[24]

On the same day that Governor Harris addressed the general assembly in Nashville, Representative Emerson Etheridge offered a slightly different solution on the floor of the United States House of Representatives. This native of Dresden, Tennessee, proposed protecting slavery by placing specific restrictions on the ability of Congress to interfere with the institution in any state, in any federal installation in slave states, and in the District of Columbia. He further suggested forbidding Congress from prohibiting "the removal or transportation of slaves from one slave state to another." Etheridge proposed dividing the Mexican Cession (excluding the state of California) along the Missouri Compromise line of 36°30' barring slavery to the north and allowing—but not protecting it—to the south.[25] By all appearances, Congressman Etheridge acted independently of both Governor Harris and Senator Johnson. While similar in some respects, his proposal differed significantly from amendments being framed in Nashville and at the other end of the United States Capitol.

Representative George Gantt from Maury County in the central portion of the state was the last (on January 11) to present an amendment before the general assembly developed its "plan of adjustment." Gantt suggested that a convention of the "other Slave States," meet in Louisville, Kentucky, for the purpose of adopting "a basis of settlement, upon which, if possible, the Union may be reconstructed." The basis of settlement, according to Gantt should include a "declaratory amendment to the Federal Constitution" that "African slavery, as it exists in the slave States, is property," and entitled to protection afforded "every other species of property." Gantt further stipulated that if northern states refused to return fugitive slaves they must pay double the value of the slave (an idea proposed earlier by both Andrew Johnson and Governor Harris), and that slaves would be "rendered secure" when traveling or "sojourning" through non-slaveholding states with their owners. Finally, Gantt dealt with the western territory by dividing it at the 36°30' parallel and declaring that "south of said line, slavery shall exist, and in all the north of it shall be forever prohibited." Like Governor Harris's amendment, Gantt's division of the territory extended to the Pacific Ocean.[26]

When George Gantt introduced his amendment in January, his fears for the future were representative of most white southerners—protecting the institution of slavery. Tennessee is "vitally interested in slavery as a political institution, and in slaves as property," Gantt argued. With the inauguration of a "Black Republican" on March 4, the power of the federal government, he reasoned, would be focused on initiating its demise. "It cannot be doubted for a moment that this power will be used to the prejudice of slave property, which will then be exposed to its attacks." Instead of being nurtured, "it will be outlawed—treated as a sin—dealt with as a wrong." Unless the Constitution were amended to provide adequate protection for this unique type of property, Gantt warned, Tennessee would be driven to "unite her destiny with her sister Slave States in a Southern Union."[27] Tennessee delayed leaving the Union, not because her grievances were different from those of South Carolina or Georgia or Mississippi, but because her state legislature contained a higher percentage of Unionists who treated secession with more caution.

Tennessee, in many ways, was representative of the eight border states. Divided on the issue of how to respond to the election of Abraham Lincoln, those states agreed that slavery was under attack but could not agree on the best remedy. Ultimately, although the seven lower South states understood the election of Lincoln to be sufficient cause for leaving the Union, the eight remaining slave states decided to wait until the Lincoln administration formally acted aggressively against the institution of slavery or, to use the term in vogue over Secession Winter, attempted to "coerce" the southern states.

Tennessee's senator Andrew Johnson emerged as the state's most vocal and adamant Unionist. Two days before Lincoln's inauguration, Johnson described secession as a conspiracy, and making war upon the United States "treason." "Show me," he challenged from the Senate floor, "who has fired on our flag, has given instructions to take our forts and our custom-houses, our arsenals, and our dock-yards, and I will show you a traitor. [Applause in the galleries.]"[28] Johnson was reminding his listeners that shortly after the secession of South Carolina, the Deep South states had moved to "liberate" federal property within their borders. Throughout the South, state militias seized federal forts, arsenals, armories, custom houses, and the United States Mint in New Orleans following Lincoln's election.[29]

Two weeks after Governor Harris presented his solution to the election of Lincoln, the general assembly responded with its own amendment—a "plan of adjustment"—expanding Harris's five proslavery articles to nine. The legislature's proposal included all of the governor's suggestions, but added four of its own. It distanced itself from Harris's proposal to divide the state of California at 36°30' by recommending that the line through the territories terminate at the eastern state line of California. Its most sweeping article included a "declaratory amendment that African slaves . . . shall be recognized as property, in the States where slavery exists," in the District of Columbia, while in transit, and in federal installations in slave states. The legislators also included provisions for protecting slaves being transported between slave states and non-slave states or territories, for labeling as fugitives those who commit crimes in one state and "escape therefrom to other States," and a final provision that "it is the duty of each State to suppress armed invasions of another State." The last article was a clear reference to the John Brown raid on Harpers Ferry a year and half earlier, and members of his band who had escaped to free states.[30]

Upon approval of those "propositions" to amend the United States Constitution by the house (on January 21) and senate (on January 22), Tennessee's general assembly sent copies to all of the slaveholding states.[31] A week later, Congressman James M. Quarles, from Clarksville, presented Tennessee's resolutions to the House of Representatives in Washington, and early in February they became part of the deliberations of the Washington Peace Conference, brought there by Tennessee's twelve-man delegation.[32] Although an element in the secession deliberations, Tennessee's proposals brought nothing new or creative to the table. Like John Crittenden's amendment, they covered all of the major points of disagreement over the future of slavery. And like Crittenden's, the proposals attempted to solve the problem of slavery in the territories by reestablishing the 36°30' Missouri Compromise line, a solution opposed by radical Republicans and radical Democrats alike. Just as the territorial problem split the Democratic Party during the election of 1860, it continued to plague every attempt to solve it via constitutional amendments.

As the Tennessee General Assembly debated secession and proposed solutions to the crisis created by the departure or pending departure of the seven south Atlantic and Gulf Coast states, a similar exchange of views was taking place in the United States House of Representatives in Washington. Tennessee's delegation to Washington consisted of three Democrats and seven members of the Opposition Party. The Opposition Party had developed during the latter years of the 1850s as the old Whig Party collapsed in the aftermath of the Kansas-Nebraska Act. Oppositionists attempted to occupy a middle ground between Democrats and Republicans by advocating for the expansion of roads, banks, canals, and railroads.[33] The party was popular in the South because it allowed pro-Union supporters to rally around a party that did not directly challenge the Democratic position on slavery. In 1858, Oppositionists elected nineteen members to the US House of Representatives from Georgia, Kentucky, North Carolina, Virginia, and Tennessee. The appeal of a centrist party was most evident in Tennessee which sent seven of the nineteen delegates to Congress. Tennessee's Oppositionists hailed, not surprisingly, from the eastern and central parts of the state with Emerson Etheridge being the lone exception coming from the Ninth District in the far western reaches of the state.

Between the middle of January and Inauguration Day, nine of the state's ten delegates offered their opinion on the state of the country, and they provide a clear window into the issues that were roiling not only Tennessee but the nation as a whole.[34] Just as Andrew Johnson and Alfred O. P. Nicholson locked horns in the Senate, Emerson Etheridge and William T. Avery offered opposing opinions in the House. Speaking on January 23, Representative Etheridge termed secession "utter madness and folly." He listed all the "dangers" perceived by his colleagues who favored disunion, including northern opposition to slavery, nonexecution of the 1850 Fugitive Slave Act, potential abolition of slavery, and that some northerners favored "social and political equality of the negro." Secession, he dramatically pronounced, would solve none of those issues. The "evils" perceived by white southerners were the result of "misrepresentation, perversion, and falsehood. . . ." If all attempts at compromise failed, Etheridge would return to Tennessee and confront disunion "with a torch in one hand and a sword in the other."[35]

A week later, William Tecumseh Avery challenged Etheridge's interpretation of events. Quoting from Republican newspapers that praised his speech, Avery found it "extraordinary and unnatural" that a southerner would "champion the cause of the sworn enemies of his section." He disputed Etheridge's claim "that the North has been guilty of no wrong" to justify secession, arguing that just a week before, Tennessee's general assembly had approved a constitutional amendment as an ultimatum in response to northern misdeeds. "Do not these resolutions point to wrongs? and that these wrongs must be righted, and that speedily?" Avery maintained that the South had much to fear from the Republican Party and that only by protecting slavery in the federal constitution could Tennessee remain in the Union. "My first and highest allegiance is to my State," he concluded, and pledged that "the brave men of Tennessee" would "resist unto the death any invasion of the soil of the South."[36]

Over the next six weeks, the other Tennessee representatives (with the exception of John Vines Wright from the Seventh Congressional District) joined the fray. The common themes were Republican "hatred" of slavery, secession being (or not being) the solution to the nation's ills, the fear of abolition and equality of the races, constitutional compromise, and coercion of the South on the part of the North. Representative Robert Hatton, for example, argued that southern people believed the Republican Party intends "to destroy the institution of slavery in the States." Whether true or not, Hatton thought it would do no harm to preserve slavery in the Constitution simply to allay southern fears.[37] James H. Thomas echoed the common belief that Republicans, and Lincoln in particular, hated slavery and that Lincoln was specifically selected as a presidential candidate "because of his hatred of slavery."[38] Whatever their definition of the problem, however, all of Tennessee's representatives supported constitutional compromise.

Hoping for concessions, four representatives warned the North against any form of belligerency against the seceded states. Like all of the eight slave states that remained in the Union, Tennessee's delegation did not believe the mere election of Lincoln warranted secession. At the same time, they generally presumed that any attempt on the part of the Lincoln administration to prevent states from leaving or forcing them to return would constitute an act of war. For Thomas, any attempt to enforce federal laws in the seceded states would equate to oppression on the part of the government. "That is the sort of coercion which George III attempted to put in force against the revolted American colonies."[39] Because many white southerners believed Lincoln would eventually invade the South to bring the seceded states to heel, talk of coercion was prevalent not just in Tennessee, but throughout the newly formed Confederacy. Federal military reprisals against the South were greatly anticipated and even predicted, but did not evolve as expected. The spark that eventually lit the tinderbox the United States had become, came from Charleston and not Washington. But not yet.

Lincoln's inaugural address on March 4, was an attempt to calm the waters and convince secessionists that the incoming president had no designs on slavery in the states where it already existed. Early in his speech, he famously repeated a statement he had used earlier: "I have no purpose, directly or indirectly, to interfere with the institution of slavery in the states where it exists. I believe I have no lawful right to do so, and I have no inclination to do so." His focus on opposition to the extension of slavery rather than to the existence of the institution irritated abolitionists, but assured Unionists in the Upper South that he intended no harm to slavery within states. His endorsement of the Corwin Amendment which had just passed the Senate that morning, furthered their belief that the Republican Party was not the abolitionist party southern fire-eaters wanted to believe it was.[40]

On the other hand, Lincoln was unable to appease secessionists. He neither acknowledged that slavery was protected in the Constitution, nor that secession was legitimate. Additionally, he affirmed that he intended to "hold, occupy, and possess the property, and places belonging to the government, and to collect the duties and imposts; but beyond what may be necessary for these objects, there will be no invasion, no using of force against, or among the people anywhere." Enough southerners took Lincoln's speech as a declaration of war that two days later the Confederate Congress authorized the raising of 100,000 troops.[41]

For all the speculation about compromise, and admonitions against coercion, the national political scene was relatively quiet for the five weeks following Lincoln's inauguration. Congress was out of session, the Tennessee General Assembly had adjourned on February 4, and the Washington Peace Conference had concluded its deliberations by the end of that month. Arkansas voters had approved a state convention, but elected a majority of Union men to represent them, and it had adjourned without action on March 21.[42] Missouri had voted almost unanimously against secession on March 19 and adjourned three days later; only Virginia's convention remained in session working feverishly to craft a compromise amendment satisfactory to Unionists and disunionists alike.[43]

Meanwhile, seven Deep South states had formed the Confederate States of America in Montgomery, Alabama, designed a constitution, and adjourned their new congress on March 16.[44] While war was much talked about, no act of aggression or coercion had occurred. Then Confederate guns shattered the uneasy calm in the early morning hours of April 12 as they bombarded the federal bastion of Fort Sumter in Charleston Harbor. President Jefferson Davis and his cabinet had grown weary of the status quo, and decided to force the issue. The Confederate president authorized an attack on the fort if Major Robert Anderson, commander of Fort Sumter, did not immediately surrender his troops. Anderson refused. The bombardment began in spite of Davis and his cabinet knowing that Anderson was running low on supplies and would have to surrender in a few days.[45]

In answer to the fall of Fort Sumter, President Lincoln issued a call on April 15, to the nation's governors for 75,000 state militia troops to "re-possess the forts, places, and property which have been seized from the Union." The president emphasized that the "utmost care" would be observed to "avoid any devastation, any destruction of, or interference with, property, or any disturbance of peaceful citizens in any part of the country."[46] Governor Harris retorted two days later that "Tennessee will not furnish a single man for purposes of coercion but 50,000 if necessary for the defense of our rights and those of our southern brothers."[47] The next day he called the general assembly back into special session. The precipitate action on the part of the Confederacy and Lincoln's response stimulated Tennessee's secessionist impulses fundamentally altering the political equation. As historian Jonathan M. Atkins observed, the president's call for troops demonstrated to Tennesseans in the central and western parts of the state that the "Black Republicans" intended to "coerce the seceded states back into the Union and to create a military dictatorship."[48]

Harris's opening address to the legislature on April 25, left no doubt regarding his position. Lincoln's request for troops could only be read as a declaration of war; an "internecine war between the people of the slave and non-slave owning States." Offering no opinion on the constitutional right of secession, Harris instead invoked the words of the Declaration of Independence that when "any form government becomes destructive of the ends for which it was created, it is the right of the people to alter and abolish it." Blaming the coming war on the "disordered moral sentiment of the North," the governor recommended that the legislators draw up an edict declaring the "independence of the State of Tennessee of the Federal Union."[49]

As the legislature debated the governor's request over the next ten days, Jefferson Davis dispatched former US Representative Henry W. Hilliard to Tennessee with instructions to encourage the state to join the southern Confederacy. He arrived on April 29 and was "warmly" greeted by Governor Harris who arranged for Hilliard to address the general assembly the following day.[50] As the Confederate national flag flew from private dwellings and public buildings alike throughout Nashville, Hilliard spoke at length to the assembled legislators denouncing Lincoln for amassing an army with which he intended to "invade" the South. He urged the legislature to join the government in Montgomery and, in closing, appealed to the gallant history of the state: "Will Tennessee, with her heroic sons, whose battles and victories have illustrated the State, join us, and help us to repel an invasion which is monstrous on this continent, and in this nineteenth century?"[51]

Obviously impressed by Hilliard's impassioned plea to join the Confederate cause, the general assembly responded by quickly approving (on May 1) a resolution that authorized Governor Harris to "appoint three Commissioners on the part of Tennessee, to enter into a Military League with the authorities of the Confederate States . . . having in view the protection and defence of the entire South against the war that is now being carried on against it."[52]

After setting the stage for a military alignment with the Confederacy, the general assembly then responded to Governor Harris's address on the 25th by developing two ordinances: one that formally separated the state from the Union, and a second adopting and ratifying the Provisional Constitution of the Confederate States of America. Both were to be set before the voters of the state on June 8, with ballots to be marked "Separation" or "No Separation" and "Representation" or "No Representation."[53]

The next day, May 7, it adopted the *Convention Between the State of Tennessee and the Confederate States of America* which it had authorized a week earlier. Over the previous seven days, Governor Harris had appointed Gustavus A. Henry (an attorney from Clarksville), George W. Barrow (an attorney from Nashville), and Archibald W. O. Totten (a former Tennessee Supreme Court justice) to meet with secession commissioner Henry Hilliard to develop the agreement. This remarkable document committed the state to supporting the Confederacy a full month before the voters were to be given the responsibility of making that decision. Designed to effect a "speedy admission into the Confederacy," the accord contained three parts. The first placed the "whole military force" of the state under the control of Jefferson Davis while the second turned over to the "Confederate States, all the public property acquired from the United States," and the third made the government in Montgomery responsible for any expenditures made by Tennessee "before she becomes a member of said Confederacy." A final clause, most significantly, gave final "approval and ratification" of the treaty, not to the voters, but to the "proper authorities of both Governments respectively."[54] As historian James W. Fertig observed several decades later, the specific wording of the *Convention Between the State of Tennessee and the Confederate States of America* "made the vote of the people superfluous."[55] Given the state's repudiation of secession on February 9, the general assembly's willingness to join militarily with the seceded states represented a significant departure from the will of the people. The legislature clearly believed the voters would uphold, on June 8, their alliance with the Confederacy. As it turned out, the Confederate government in Montgomery also preempted the state's ratification vote by quickly approving the Hilliard convention and then unanimously admitting Tennessee to statehood on May 17, a full three weeks before the scheduled popular vote.[56]

To ensure that the upcoming vote endorsed the legislators' alliance with the Confederacy, the general assembly promptly produced an open letter to the citizens of the state designed to rationalize its actions and persuade them to concur. Akin in many ways to the declarations of secession composed by the conventions in South Carolina, Georgia, Mississippi, and Texas, the "Legislative Address to the People of Tennessee" was both a justification for secession and an explanation of the state government's commitment to disunion.

Like the governor, the legislators "steered clear of the mooted question of secession" and invoked the right of revolution from the state's 1834 constitution which declared the right "to alter, reform, or abolish our form of government in such manner as we think proper." Unlike other states that joined the Confederacy, Tennessee did not attempt to justify its action by claiming the compact form of government whereby any state may lawfully and peacefully withdraw from the Union.[57] Instead, the legislators summoned up the ideals of the Declaration of Independence and "submitted a revolutionary document."[58]

In many ways, the address was a call to arms summoning the sons of the state to "drive the invaders from her soil, and to give to her the rights that traitors and usurpers are seeking to destroy." Theirs was a sacred cause, a battle for the "inalienable rights of man." The legislators hoped that their reference to Lincoln as a "usurping tyrant and false hearted hypocrite" that threatened the South's way of life would be enough to sway the scheduled vote on June 8. The letter concluded with the assumption that separation from the United States was an accomplished fact: "Tennessee has taken her position and has proudly determined to throw her banners to the breeze, and will give her strength to the sacred cause of the WHITE MAN OF THE

SOUTH."[59] While the "Address to the People" was an urgent plea for the voters to endorse the legislators' action, disunion for Tennessee had already taken place. As state historian Robert H. White observed in 1959, Governor Harris and the general assembly had not waited for the June 8 referendum. Weeks before the vote, the issue had been "settled in favor of separation."[60]

While the governor and legislators were making common cause with the Confederacy and planning for war (having called up 55,000 volunteers for the "defence of the State"), Unionists in East Tennessee gathered to object to the precipitate action of the state government. Shortly after the "Address to the People" was printed and circulated, prominent Knoxville citizens called for a convention to meet in Knoxville on May 30–31, to determine a different course for the state. Attorneys Oliver P. Temple and Connally Trigg, and newspaper editor William G. "Parson" Brownlow were among the central organizers of the gathering. When the 462 delegates met in Knoxville on May 30 they quickly elected US Representative Thomas A. R. Nelson as president. Nelson, in turn, appointed a business committee of twenty-six men who were charged with drawing up a series of resolutions reflecting the disapproval of the assembled with the response of the state government to the events at Fort Sumter.[61]

Less than twenty-four hours later, the committee presented its report which was unanimously accepted. Among the twelve points of concern noted, the committee's assessment found that: 1) the general assembly had no authority to enter into a military league with the Confederate States of America, 2) that in so doing, it disregarded the rights of the people who overwhelmingly voted for Union in the February canvas, and 3) that the "evils" confronting the state were "the legitimate offspring of the ruinous and heretical doctrine of secession." The general tone of the challenge to the legislature was that until the will of the people was assessed on June 8, the general assembly should have been guided by the February vote against secession. After listening to a three-hour speech by Senator Andrew Johnson in support of the convention's purpose, the delegates promptly adjourned to await the results of the June 8 referendum."[62]

Any concerns Governor Harris and the general assembly might have had that voters would not follow their lead were allayed when the results of the popular vote were tallied. Tennessee's white male voters opted for secession by an overwhelming majority—68 to 32 percent. In East Tennessee, however, the vote was reversed with 69 percent voting for "No Separation."[63] The huge reversal in sentiment from the February plebiscite combined with three counties (Franklin, Lincoln, and Humphreys) reporting not a single Unionist vote suggested more than perfunctory electoral fraud. Historian Robert White later observed that "the lopsided vote in certain counties seems to indicate that chicanery may have been 'present and voting.'"[64] Parson Brownlow, editor of the Knoxville *Whig*, voiced even stronger convictions. "The election in Middle and West Tennessee has been a perfect *farce*. There was the show—an empty show—of a popular vote upon the ordinance of secession, when the military forces stationed at important points, intimidated timid men, and, themselves voted, in and out of the state, in violation of the Constitution, and of every law enacted in pursuance thereof."[65]

Convinced that fraud had, indeed, influenced the outcome of the election, Representative Thomas A. R. Nelson called for the East Tennessee Convention to reassemble on June 17 at Greeneville having determined that Knoxville was no longer a safe place for Unionists.[66] On June 20, the business committee presented a "Declaration of Grievances" which the convention, after much heated debate and with many changes, finally adopted. The "Declaration" charged secessionists with voter intimidation, vote suppression, and duplicity. "The secession cause," it proclaimed, "has thus been sustained by deception and falsehood as to the action of Congress; by false dispatches as to battles that were never fought and victories that were never won; by false accounts as to the purposes of the President; by false representations as to the views of Union men, and by false pretenses as to the facility with which the secession troops would take possession of the Capitol and capture the highest officers of the Government." The convention concluded its proclamation with six resolutions declaring that the people of East Tennessee desired peace and avoidance of civil war, that the action of the general assembly in adopting the military league with the Confederate States was unconstitutional, and that they be allowed to "form and erect a separate State."[67]

That afternoon, the convention approved a "memorial" (in accordance with Article III, Article IV, Section 3 of the United States Constitution), requesting the general assembly's approval in the formation of a separate state. Seeking a peaceful means of resolving the great disparity in its vote for "No Separation" in the June election from that of West and Central Tennessee, the petition proposed to "effect a separation amicably, honorably, and magnanimously, by a settlement of boundaries so as to divide East Tennessee" from the rest of the state. To present the appeal to the legislature, the convention appointed Oliver P. Temple, John Netherland, and James P. McDowell as commissioners. The response from the general assembly was negative as expected. The house and senate committees, to which the petition had been referred, doubted that the memorial represented the true sentiment of the people of East Tennessee, especially since the convention delegates had been elected before the June 8 referendum. As in many elections in the past, the report lectured, the minority had "uniformly acquiesced" in the decisions of the majority. Not wanting to consider the request further, the committees concluded that "the question can be better disposed of by our successors. . . ."[68]

The displeasure of East Tennessee citizens with secession continued throughout the war although in muted form as the Confederacy greatly increased military presence there following the June vote. The Chattanooga-Knoxville-Greeneville-Bristol corridor was of critical importance to the South because it contained the most direct railroad line connecting Mississippi, Alabama, and Georgia to Virginia. Because of the strategic military importance of East Tennessee, it remained under Confederate control until late 1863, but was never fully brought to heel. Guerilla warfare and sabotage against the Confederate "army of occupation" marked the area while approximately thirty thousand East Tennesseans joined the United States Army.[69]

〈〈〈 〉〉〉

With its pro-separation vote on June 8, 1861, Tennessee became officially the last state to join the Confederacy. While the state's path to disunion was different from the other states to join the Confederacy, its reasons for feeling the need to secede were identical—preserving slavery and white supremacy. As the speeches of Tennessee's representatives in Congress and the general assembly made clear, fear of a Republican assault on the South's peculiar institution and the concomitant loss of racial superiority drove the state's secessionist ideology.[70] The nine constitutional amendments proposed by Tennesseans over Secession Winter, all designed to preserve slavery at the national level beyond the reach of state or congressional authority, are telling in this regard.

In the end, Senator Andrew Johnson and Representative William Stokes were correct, secession would (and did) lead to the abolition of slavery. Begun as an effort to preserve and expand the enslavement of African Americans, the war moved Republicans (and Lincoln) to become abolitionists and pursue the destruction of the institution as a war measure.[71] With the demise of the Confederacy, the world for white southerners had, indeed, turned upside down. Among the unintended consequences of the war were the 1865 election of the iconoclast and Unionist (and arch-enemy of Isham Harris) William G. Brownlow as governor, and the ratification of the Thirteenth Amendment on April 5, 1865, by the state's Thirty-Fourth General Assembly. Tennessee became only the third former state of the Confederacy to approve the national abolition of slavery (after Virginia and Louisiana).[72] In his first address to the Tennessee legislature, Governor Brownlow urged the assembled to "strike down the monster institution (slavery)" which had caused the "most wicked, uncalled for and bloody war known to the history of the civilized world." Calling secession an "abomination," Brownlow listed at length the misery and hardship caused by a war brought about by an attempt to enlarge slavery's power and "perpetuate its existence."[73] Those listening to Governor Brownlow on April 6, 1865, needed only to think back to Governor Harris's opening address to the legislature on January 7, 1861, to understand the extent to which secession had achieved the exact opposite of what secessionists had envisioned.

Epilogue

Tennessee's secession might seem unusual given its overwhelming vote against separation in February. During the four months between the February 9 referendum when the state voted 80 percent for Union and the June 8 vote when almost 70 percent favored leaving, opinions on the crisis had obviously shifted. What caused that sudden reversal? A number of factors contributed to Tennessee finally joining her southern sisters in the Confederacy. In February, Tennessee's neighbors of Virginia, North Carolina, and Arkansas were still in the Union and not seriously contemplating secession. By June, those three states had aligned themselves with the new secessionist government in Richmond (only recently moved there from Montgomery). While Kentucky and Missouri had decided to cast their lot with the United States, white male voters from Memphis to Knoxville felt increased political pressure from the eastern, western, and southern borders of the state.

Governor Harris certainly played a role in persuading the populace that their cherished institution of slavery was threatened. Back in January, he had stoked their fears that the Republican Party threatened slavery and the South's way of life based on the retention of white supremacy. Not only had the northern people, he warned, made war upon slavery and slave owners, but also the president elect had "asserted the equality of the *black* with the *white race.*" (Italics in the original.) Harris sowed the seeds for the state's secession by raising the specter of the federal government, under the control of the upstart Republican Party, forcing its dogmas upon the white South. Tennessee would resist, he maintained, "any attempt upon the part of the others to hold, by means of a military force, an unwilling sovereignty as a member of a common Union." "Coercion," or more specifically, federal interference with southern norms, was raised repeatedly by other elected officials from Tennessee. State Representatives Joseph J. Beaty, William E. B. Jones, and James L. Thompson all warned against federal use of force in their speeches to the general assembly, as did US Representatives James H. Thomas, William T. Avery, and Horace Maynard in Washington.

Once the United States detachment at Fort Sumter surrendered and Lincoln issued his call for troops, the governor intensified his rhetoric in response to the "encroachment of Abolition power." Likening the southern cause to that of "our revolutionary fathers," he castigated Lincoln's actions in terms of an "unholy mission," as "low duplicity," and "dishonorable and treacherous." Making no mention of the Confederacy's bombardment of a federal fort or its earlier thwarting of the re-supply mission of the *Star of the West*, Harris spoke only of an "unprovoked and tyrannical usurpation of a people." Lincoln was elected "upon avowed purposes of hostility to the South," and his call for troops was only further demonstration of that hostility. With their governor shaping his message in this manner, making Tennessee a victim of governmental aggression, it is not surprising the June vote reflected the fears he engendered.

Additionally, the failure of any significant constitutional compromise diminished hope for a political solution. The most contentious issue confronting the nation's elected officials was that of dealing with slavery in the western territories. To forestall secession, southern Democrats needed Republicans to agree that slaves taken into the West would be free from congressional interference. That was the only guarantee the South had to have, and it was the only concession Republicans could not make because the central plank of their 1860 platform was opposition to the extension of slavery. They could not negotiate their stance on the issue without repudiating the core principle upon which the party was founded in 1854.

Amending the United States Constitution to protect slavery was actively promoted, as evidenced by the nine proposals offered by Tennessee officials. Of the fifty-nine articles suggested, most dealt with safeguarding slavery in the western territories, the District of Columbia, and in federal installations in southern states; and enhancing the 1850 Fugitive Slave Act. None of these, however, were included in the only congressional compromise possible—the Seward/Adams/Corwin amendment that prohibited Congress from interfering with slavery in the states where it already existed. As significant as this change was in establishing, for the first time, specific constitutional protections for slavery, it fell far short of protecting slavery in the territories which virtually every Tennessee amendment had proposed, and came too late to affect southern sentiments. Compromise, as far as Tennesseans were concerned, had failed.

A major factor in the reversal of public opinion in Tennessee undoubtedly was the legislature's "Address to the People" on May 9. Filled with exaggerations and overstatements, the message was persuasive in that it cast the state, much as in Governor Harris's April 25 message, as a victim of Lincoln—a "miserable tyrant" and "barbarian chieftain"—who proclaimed "war against the South in defiance of the Constitution." Charging Lincoln with marching "against peaceful and unoffending citizens," the legislature alleged the president's plan was to "murder Southern freemen and to desecrate Southern soil," grandly embroidering on the actual language of Lincoln's call for troops. To ensure that its message resonated as deeply as possible among white voters, the legislature ended its appeal by invoking a fear of losing the underpinnings of the South's system of racial inequality: "Tennessee has taken her position and has proudly determined to throw her banners to the breeze, and will give her strength to the sacred cause of freedom for the WHITE MAN OF THE SOUTH." With ten thousand copies of the address distributed across the state, Tennessee's voters—except those occupying the eastern mountains—acknowledged the presumed threat and voted for secession.

It must be assumed that John Bell's shift from a Unionist to a conditional secessionist following Lincoln's April 15 proclamation also played a role in moving the state toward disunion. Bell garnered all twelve of Tennessee's electoral votes as a result of the 1860 election, narrowly besting John Breckinridge. (Stephen Douglas was favored by only 8 percent of the state's voters; Abraham Lincoln was not included on the ballot.) A week after Lincoln called for troops to "suppress" the southern rebellion, Bell delivered a speech in Nashville that announced his dismay over the president's action and his belief that "we have new grounds for distrust and alarm." Not yet willing to declare fully for secession, Bell clung to the illusion that Tennessee and Kentucky could somehow remain neutral. In any event, he suggested that "no invasion of the South will be attempted until after Congress have assembled [scheduled for July 4], and then it will scarcely be considered safe to enter upon a Summer campaign with troops drawn from the North, and not inured to the exposure and hardships of service in the field."[74]

Bell's tempered view of Lincoln's intentions, however, also included rather dire predictions. While he indicated that war was not imminent, he did proclaim that "the North now appears resolved to wage war against the South." By labeling Lincoln's likely war against the South as "wanton, wicked, and aggressive," Bell aligned himself much more with the Breckinridge faction of voters than his own former Unionist followers. "No confident reliance could be placed," he counseled, "upon the pacific disposition of the Administration." Every report from the North brought news of the "intense and increasing excitement in that section and the united and determined purpose to wage a war for the subjugation of the South." Bell's prophecy of northern aggression, no matter how guarded or qualified, surely influenced many of his supporters to shift, as did Bell himself, from Unionism to a more favorable view of disunion.[75]

The extent of voter manipulation and intimidation in the June referendum, especially in West Tennessee, has been well documented by historian Derek Frisby who observed that secessionists, stunned by the February vote in favor of Unionism, determined to redouble their efforts to carry the state out of the Union. A "coordinated campaign of fear and repression" brought Tennessee "to the precipice" by April. While Lincoln's call for troops converted many conditional Unionists into reluctant Confederates, secessionist-organized intimidation continued throughout the next six weeks.[76] The extent of secessionist interference with the election was also chronicled by historian William L. Barney who noted that disunion vigilance committees banished northern newspapers, shut down Unionist editors, and "ransacked mail to ferret out the disloyal."[77] On the other hand, Stephen V. Ash, in his examination of Middle Tennessee, concluded that "there is no good evidence that slaveholding aristocrats for their own selfish purposes tricked, cajoled, or browbeat the ignorant, ingenuous common folk into following them out of the Union." Lincoln's singular call for troops in April became "a mortal threat to their racist, slaveholding society," and caused slaveholder and nonslaveholder alike to march "shoulder to shoulder into the ranks of the rebels."[78]

By early June, after ten southern states had proclaimed their independence, after the governor and the general assembly had repeatedly warned of the dangers of a "new and coercive Government," after hearing their elected officials admonish them that nothing less than the future of slavery was on the line, Tennessee's voters opted to join the southern Confederacy rather than remain in the Union. Oliver Perry Temple's explanation was simple: "When the people found themselves deserted by those they were accustomed to follow, they naturally lost heart and courage, and in the mad excitement and terror of the hour, they followed their panic-stricken leaders over into the camp of secession."[79]

Without question, Lincoln's call for seventy-five thousand troops in response to the attack of Fort Sumter pushed Tennessee over the edge as it had for Arkansas, Virginia, and North Carolina. As historian Annette Gordon-Reed has observed, "Fort Sumter changed the calculus."[80] With Lincoln's April 15 request for assistance to quell the rebellion, Tennessee moved decidedly toward secession. Senator Alfred Nicholson, consistently an advocate for southern rights, emphasized the looming threat Tennessee faced when writing a friend that "it is no longer the negro question but a question of resistance to tyranny."[81]

Bombarded by secessionist rhetoric from their governor and general assembly, and moved by secessionist actions of both between April 25 and May 7, the state's voters reflected on the events of the previous month and determined that Senator Nicholson had been correct all along. The Republican Party was engaged in a war against slavery and Lincoln's request for troops proved it. The campaign of fear and distortion had had its desired effect. By the time of the June vote, white Tennesseans knew that the future of white supremacy and slavery were the issues at stake and cast their ballots accordingly.

Sources

The long-threatened breakup of the Union over Secession Winter was remarkably well documented at both the national and state level. Debates from the second session of the Thirty-Sixth Congress occupy 2,000 pages in its original typescript preserved in the Library of Congress and are easily accessed online: http://memory.loc.gov /ammem/amlaw/lwcglink.html#anchor36. Printed with ten-point type on three columns per page, the *Congressional Globe* for those three months provides a front-row, balcony seat for those attracted by the details of the sectional drama as it played out over the winter of 1860–1861. The proceedings of ten state secession conventions were all published in either 1861 or 1862 (Texas waited until 1912) and can be found in the original or facsimile format. Some have been digitized and can be read online. The proceedings of the Tennessee General Assembly and the public acts it approved can likewise be found online at https://www.hathitrust.org/. With the journal of the Washington Peace Conference contributing 621 pages of day-by-day deliberations, the official record of Secession Winter amounts to over 8,000 pages.

The documents that follow illustrate Tennessee's political divisions, divisions that separated Democrats from Oppositionists and, in the case of Senators Johnson and Nicholson, Democrats from Democrats. They offer windows into the sectional crisis as it played out in one Upper South state. As concern for the future of the South's peculiar institution intensified following Lincoln's election and the march toward secession by seven Deep South states, these speeches, resolutions, proposed constitutional amendments, and declarations provide a framework for understanding the state's initial distaste for disunion and its ultimate rush to join the Confederacy.

I wish to extend heartfelt appreciation to Sam D. Elliott and Jonathan M. Atkins who reviewed this effort in draft and offered detailed and critical comments. Their critique and thoughtful advice strengthened the manuscript and saved me from several embarrassing errors. Scot Danforth supported this project from the beginning for which I am most grateful. Exercising his considerable editorial skills, Jon Boggs made the text more readable.

Editor's Note

In order to bring clarity to Tennessee's move toward secession, I have included the most relevant documents created by her elected officials. Although extensive newspaper articles and editorials exist that illuminate Secession Winter, it was the elected officials who had their fingers quite literally on the trigger. They and they alone were responsible for the decision to leave or stay. The speeches have been edited to include the significant portions and omit redundant or tangential material. To signal omitted sections for readers, I have included brief comments within braces, i.e., {}. Because many of the documents contain brackets inserted by the original compilers and editors such as "[Applause in the galleries]," my explanatory additions are also contained within braces. In some cases, documents contain asterisks as ellipses in the original. Those have been retained. Quoted material within the documents has been identified and cited as appropriate; the origins of some quotes could not be established.

TENNESSEE SECEDES

CHAPTER ONE

US Senators Andrew Johnson and Alfred Osborn Pope Nicholson

Andrew Johnson (Democrat)
December 19, 1860

Tennessee's two Democratic senators, Andrew Johnson and Alfred O. P. Nicholson, represented opposite ends of the state's political spectrum. Johnson, from East Tennessee, opposed secession calling it, like Andrew Jackson three decades earlier, "treason." On the other hand, Nicholson, from central Central Tennessee, believed that the elevation of a Republican to the White House alone justified separation. Lincoln's election, based on the Republican platform, was "tantamount to a declaration of war" against the South.

Andrew Johnson (1808–1875) had extensive political experience beginning as mayor of Greeneville, Tennessee (1834–1838), two terms in the Tennessee House of Representatives (1835–1841), Tennessee Senate (1841–1843), and the US House of Representatives (1843–1853). He served as governor of Tennessee (1853–1857) and then as a US Senator from 1857 to 1862 when he was appointed military governor of the state by President Lincoln.

Speaking the day before South Carolina seceded, Senator Johnson began by arguing against the constitutional right of any state to secede "without the consent of the other States." As evidence, he cited James Madison, Thomas Jefferson, Justice John Marshall, and, at length, Andrew Jackson. Of the latter, he quoted him writing in 1833: "Secession, like any other

revolutionary act, may be morally justified by the extremity of
oppression; but to call it a constitutional right, is confounding
the meaning of terms, and can only be done through gross error,
or to deceive those who are willing to assert a right but would
pause before they made a revolution, or incurred the penalties
consequent on a failure." In his quest to calm secessionist emo-
tions, Johnson also argued against secession on practical grounds.
Employing oft used appeals over Secession Winter, he cautioned
against precipitate action because Democrats would control
Congress for the next two years (during the Thirty-Seventh
Congress) and that secession would lead to the overthrow of the
"institution of slavery."

Having traveled thus far, the question arises, in what sense are we to
construe the Constitution of the United States? I presume what is
assumed in one of Mr. Madison's letters, that the Constitution was
formed for perpetuity; that it never was intended to be broken up.
It was commenced, it is true, as an experiment; but the founders of
the Constitution intended that this experiment should go on and
on and on; and by way of making it perpetual, they provided for its
amendment. They provided that this instrument could be amended and
improved, from time to time, as the changing circumstances, as the
changing pursuits, as the changing notions of men might require; but
they made no provision whatever for its destruction. The old Articles
of Confederation were formed for the purpose of making "a perpetual
union." In 1787, when the convention concluded their deliberations and
adopted the Constitution, what do they say in the very preamble of
that Constitution? Having in their mind the idea that was shadowed
forth in the old Articles of Confederation, that the Union was to be
perpetual, they say, at the commencement, that it is to make "a more
perfect union" than the union under the old Articles of Confederation,
which they called "perpetual."

What furthermore do we find? The Constitution of the United
States contains a provision that it is to be submitted to the States

respectively for their ratification; but on nine States ratifying it, it shall be the Constitution for them. In that way the Government was created; and in that way provision was made to perfect it. What more do we find? The Constitution, as I have just remarked, provides for its own amendment, its improvement, its perpetuation, its continuance, by pointing out and by prescribing the mode and manner in which improvements shall be made. That still preserves the idea that it is to be perpetual. We find, in addition, a provision that Congress shall have power to admit new States.

Hence, in traveling along through the instrument, we find how the Government is created, how it is to be perpetuated, and how it may be enlarged in reference to the number of States constituting the Confederacy; but do we find any provision for winding it up, except on that great inherent principle that it may be wound up by the States— not by a State, but by the States which spoke it into existence—and by no other means. That is a means of taking down the Government that the Constitution could not provide for. It is above the Constitution; it is beyond any provision that can be made by mortal man.

Now, to expose the absurdity of the pretension that there is a right to secede, let me press this argument a little further. The Constitution has been formed; it has been made perfect, or, in other words, means have been provided by which it can be made perfect. It was intended to be perpetual. In reference to the execution of the laws under it, what do we find? As early as 1795, Congress passed an excise law, taxing distilleries throughout the country, and, what were called the whiskey boys of Pennsylvania, resisted the law. The Government wanted means. It taxed distilleries. The people of Pennsylvania resisted it. What is the difference between a portion of the people resisting a constitutional law, and all of the people of a State doing so? But because you can apply this term coercion in one case to a State, and in the other call it simply the execution of the law against individuals, you say there is a great distinction! We do not assume the power to coerce a State, but we assume that Congress has the power to lay and collect taxes, and Congress has the right to enforce that law when obstructions and impediments are opposed to its enforcement. The people of Pennsylvania did object; they did resist and oppose the legal authorities of the country. Was that law enforced? Was it called coercion at that day to enforce it? Suppose all the people of the State of Pennsylvania had resisted: would not the law have applied with just the same force, and would it not have been just as constitutional to execute it against all people of the State, as it was to execute it upon a part of their citizens?

{*Senator Johnson here quoted George Washington in justifying calling out the militia to suppress the Whiskey Rebellion, and explores Andrew Jackson's motivations in confronting South Carolina's 1833 nullification of a tariff. In the present instance, Johnson proclaimed that, "If she (South Carolina) makes an advance either to dispossess the Government of that which it has purchased, or to resist an execution of the revenue laws, or of our judicial system, or the carrying of the mails, or the exercise of any other power conferred on the Federal Government, she puts herself in the wrong, and it will be the duty of the Government to see that the laws are faithfully executed." Johnson then quoted from South Carolina's 1805 transfer of various parcels of land in Charleston Harbor to the federal government.*}

Here is a clear deed of cession. The Federal Government has complied with all the conditions, and has, in its own right, the land on which these forts are constructed. The conditions of the cession have been complied with; and the Government has had possession from that period to the present time. There are its forts; there is its arsenal; there are its dock-yards; there is the property of the Government; and now, under the Constitution, and under the laws made in pursuance thereof, has South Carolina the authority and the right to expel the Federal Government from its own property that has been given to it by her own act, and of which it is now in possession? By resisting the execution of the laws; by attempting to dispossess the Federal Government, does she not put herself in the wrong? Does she not violate the laws of the United States? Does she not violate the Constitution? Does she not put herself, within the meaning and purview of the Constitution, in the attitude of levying war against the United States? The Constitution defines and declares what is treason. Let us talk about things by their right names. I know that some hotspur or madcap may declare that these are not times for a government of law; that we are in a revolution. I know that Patrick Henry once said, "if this be revolution, make the most of it.[1] If anything can be treason in the scope and purview of the Constitution, is not levying war upon the United States treason? Is not an attempt to expel its soldiers treason? Is not an attempt to resist the collection of the revenue, or to expel your mails, or to drive your courts from her borders, treason? Are not these powers clearly conferred in the Constitution on the Federal Government to be exercised? What is it, then, I ask in the name of the Constitution, in the meaning of the term as there defined? It is treason, and nothing but treason; and if one State, upon its own volition, can go out of this Confederacy without regard to the effect it is to have upon the remaining parties to the compact, what is your Government worth? what will it come to? and in what will it end? It is no Government at all upon such a construction.

But it is declared and assumed that, if a State secedes, she is no longer a member of the Union, and that, therefore, the laws and the Constitution of the United States are no longer operative within her limits, and she is not guilty if she violates them. This is a matter of opinion. I have tried to show, from the origin of the Government down to the present time, what this doctrine of secession is, and there is but one concurring and unerring conclusion reached by all the great and distinguished men of the country. Madison, who is called the Father of the Constitution, denies the doctrine. Washington, who was the Father of his Country, denies the doctrine. Jefferson, Jackson, Clay, and Webster, all deny the doctrine; and yet all at once it is discovered and ascertained that a State, of its own volition, can go out of this Confederacy, without regard to consequences, without regard to the injury and woe that may be inflicted on the remaining members from the act!

Suppose this doctrine to be true, Mr. President, that a State can withdraw from this Confederacy; and suppose South Carolina has seceded, and is now out of the Confederacy; in what an attitude does she place herself? There might be circumstances under which the States ratifying the compact might tolerate the secession of a State, she taking the consequences of the act. But there might be other circumstances under which the States could not allow one to secede. Why do I say so? Some suppose—and it is a well-founded supposition—that by the secession of a State all the remaining States might be involved in disastrous consequences; they might be involved in war; and by the secession of one State, the existence of the remaining States might be involved. Then, without regard to the Constitution, dare the other States permit one to secede when it endangers and involves all the remaining States? The question arises in this connection, whether the States are in a condition to tolerate or will tolerate the secession of South Carolina. That is a matter to be determined by the circumstances; that is a matter to be determined by the emergency; that is a matter to be determined when it comes up. It is a question which must be left open to be determined by the surrounding circumstances, when the occasion arises.

But conceding, for argument's sake, the doctrine of secession, and admitting that the State of South Carolina is now upon your coast, a foreign Power, absolved from all connection with the Federal Government, out of the Union: what then? There was a doctrine inculcated in 1823, by Mr. Monroe, that this Government, keeping in view the safety of the people and the existence of our institutions, would permit no European Power to plant any more colonies on this continent.[2] Now, suppose that South Carolina is outside of the Confederacy, and this Government is in possession of the fact that she is forming an alliance with a foreign Power—with France, with England, with Russia, with Austria, or with all of the principal Powers of Europe; that there is to be a great naval station established there; an immense rendezvous for their army, with a view to ulterior objects, with a view of making advances upon the rest of these States: let me ask the Senate, let me ask the country, if they dare permit it? Under and in compliance with the great law of self-preservation, we dare not let her do it; and if she were a sovereign Power to-day, outside of the

Confederacy, and was forming an alliance that we deemed inimical to our institutions, and the existence of our Government, we should have a right to conquer and hold her as a province—a term which is so much used with scorn.

{*Senator Johnson spent much time here elaborating on his earlier comment regarding the Monroe Doctrine pointing out that new territories have been added to the United States over the decades in order to strengthen the nation and keep foreign nations at arm's length. If South Carolina or another southern state were to secede and then "form an alliance with France and with England" for protection, should, he asked, the United States permit such an act? His answer: "I do not believe that we can."*}

I have referred to these extracts to show the policy intended to be pursued by our seceding sisters. What is the first threat thrown out? It is an intimidation to the border States, alluding especially, I suppose, to Virginia, Maryland, Kentucky, and Missouri. They constitute the first tier of the border slave States. The next tier would be North Carolina and Tennessee and Arkansas. We in the South have complained of and condemned the position assumed by the Abolitionists. We have complained that their intention was to hem slavery in, so that, like the scorpion when surrounded by fire, if it did not die from the intense heat of the scorching flames, it would perish in its poisonous skin. Now, our sister, without consulting her sisters, without caring for their interest or their consent, says that she will move forward; that she will destroy the Government under which we have lived, and that hereafter, when she forms a Government or a Constitution, unless the border States come in, she will pass laws prohibiting the importation of slaves into her State from those States, and thereby obstruct the slave trade among the States, and throw the institution back upon the border States, so that they will be compelled to emancipate their slaves upon the principle laid down by the Abolition party. That is the rod held over us!

I tell our sisters in the South that so far as Tennessee is concerned, she will not be dragged into a southern or any other confederacy until she has had time to consider; and then she will go when she believes it to be her interest, and not before. I tell our northern friends, who are resisting the execution of the laws made in conformity with the Constitution, that we will not be driven on the other hand into their confederacy, and we will not go into it unless it suits us, and they give us such guarantees as we deem right and proper. We say to you of the South, we are not to be frightened and coerced. Oh, when one talks about coercing a State, how maddening and insulting to the State; but when you want to bring the other States to terms, how easy to point out a means by which to coerce them! But, sir, we do not intend to be coerced.

We are told that certain States will go out and tear this accursed Constitution into fragments, and drag the pillars of this mighty edifice down upon us, and involve us all in one common ruin. Will the border States submit to such a threat? No. If they do not come into the movement, the pillars of this stupendous fabric of human freedom and greatness and goodness are to be pulled down, and all will be involved in one common ruin. Such is the threatening language used. "You shall come into our confederacy, or we will coerce you to the emancipation of your slaves." That is the language which is held over us.

There are many ideas afloat about this threatened dissolution, and it is time to speak out. The question arises in reference to the protection and preservation of the institution of slavery, whether dissolution is a remedy or will give to it protection. I avow here, to-day, that if I were an Abolitionist, and wanted to accomplish the overthrow and abolition of the institution of slavery in the southern States, the first step that I would take would be to break the bonds of this Union, and dissolve this Government. I believe the continuance of slavery depends upon the preservation of this Union, and a compliance with all the guarantees of the Constitution. I believe an interference with it will break up the Union; and I believe a dissolution of the Union will, in the end, though it may in some time to come, overthrow the institution of slavery. Hence we find so many in the North who desire the dissolution of these States as the most certain and direct and effectual means of overthrowing the institution of slavery.

{Johnson spoke at length here against the dangers of secession, arguing that "if there is one division of the States, will there not be more than one?" Where are we drifting? he asked. "What kind of breakers are ahead? Have we a glimpse through the fog that develops the rock on which the vessel of State is drifting? Should we not consider maturely, in giving up this old Government, what kind of government is to succeed it?"}

Why should we go out of the Union? Have we anything to fear? What are we alarmed about? We say that you of the North have violated the Constitution; that you have trampled under foot its guarantees; but we intend to go to you in a proper way, and ask you to redress the wrong, and to comply with the Constitution. We believe the time will come when you will do it, and we do not intend to break up the Government until the fact is ascertained that you will not do it. Where is the grievance; where is the complaint that presses on our sister, South Carolina, now? Is it that she wants to carry slavery into the Territories; that she wants protection to slavery there? How long has it been since, upon this very floor, her own Senators voted that it was not necessary to make a statute now for the protection of slavery in the Territories? No longer ago than the last session. Is that a good reason? They declared, to the resolutions adopted by the Senate, that when it was necessary they had the power to do it; but that it was not necessary then. Are you going out for a grievance that has not occurred, and which your own Senators then said had not occurred? Is it because you want to carry slaves to the Territories? You were told that you had all the protection needed; that the courts had decided in your behalf, under the Constitution; and that, under the decisions of the courts, the law must be executed.

{There ensued a debate among Johnson, Mississippi's Jefferson Davis, and Texas's Louis T. Wigfall over the meaning of a set of resolutions first proposed by Davis in February 1860 designed to protect slavery. The proposition at issue was one that held that if slavery in the territories needed additional protection, it would

I was going to say that the want of protection to slavery in the Territories cannot be considered a grievance now. That is not the reason why she is going out, and going to break up the Confederacy. What is it, then? Is there any issue between South Carolina and the Federal Government? Has the Federal Government failed to comply with, and carry out, the obligations that it owes to South Carolina? In what has the Federal Government failed? In what has it neglected the interest of South Carolina? What law has it undertaken to enforce upon South Carolina that is unconstitutional and oppressive?

If there are grievances, why cannot we all go together, and write them down, and point them out to our northern friends after we have agreed on what those grievances were, and say, "here is what we de- mand; here our wrongs are enumerated; upon these terms we have agreed; and now, after we have given you a reasonable time to consider these guarantees in order to protect ourselves against these wrongs, if you refuse them, then, having made an honorable effort, having ex- hausted all other means, we may declare the association to be broken up, and we may go into an act of revolution." We can then say to them, "You have refused to give us guarantees that we think are needed for the protection of our institutions and for the protection of our other inter- ests." When they do this, I will go as far as he who goes the furthest.

I tell them here to-day, if they do not do it, Tennessee will be found standing as firm and unyielding in her demands for those guar- antees in the way a State should stand, as any other State in this Confederacy. She is not quite so belligerent now. She is not making quite so much noise. She is not as blustering as Sempronius was in the council of Addison's play of Cato, who declared that his "voice was still for war."[4] There was another character there, Lucius, who was called upon to know what his opinions were; and when he was called upon, he replied that he must confess his thoughts were turned on peace; but when the extremity came, Lucius, who was deliberative, who was calm, and whose thoughts were upon peace, was found true to the interests of his country. He proved himself to be a man and a soldier; while the other was a traitor and a coward. We will do our duty; we will stand upon principle, and defend it to the last extremity.

We do not think, though, that we have just cause for going out of the Union now. We have just cause of complaint; but we are for remaining in the Union, and fighting the battle like men. We do not intend to be cowardly, and turn our backs on our own camps. We intend to stay and fight the battle here upon this consecrated ground. Why should we retreat? Because Mr. Lincoln has been elected President of the United States? Is this any cause why we should retreat? Does not every man, Senator or otherwise, know that if Mr. Breckinridge had been elected, we should not be to-day for dissolving the Union. Then what is the issue? It is because we have not got our man. If we had got our man, we should not have been for breaking up the Union; but as Mr. Lincoln is elected, we are for breaking up the Union! I say no. Let us show ourselves men, and men of courage.

How has Mr. Lincoln been elected, and how have Mr. Breckinridge and Mr. Douglas been defeated? By the votes of the American people, cast according to the Constitution and the forms of law, though it has been upon a sectional issue. It is not the first time in our history that two candidates have been elected from the same section of country. General Jackson and Mr. Calhoun were elected on the same ticket; but nobody considered that cause of dissolution. They were from the South. While I oppose the sectional spirit that has produced the election of Lincoln and Hamlin, yet it has been done according to the Constitution and according to the forms of law. I believe we have the power in our own hands, and I am not willing to shrink from the responsibility of exercising that power.

How has Lincoln been elected, and upon what basis does he stand? A minority President by nearly a million votes; but had the election taken place upon the plan proposed in my amendment of the Constitution, by districts, he would have been this day defeated. But it has been done according to the Constitution and according to law. I am for abiding by the Constitution; and in abiding by it I want to maintain and retain my place here and put down Mr. Lincoln and drive back his advances upon southern institutions, if he designs to make any. Have we not got the brakes in our hands? Have we not got the power? We have. Let South Carolina send her Senators back; let all the Senators come; and on the 4th of March next we shall have a majority of six in this body against him. This successful sectional candidate, who is in a minority of a million, or nearly so, on the popular vote, cannot make his Cabinet on the 4th of March next unless this Senate will permit him.

Am I to be so great a coward as to retreat from duty? I will stand here and meet the encroachment upon the institutions of my country at the threshold; and as a man, as one that loves my country and my constituents, I will stand here and resist all encroachments and advances. Here is the place to stand. Shall I desert the citadel, and let the enemy come in and take possession? No. Can Mr. Lincoln send a foreign minister, or even a consul, abroad, unless he receives the sanction of the Senate? Can he appoint a postmaster whose salary is over a thousand dollars a year without the consent of the Senate? Shall we desert our posts, shrink from our responsibilities, and permit Mr. Lincoln to come with his cohorts, as we consider them, from the North, to carry off everything? Are we so cowardly that now that we are defeated, we shall do this? Yes, we are defeated according to the forms of law and the Constitution; but the real victory is ours—the moral force is with us. Are we going to desert that noble and that patriotic band who have stood by us at the North? who have stood by us upon principle? who have stood by us upon the Constitution? They stood by us and fought the battle upon principle; and now that we have been defeated, not conquered, are we to turn our backs upon them and leave them to their fate? I, for one, will not. I intend to stand by them. How many votes did we get in the North? We got more votes in the North against Lincoln than the entire southern States cast. Are they not able and faithful allies? They are; and now, on account of this temporary defeat, are we to turn our backs upon them and leave them to their fate, as they have fallen for us in former controversies?

{*Senator Johnson concluded his speech with a final appeal to southern senators to maintain the Union and not secede: "Shall we give all this up to the Vandals and the Goths? Shall we shrink from our duty, and desert the Government as a sinking ship, or shall we stand by it?" After expressing his commitment to support the country as long as possible, he ended by encouraging his colleagues: "Then, let us stand by the Constitution; and in preserving the Constitution we shall save the Union; and in saving the Union, we save this, the greatest Government on earth."*}

Source: *Congressional Globe*, 36th Cong. 2nd Sess., 134–43.

ALFRED OSBORN POPE NICHOLSON (DEMOCRAT)
December 24, 1860

Alfred O. P. Nicholson (1808–1876) had a varied career as an attorney, newspaper editor, and politician. After serving in the Tennessee House of Representatives (1833–1839), he was appointed US Senator (1840–1842), elected to the state senate (1843–1845), and then edited the Nashville Union *from 1844 to 1846. During the early 1850s, Nicholson was the printer for the United States House of Representatives and edited the* Washington Union, *the official newspaper of the Democratic Party. In 1858, he was elected to the US Senate and served from 1859 until 1861 when he was formally expelled on July 11 for supporting the southern rebellion.*

Senator Nicholson began this lengthy speech by quoting from an earlier address to the Senate by Benjamin Franklin Wade (1800–1878), a Republican from Ohio who argued that the South's concerns regarding the motivations of the Republican Party were unfounded. Wade maintained that the people of the South were being misled into believing that Republicans were "their mortal enemies, and stand ready to trample their institutions under foot." The Ohio senator cautioned the South against taking precipitate action to secede "on a bare groundless suspicion."[5]

It seems then, Mr. President {the president of the Senate} that this gloom which hangs over the country, and which is seen and felt by us all, and freely admitted by the Senator himself, has no better foundation, in his estimation, than the groundless suspicion that the party soon to take possession of the Government intends to do something wrong. Is it possible that this feeling which pervades the whole country; which manifests itself in all our intercourse; which is seen in the countenances of all men; and which indicates the fearful looking for of some sad calamity that is about to befall the country, is only the result of an idle delusion? Is it possible that this wide-spread, disastrous, pecuniary and commercial revulsion that has taken place; this destruction of private and public credit which within the last sixty days has diminished the actual value of the estates of men in this country from twenty-five to fifty per cent., is it possible, I say, that all these consequences, these apprehensions, these dangers, are the fruits of an idle, baseless, groundless suspicion on the part of southern men? If it be so, then it becomes us all with promptness and fairness and candor, at once to relieve the country from so strange and so ruinous a delusion.

But, while the Senator can find no better ground for this wide-spread feeling of alarm and danger, he concedes that southern men are not so much to blame. He concedes that we *believe* that the Republican party are our mortal enemies, and, believing that, he does not think we are so much to blame; but in the next breath he says we believe this upon unfounded information; that we listen to none but the mortal enemies of the Republican party at the North, and that we will not hear that party itself. I suppose the Senator alludes to those in the North as mortal enemies who stand opposed to the Republican party. As a matter of course, he embraces within this designation the Democratic party of the North. While I freely concede that he is right in saying that we of the South believe his party our mortal enemies, I deny that

that conviction is made on our minds from information, either true or false, derived exclusively or mainly even, from our friends of the North.

We have for them the highest appreciation. In regard to them, it is my pleasure to say, that in the South we have for years confided in them as faithful friends and true patriots. We have regarded them as standing as a barrier between our rights and interests and the aggressions of our enemies; and but for their faithful and efficient exertions and devotion to the constitutional rights of all sections, this crisis which is now upon us would have come years ago. It would at least have come in 1856. My only regret is that they have not been able still to stem the current of sectionalism and fanaticism that has overwhelmed them and brought full into our view the terrors of a dissolving Union. Whatever may come in the future—though this Union may be dissolved; though we may separate into two confederacies—there is one thing that will always be remembered by southern men; and that is the fidelity and bravery and disinterestedness with which northern men have stood by and sustained and defended our rights, until the power of sectionalism has at last crushed them down.

But, Mr. President, it is true, as assumed by the Senator from Ohio, that there does exist in the South a deep and wide-spread conviction that the Republican party is the mortal enemy of the institutions and rights of the South. That conviction, as I have said, does not arise from the misrepresentations, as some have said, of northern national men, of whatever party, but it has been produced by stubborn facts, and by information derived from the most authentic and reliable sources. It comes from the leading men of the Republican party; from their speeches made here and elsewhere; from the acts of their Legislatures; from all the sources, authentic and reliable, from which the truth as to public sentiment is to be ascertained. Among those from whom, and by whom, this conviction has been produced on the southern mind, there are few, if any, who have contributed more than the Senator from Ohio himself. His own speeches here and elsewhere have made the impression at the South that, so far as his opinions are concerned, (and we regard him as a representative man,) that portion of the northern people represented in sentiment by him, are our mortal enemies. The people of the South know the characters of the leading men of the North of all parties. I tell the distinguished Senator from Ohio that in the South we regard him not only as a representative man, as a strong-minded man, but a bold, blunt, brave man; a man of candor; and when he speaks, when he tells the country that there is now "*really no union* between the North and the South;" that there is a "*bitter rancor*" of feeling existing between the two sections that does not characterize the feeling existing between any other two foreign Governments; when he says that "the only salvation of this Union is to be found in divesting it entirely from all taint of slavery, what are we to infer but that he and those whose opinions he represents are the mortal enemies of interests and rights with which our lives and our happiness and our all are identified?

I have alluded, Mr. President, to the evidence of a hostile feeling in the North against the South furnished by the Senator from Ohio, because he has assumed that the only evidence on which the southern mind relies for its convictions on this subject is derived from the enemies of Republicanism in the North. I could pile up the proof, in refutation of his remark, by referring to the declarations of other representative and leading men of the Republican party, in this body and in the other House, and out of them; by referring to the facilities well known to be constantly furnished to the free States for the escape of fugitive slaves; by referring to the difficulty and danger of executing the fugitive slave law; by referring to the statutes passed by many of the free State Legislatures for the acknowledged purpose of obstructing the successful execution of a plain obligation imposed by the Constitution; by referring to the well-known fact that anti-slavery societies are tolerated in the free States, when the avowed purposes of their association are to scatter incendiary publications through the South, tending directly to the production of discontent, rebellion, and insurrection among the slaves; but I forbear. It is only necessary to allude to the facts to repel the allegation of the Senator from Ohio, that our convictions as to the hostility of his party are unfounded, and based only on the information derived from the enemies of his party in the North.

But, Mr. President, without going outside of the most authentic sources of information, relying upon no facts stated by the friends of the South at the North; but upon the acknowledged evidences furnished by the Republican party itself, I shall proceed to state, as briefly as possible, what I understand to be the complaints of the South.

Mr. President, in regard to the sentiments of a majority of the northern people upon the subject of slavery as an abstract proposition, either morally or politically, I presume there can be no diversity of opinion. Looking to all the sources of information that are reliable, I understand these propositions to present fairly the sentiment of the northern mind—I mean the prevailing sentiment—in reference to the subject of slavery.

1. That slavery, as it exists in the southern States, is a moral as well as social and political evil.

2. That the owners and their slaves are created equal; that they are endowed alike with the inalienable rights of life, liberty, and the pursuit of happiness; and that to secure these rights equally to both governments are instituted, deriving their just power from the consent of the governed.

3. That as the owners and their slaves are created equal, and the former cannot rightfully acquire or hold domain over, or property in, the latter without his consent.

Now, Mr. President, these I understand to be the prevalent sentiments of the northern mind in reference to the question of slavery, viewed either socially, morally, or politically.

{*Senator Nicholson continued here to offer comments to the effect that differences over slavery were present in the Constitutional Convention, but that the founders believed every man had the right to enjoy "his own conscientious conviction."*}

What we now complain of is, that in the year 1856 these questions known to be questions of antagonism, morally and socially, if not politically, incapable of reconciliation between the North and South, were seized upon by political leaders at the North and incorporated as the basis, as the "central idea," of a political association which, rising upon the strength of this prevailing sentiment at the North, has finally taken possession of the Government of the country. Mr. President, the first fatal stab to this Union was made at the Philadelphia convention, in 1856, when these propositions were incorporated as a part of the Republican platform. There was the birth of Republicanism, and there was the birth of organized sectionalism; its legitimate fruits are agitation, dissension, alienation, and, finally, disunion, in some form or another. In my honest conviction, there is to be found the true origin of disunionism, and there the real responsibility for that catastrophe.

Mr. President, I desire now to turn the attention of the Senate to the Republican platform, for the purpose of showing that the surprise which is expressed here at the prevalence of the feeling of resistance in the South ought to have no existence. The resolution in that platform to which I particularly refer is this:

> *Resolved*, That, with our republican fathers, we hold it to be a self-evident truth that all men are endowed with the inalienable rights to life, liberty, and the pursuit of happiness; and that the primary object and ulterior designs of our Federal Government were to secure these rights to all persons within its exclusive jurisdiction; that as our republican fathers, when they had abolished slavery in all our national territory, ordained that no person should be deprived of life, liberty, or property, without due process of law, it becomes our duty to maintain this provision of the Constitution, against all attempts to violate it for the purpose of establishing slavery in any Territory of the United States, by positive legislation, prohibiting its existence or extension therein. That we deny the authority of Congress, of a Territorial Legislature, of any individual or association of individuals, to give legal existence to slavery in any Territory of the United States while the present Constitution shall be maintained.[6]

There, Mr. President, in my estimation, is the incorporation into a political platform of principles which make up an issue between the

North and the South which I fear is wholly irreconcilable. There is sectionalism in its length and breadth; and I regret to add, sectionalism largely impregnated with fanaticism. Who was the author of that platform? I think I have seen it stated recently that a distinguished gentleman, late a member of Congress from Ohio, Mr. Giddings,[7] claims the honor of having inserted this plank in the Republican platform. It is a plank in that platform worthy of that prominent man's known hostility to southern institutions. He has succeeded in incorporating a principle which, sooner or later, must result in the destruction of our Federal system of government, unless we can return, in truth and in honesty, to the real sentiments and patriotism of our fathers who framed it.

Mr. President, when the principle was incorporated into the Republican platform, there was a distinguished citizen of the State of New York, then, or soon after, a candidate for the Presidency, who spoke words of warning on this subject which it will now be of use to recur to for more purposes than one—I allude to Mr. Fillmore.[8] In his criticisms upon this party and its organization, he stated in plain, simple, and few words, the truth, the whole truth, and the end of this sectional organization. Listen to him:

> But we now see a party organized in the North for the first time selecting candidates for President and Vice President exclusively from the northern states, with the avowed intention of electing them to govern the South as well as the North.

And again:

> The North is, beyond all question, the most populous, the most wealthy, and has the most voters; and therefore has the power to inflict this injustice upon the South. But we can best judge of its consequences by reversing the case. Suppose the South was the most populous, the most wealthy, and possessed the greatest number of electoral votes; and that it should declare that, for some fancied or real injustice done at the North, it would elect none but a President and a Vice President of slaveholders from the South

to rule over the North: do you think, fellow-citizens, you would submit to this injustice? ["No!" "No!"] No, truly you would not; but one universal cry of "no!" would rend the skies! And can you suppose your southern brethren less sensitive than yourselves, or less jealous of their rights? If you do, let me tell you that you are mistaken; and you must therefore perceive that the success of such a party, with such an object, must be . . .

What?

a dissolution of the Union.

There, Mr. President, is the truth spoken in plain, unmistakable words. What is the complaint? It is that the majority of the people of one section of the Union, having the numerical power to obtain possession of the Government, form themselves into a political organization upon principles that exclude the minority section from cooperation, for the purpose of governing that minority section.

{*Senator Nicholson here elaborated on Millard Fillmore's concerns about the formation of the Republican Party and the development of its 1860 platform.*}

What, then, is it in this platform to which we take exception? The first thing is, that it recognizes the general principle that ALL men are created equal; and, in recognizing this, asserts, as a fact, that Governments are made for the purpose of securing alike the rights of life and liberty and the pursuit of happiness to the slave and to his owner.[9] That general principle, if applied in the States, would liberate four million slaves. This is a necessary deduction from the assertion of the principle of the equality of the two races. But the Republican party, I must do them the justice to say, do not in their platform make the application of this general principle to the States. They confine it to those places within which Congress has, according to the platform of 1856, "exclusive jurisdiction." Then, the position is this: you concede that in the States we have a right to enjoy this property, and you profess to be willing that this constitutional guarantee shall be maintained; yet, in so doing, you avow a principle to be applied to all other places within which Congress has jurisdiction, which principle fixes a stigma on every southern man who is the owner of a slave; which principle would, if applied, (and which, if you had the power, it is fair to infer, you would apply,) would set free every slave in the South. Without undertaking to say that this would be done without regard to other consequences than the loss of property, yet to a southern mind these other consequences are so frightful, that when a party plants itself on a principle so alarming and so destructive, if carried out into all its legitimate results, we can but feel that our security is small when all we have to repose upon is the professions of that party that it will regard our rights within the States, when the same party tells us that rights which we regard the same outside of the States, it intends to disregard. This party promises us, as the inducement to our repose, that our rights of property slaves shall not be interfered with in the States *because* the Constitution recognizes those rights. But they refuse to extend that promise to our rights of property in slaves outside of the States, although, upon the authority of the high judicial tribunal of the country for deciding constitutional questions, we have exactly the same rights outside of the States, within the jurisdiction of the Federal Government, as the owners of any other species of property have. They concede our rights in the one case, because they are expressly recognized by the Constitution; they deny them in the other, and in so doing, repudiate the authoritative adjudication of the Supreme Court.

But, suppose this general principle be carried out within those where Congress has jurisdiction: then it will be carried out in this District, for here Congress has jurisdiction; it will be carried out in the forts and arsenals, for Congress there has jurisdiction; it will be carried out in the Territories, for Congress there has jurisdiction. Suppose a State makes application for admission into the Union with the recognition of slavery in its constitution: is not that another case within your jurisdiction? And do you not stand, at least by implication from the principle you assert, pledged to reject the admission of such a State?

These are vital points with southern men. Suppose your party gets possession of both branches of Congress: then, under this platform, and under your pledge to carry out this general principle of yours, what guarantee have we, what hope have we, that this District will not at once be visited with your power? And so of the forts and arsenals within the slave States. We know that in the Territories you would at once erect an impassable barrier. We believe that you would exclude every other slave State from the Union. Will any fair-minded man deny that these measures, in their practical consequences, work not only to the prevention of the spread of slavery, but to its final extinguishment in the States where it now exists? Will any candid man deny that these principles and measures are expected and intended by the Republican party to result in the universal emancipation of the slaves?

But, Mr. President, while these measures, if carried out into practice under the feeling that you manifest, look, as we honestly believe, to a period when they will result naturally, legitimately, and necessarily, without any violence upon the Constitution, according to your mode of construing it, in the final extinction of slavery,—a more fearful aspect of the case is presented when it is remembered that, without any violation of the Constitution, the operation of these measures is to swell the already formidable disparity between the two sections, by increasing the number of free States. The same power that will enable you to carry out these measures will enable you to hasten the introduction of the free States to the number that will enable you to adopt such amendments to the Constitution as your party may desire. Is it strange to you that southern men, looking to the final catastrophe which they believe is the ultimate end of your organization, shall look to the period when you obtain the power to make these amendments as the end of the institution of slavery?

Mr. President, these, in my estimation, are the grounds on which the southern mind is now resting, and upon which the southern people have come to the settled conviction that the election of Mr. Lincoln to the Presidency, on the principles laid down in the Republican platform, is tantamount to a declaration of war against an institution which, in the South, is identified with all our interests, with all our happiness, with all our prosperity, socially, politically, and materially. This is our conviction and this conviction is strengthened when we turn to the antecedents, politically, of the candidate whom you have succeeded in electing. Against him personally, I have not a word to say. He may be all that his friends represent him, and I shall not controvert it; but the point is, is he a fair representative in his antecedents of these principles and these measures which we look upon as threatening our institutions. When I turn to his record, I find a most remarkable coincidence in all respects between his position, as deliberately and frequently repeated by him, and the principle to which I have referred as constituting the "central idea" of the platform of the Republican party. Upon a careful examination of Mr. Lincoln's sentiments, as declared again and again in his celebrated controversy, in 1858, with Judge DOUGLAS, and other speeches of his published and relied upon by his friends in the late contest, in the volume which is before me, I come to the conclusion that he entertains these opinions: He hates slavery as much as an Abolitionist hates it; he says so in so many words. He believes that the slave has the same right to be protected in his life, LIBERTY, and pursuit of *happiness*, as his owner. He believes that man cannot have property in man without his consent; that is Mr. Lincoln's "central idea," his "sheet-anchor" of Republicanism. He believes that slavery is a social, moral, and political evil. He desires its ultimate extinction. He looks to the Republican party to adopt and carry out such a policy, not inconsistent with the Constitution as he construes it, as will induce the public mind to repose on the conviction that slavery will be finally extinguished. He believes that such a policy is compatible with the continued existence of the Federal Union. He believes the Constitution can be so construed, administered, and executed, that it will be, if not the instrument, at least no obstruction to the final extinction of slavery.

Now, Mr. President, in the triumph of the Republican party they have placed in the presidential chair a President who entertains these views, in strict accordance, I agree, with the principles and sentiments which characterize his party. In all seriousness and earnestness, I ask gentlemen on the other side if it is surprising that the southern mind is moved, is disturbed, is alarmed at the triumph of a party entertaining these opinions and at the election of a candidate avowing these sentiments?

The whole impact and purport, therefore, of your triumph is plainly this: that you have formed and intend to perpetuate a political organization which must, from its principles, be confined to one section, and that the stronger section, with the avowed purpose of so construing and administering the Constitution as finally to extinguish the institution of slavery.

{*Senator Nicholson continued here with a series of questions contemplating the future of the South "under the permanent domination of the Republican party."*}

We are asked to repose quietly, because the President elect is said to be a conservative man. I do not believe he intends to violate the Constitution, as he construes it; but where is the necessity of his violating it? The measures that he proposes to carry out, and that party stand pledged to carry out, require no violation of the Constitution, as they construe that instrument, for their ultimate success. It is only a matter of time. The end may be hastened under the administration of a fanatical President, and a fanatical Congress, or it may be delayed with a more conservative President and Congress; but the result is fixed; it is inevitable. Mr. Lincoln desires to place this Government in a condition in which the public mind will repose upon the conviction that the institution of slavery is finally to be extinguished. What sort of appeal is that to southern men, whose interests and happiness are identified with this institution? What sort of appeal is it to those men in the extreme South, where not only all they have is identified with this institution and is involved in it, but where the lives of themselves and their families are constantly liable to be destroyed and sacrificed by some misguided fanatic or monomaniac, who, feeling restive and unwilling to await the slow process of the Republican mode of liberating the slaves, chooses to resort to the torch and to insurrection? Is it not a most astonishing appeal to make to them, to say to them, "We expect you to repose quietly upon the conviction that in five years, ten years, twenty years, or thirty years, all that you have is to be swept away?"

Repose is the great object desired by the South. It is essential to the peace, happiness, and prosperity of her people. To them the constant agitation of the slavery question is full of danger. It was to secure repose that the South sought for years, and with earnestness, to secure the recognition of congressional non-intervention as the established policy of the country. Although this principle has been declared by the Supreme Court to be the true intent and meaning of the Constitution, we have failed to secure repose, because the Republican party repudiated that solemn adjudication, and resolved to continue the agitation of the question until its reversal could be secured. We can never have repose until the right to hold slaves as other property is placed beyond discussion and agitation. This can only be accomplished by an express constitutional recognition of that right. It is for that reason that the South now demands this express recognition as a necessary condition to a final and satisfactory settlement of the issue between the North and the South, and to the preservation and perpetuation of the Federal Union.

{*Senator Nicholson introduced his regret that the "extreme southern States" did not delay their leaving until a general consultation could have occurred "representing fairly and honestly the sentiments of each State." Since he acknowledged that that was not going to happen, he reiterated his solution—demand—that there must be a constitutional guarantee that recognizes "distinctly and fully the right of the southern man to his slave as property."*}

Our extreme southern brethren disagree with us as to the best mode of meeting the crisis. I am willing to believe that all of us are aiming at the same end. I am not willing yet to believe that the policy adopted by them has been resorted to from a feeling of disunion *per se*; but I regard them as viewing separate secession as the best means of awaking the sentiment of the whole North, and of the whole country, to the real danger, and the importance of a satisfactory adjustment. While I differ with them in that policy, I am not prepared to pronounce judgment of censure and condemnation upon them. They are sovereign independent States. It is their right to do on this subject as their judgments dictate. But having taken their course, the duty devolves upon us who live in the middle and border States to take our course.

Our people are not prepared—at least I can speak for my own State—until every reasonable effort is exhausted, to resort to the last remedy. What, then, shall we do? In my judgment, the middle and border States have a plain duty marked out. I think it is their duty to meet together in consultation, in the most solemn manner that such consultation can be gotten up, and to present to the North their demand for guarantees on these questions. Will the North not grant them? Judging from what I see here; judging from the efforts now being made by leading organs of the Republican party to prevent even the inauguration of propositions to be submitted to the States on this question, I confess that I scarcely see a ray of hope of anything being accomplished; but if there is any hope, it is in an appeal to the people themselves. I think the middle and border States ought to make that appeal. What will that demand be? Mr. President, I am bound as a man of candor, to say that one essential feature in that guarantee must be the constitutional recognition of our right to property in slaves in the Territories; and that this right of property shall never be disturbed by any future amendment of the Constitution.

Now, I know that presents the great point of difference between us. It was the great point of difference when our Government was formed. Our fathers had patriotism enough to settle it. We have lived happily, and prosperously, and grown great under that settlement for over sixty years. Why can we not settle the same question again? Why will the northern mind refuse to do it? Is it a matter of conscience that we ask them to surrender? Was it not a matter of conscience with our fathers that slavery was a social and moral evil? And yet they could settle it. They could concede the right of property in slaves, without doing violence to their consciences. They could authorize the increase of the number of slaves by new immigrations for twenty years. They could provide for the existence of this right of property, even outside of the slave States, when the slaves escape into a free State. Will any one presume to say that our fathers were less conscientious than we are? Yet, I am told that if the recognition of our right of property in slaves be the *sine qua non* of our demand, then all is hopeless. I think that may be the sentiment of gentlemen who have ridden upon the current of sectionalism into power, and now occupy official places; but I prefer, at least, before I give up all hope, to see whether or not, on an appeal to the popular sovereignty of the North, there is not patriotism enough there again to make this concession as our fathers did, and to close up and settle forever this question of agitation between the two sections.

These, Mr. President, are my views as to our duty in the present crisis, entertained from a deep sense of their correctness, as well as from an ardent attachment to this Government, and a most determined opposition to seeing it destroyed until every reasonable effort to maintain it upon principles of justice and equality shall be exhausted.

{*Senator Nicholson concluded his speech with allusions to the "horrors of a civil war" and an appeal to a peaceful separation: "If we cannot agree to live together in harmony as brothers of one Confederacy, let us separate in peace, showing, by our justice to each other in the act of separation, that we are determined so to live as neighbors that the hope of a future reconstruction of our Confederacy, and of the resurrection at no distant day of our Federal Union to an immortality of grandeur and prosperity, may not be forever destroyed."*}

Source: *Congressional Globe*, 36th Cong. 2nd Sess., 185–89.

CHAPTER TWO

GOVERNOR ISHAM GREEN HARRIS (DEMOCRAT) ADDRESS TO THE GENERAL ASSEMBLY

January 7, 1861

Isham Green Harris was born in 1818 in Franklin County, Tennessee. He read for, and was admitted to the bar, and began practicing law in Paris, Henry County, in 1841. He quickly entered politics. First elected to the state senate, he then served two terms in the US House of Representatives from 1849 to 1853. Moving to Memphis, he ran for the governorship and was elected in 1857, 1859, and 1861. With the occupation of Nashville by United States troops in February 1862, he joined the Confederate Army of Tennessee as a volunteer aide and served until the end of the war.[1] In 1865, the general assembly declared him guilty of treason whereupon he fled to Mexico and then England, returning in 1867. In 1877, Harris was elected to the US Senate, a position he held until his death in 1897.

In this speech to Tennessee's general assembly, Governor Harris reiterated many of the standard charges against the northern states, Republican Party, and abolitionists. The "antislavery cloud" had grown to "colossal proportions" and threatened the security of Tennessee and the South. He reminded the assembled that while slaves were recognized as property in the Constitution, the "distempered public opinion" in the North was "deliberately nullifying and setting at defiance" the constitutional requirement for returning fugitive slaves. To ignore the long list of aggressions against the institution of slavery would be fatal. "The people of the South must prepare either to abandon it, or to fortify and maintain it." Not wanting to recommend secession without an attempt at compromise, Harris proposed a constitutional amendment of five parts designed to protect slavery across the New Mexico Territory, in the District of Columbia, and in federal installations throughout the slave-owning states. He advocated strengthening the fugitive slave clause, and allowing slave owners safe passage while traveling—"temporarily sojourning"—through any of the states in the Union. Barring the adoption of this amendment, Harris lectured, "there is no hope of peace or security in the government." The governor ended his address by warning against the potential for military aggression on the part of the incoming Lincoln administration against the seceding states. Any attempt upon the part of the federal government to hold "an unwilling sovereignty as a member of a common Union, must inevitably lead to the worst form of internecine war."

Gentlemen of the Senate, and House of Representatives:

The ninth section of the third article of the Constitution, provides that, on extraordinary occasions, the Governor may convene the General Assembly. Believing the emergency contemplated, to exist at this time, I have called you together. In welcoming you to the capitol of the State, I can but regret the gloomy auspices under which we meet. Grave and momentous issues have arisen, which, to an unprecedented degree, agitate the public mind and imperil the perpetuity of the Government.

The systematic, wanton, and long continued agitation of the slavery question, with the actual and threatened aggressions of the Northern States and a portion of their people, upon the well-defined constitutional rights of the Southern citizen; the rapid growth and increase, in all the elements of power, of a purely sectional party, whose bond of union is uncompromising hostility to the rights and institutions of the fifteen Southern States, have produced a crisis in the affairs of the country, unparalleled in the history of the past, resulting already in the withdrawal from the Confederacy of one of the sovereignties which compose it, while others are rapidly preparing to move in the same direction. Fully appreciating the importance of the duties which devolve upon you, fraught, as your action must be, with consequences of the highest possible importance to the people of Tennessee, knowing that, as a great Commonwealth, our own beloved State is alike interested with her sisters, who have resorted, and are preparing to resort, to this fearful alternative. I have called you together for the purpose of calm and dispassionate deliberation, earnestly trusting, as the chosen representatives of a free and enlightened people, that you will, at this critical juncture of our affairs, prove yourselves equal to the occasion which has called for the exercise of your talent and patriotism.

A brief review of the history of the past is necessary to a proper understanding of the issues presented for your consideration.

Previous to the adoption of the Federal Constitution, each State was a separate Government—a complete sovereignty within itself—and in the compact of union, each reserved all the rights and powers incident to sovereignty, except such as were expressly delegated by the Constitution to the General Government, or such as were clearly incident, and necessary, to the exercise of some expressly delegated power.

The Constitution distinctly recognizes property in *slaves*—makes it the duty of the States to deliver the fugitive to his owner, but contains no grant of power to the Federal Government to interfere with this species of property, except "the power coupled with the duty," common to all civil Governments, to protect the rights of *property*, as well as those of *life* and *liberty*, of the citizen, which clearly appears from the exposition given to that instrument by the Supreme Court of the United States in the case of Dred Scott *vs*. Sandford. In delivering the opinion of the Court, Chief Justice Taney said:

"Now, as we have already said in an earlier part of this opinion, upon a different point, *the right of property in a slave is distinctly and expressly affirmed in the Constitution.*

"And no word can be found in the Constitution which gives Congress a greater power over slave property, or which entitles property of that kind to less protection than property of any other description. *The only power confirmed, is the power coupled with the duty, of guarding and protecting the owner in his rights.*"

This decision of the highest judicial tribunal, known to our Government, settles the question, beyond the possibility of doubt, that slave property rests upon the same basis, and is entitled to the same protection, as every other description of property, that the General Government has no power to circumscribe or confine it within any given boundary; to determine where it shall, or shall not exist, or in any manner to impair its value. And certainly it will not be contended, in this enlightened age, that any member of the Confederacy can exercise higher powers, in this respect, beyond the limits of its own boundary, than those delegated to the General Government.

The States entered the Union upon terms of perfect political equality, each delegating certain powers to the General Government, but neither delegating any power to the other to interfere with its reserved rights or domestic affairs; hence, there is no power on earth which can rightfully determine whether slavery shall or shall not exist within the limits of any State, except the people thereof acting in their highest sovereign capacity. The attempt of the Northern people, through the instrumentality of the Federal Government—their State governments, and emigrant aid societies—to confine this species of property within the limits of the present Southern States—to impair its value by constant agitation and refusal to deliver up the fugitive— to appropriate the whole of the Territories, which are the common property of all the people of all the States, to themselves; by excluding therefrom every Southern man who is unwilling to live under a government which may by law recognize the free negro as his equal; "and in fine, to put the question where the Northern mind will rest in the belief of its ultimate extinction," is justly regarded by the people of the Southern States as a gross and palpable violation of the spirit and obvious meaning of the compact of Union—an impertinent inter-meddling with their domestic affairs, destructive of fraternal feeling, ordinary comity, and well defined rights.

As slavery receded from the North, it was followed by the most violent and fanatical opposition. At first the anti-slavery cloud, which now overshadows the nation, was no larger than a man's hand. Most of you can remember, with vivid distinctness, those days of brotherhood, when throughout the whole North, the abolitionist was justly regarded as an enemy of his country. Weak, diminutive and contemptible as was this party in the purer days of the Republic, it has now grown to colossal proportions, and its recent rapid strides to power, have given it possession of the present House of Representatives, and elected one of its leaders to the Presidency of the United States; and in the progress of events, the Senate and Supreme Court must also soon pass into the hands of this party—a party upon whose revolutionary banner is inscribed, "No more slave States, no more slave Territory, no return of the fugitive to his master"—an "irrepressible conflict" between the Free and Slave States; "and whether it be long or short, peaceful or bloody, the struggle shall go on, until the sun shall not rise upon a master or set upon a slave."[2]

Nor is this all; it seeks to appropriate to itself, and to exclude the slaveholder from the territory acquired by the common blood and treasure of all the States.

It has, through the instrumentality of Emigrant Aid Societies, under State patronage, flooded the Territories with its minions armed with Sharp's rifles and bowie knives, seeking thus to accomplish, by intimidation, violence and murder, what it could not do by constitutional legislation.

It demanded, and from our love of peace and devotion to the Union, unfortunately extorted in 1819–'20, a concession which excluded the South from about half the territory acquired from France.[3]

It demanded, and again received, as a peace offering in 1845, all of that part of Texas, North of 36°30' North latitude, if at any time the interest of the people thereof shall require a division of her territory.[4]

It would submit to nothing less than a compromise in 1850, by which it dismembered that State, and remanded a territorial condition a considerable portion of its territory South of 36 30.[5]

It excluded, by the same Compromise, the Southern people from California, whose mineral wealth, fertility of soil, and salubrity of climate, is not surpassed on earth; by prematurely forcing her into the Union under a Constitution, conceived in fraud by a set of adventurers, in the total absence of any law authorizing the formation of a Constitution, fixing the qualifications of voters, regulating the time, place, or manner of electing delegates, or the time or place of a meeting of such Convention.[6] Yet all these irregular and unauthorized proceedings were sanctified by the fact that the Constitution prohibited slavery, and forever closed the doors of that rich and desirable territory against the Southern people. And while the Southern mind was still burning under a humiliating sense of this wrong, it refused to admit Kansas into the Union upon a Constitution, framed by authority of Congress, and by delegates elected in conformity to law, upon the ground that slavery was recognized and protected.[7]

It claims the constitutional right to abolish slavery in the District of Columbia, the forts, arsenals, dock-yards and other places ceded to the United States, within the limits of slaveholding States. It proposes a prohibition of the slave trade between States, thereby crowding the slaves together and preventing their exit South, until they become unprofitable to an extent that will force the owner finally to abandon them in self-defence.

It has, by the deliberate legislative enactment of a large majority of the Northern States, openly and flagrantly nullified that clause of the Constitution which provides—

"No person held to service or labor in one State under the laws thereof, escaping into another, shall, in consequence of any law or regulation therein, be discharged from such service or labor, but shall be delivered up on claim of the party to whom such service or labor may be due."

This provision of the Constitution has been spurned and trampled under foot by these "higher law" nullifiers.[8] It is utterly powerless for good, since all attempts to enforce the Fugitive Slave Law under it, are made a felony in some of these States, a high misdemeanor in others, and punishable in all by heavy fines and imprisonment.[9] The distempered public opinion of these localities having risen above the Constitution and all other law, planting itself upon the anarchical doctrines of the *"higher law,"* with impunity defies the Government, tramples upon our rights, and plunders the Southern citizen.

It has, through the Governor of Ohio, as openly nullified that part of the Constitution which provides that—

"A person charged in any State with treason, felony or other crime, who shall flee from justice and be found in another State, shall, on demand of the executive authority of the State from which he fled, be delivered up, to be removed to the State having jurisdiction of the crime."

In discharge of official duty, I had occasion, within the past year, to demand of the Governor of Ohio, *a person charged in the State (of Tennessee) with the crime" of slave stealing*, who had fled from justice and was found in the State of Ohio. The Governor refused to issue his warrant for the arrest and delivery of the fugitive, and in answer to a letter of inquiry which I addressed to him, said: "The crime of negro stealing, not being known to either the common law or the criminal code of Ohio, it is not of that class of crimes contemplated by the Federal Constitution, for the commission of which I am authorized, as the executive of Ohio, to surrender a fugitive from the justice of a sister State, and hence I declined to issue a warrant," &c; thus deliberately nullifying and setting at defiance the clause of the Constitution above quoted, as well as the act of Congress of February 12th, 1793, and grossly violating the ordinary comity existing between separate and independent nations, much less the comity which should exist between sister States of the same great Confederacy, the correspondence connected with which is herewith transmitted.

It has, through the executive authority of other States, denied extradition of murderers and marauders.

It obtained its own compromise in the Constitution to continue the importation of slaves, and now sets up a law, higher than the Constitution, to destroy this property imported and sold to us by their fathers.

It has caused the murder of owners in pursuit of their fugitive slaves, and shielded the murderers from punishment.

It has, upon many occasions, sent its emissaries into the Southern States to corrupt our slaves, induce them to run off, or excite them to insurrection.

It has run off slave property by means of the "under-ground railroad," amounting in value to millions of dollars, and thus made the tenure by which slaves are held in the border States so precarious as to materially impair their value.

It has, by its John Brown and Montgomery[10] raids, invaded sovereign States and murdered peaceable citizens.

It has justified and "exalted to the highest honors of administration, the horrid murders, arsons, and rapine of the John Brown raid, and has canonized the felons as saints and martyrs."

It has burned the towns, poisoned the cattle, and conspired with the slaves to depopulate Northern Texas.

It has, through certain leaders, proclaimed to the slaves the terrible motto, "Alarm to the sleep, fire to the dwellings, poison to the food and water of slaveholders."

It has repudiated and denounced the decision of the Supreme Court.

It has assailed our rights as guaranteed by the plainest provisions of the Constitution, from the floor of each house of Congress, the pulpit, the hustings, the school room, their State Legislatures, and through the public press, dividing and disrupting churches, political parties, and civil governments.

It has, in the person of the President elect, asserted the equality of the *black* with the *white race.*

These are some of the wrongs against which we have remonstrated for more than a quarter of a century, hoping, but in vain, for their redress, until some of our sister States, in utter despair of obtaining justice at the hands of these lawless confederates, have resolved to sever the ties which have bound them together, and maintain those rights out of the Union, which have been the object of constant attack and encroachment within it.

No one will assert that the Southern States or people have, at any time, failed to perform, fully and in good faith, all of the duties which the Constitution devolves upon them.

Nor will it be pretended that they have, at any time, encroached or attempted aggression upon the rights of a Northern sister State.

The Government was for many years under the control of Southern Statesmen, but in originating and perfecting measures of policy, be it said to the perpetual honor of the South, she has never attempted to encroach upon a single constitutional right of the North. The journals of Congress will not show even the introduction of a single proposition, by any Southern Representative, calculated to impair her rights in property, injure her trade, or wound her sensibilities. Nor have they at any time demanded at the hands of the Federal Government, or Northern States, more than their well defined rights under the Constitution. So far from it, they have tolerated those wrongs, from a feeling of loyalty and devotion to the Union, with a degree of patience and forbearance unparalleled in the history of a brave and free people. Moreover, they have quietly submitted to a revenue system which indirectly, but certainly, taxes the products of slave labor some fifty or sixty millions of dollars annually, to increase the manufacturing profits of those who have thus persistently and wickedly assailed them.

To evade the issue thus forced upon us at this time, without the fullest security for our rights, is, in my opinion, fatal to the institution of slavery forever. The time has arrived when the people of the South must prepare either to abandon or to fortify and maintain it. Abandon it, we cannot, interwoven as it is with our wealth, prosperity and domestic happiness. We owe it to the mechanic whose shop is closed, to the multiplied thousands of laborers thrown out of employment, to the trader made bankrupt by this agitation. We owe it to ourselves, our children, our self-respect and equality in the Government, to have this question settled permanently and forever upon terms consistent with justice and honor, and which will give us peace and perfect security for the present and the future.

Palliatives and opiates, in the character of legislative compromises, may be applied, affording momentary relief; but there will be no permanent safety, security, or peace, until Northern prejudice has been eradicated, and the public sentiment of that section radically changed and nationalized. To attempt the application of effective remedies before this great object has been accomplished, is like cleansing the stream while the fountain itself is poisoned.

The consequences and immense interests which are involved in the proper solution of the difficulties that surround us, the deep, lasting and vital importance of settling them upon principles of justice and equality, demand the most serious consideration of the whole people, as well as that of the public functionaries of the State. Whilst I cheerfully submit to your discretion the whole question of our federal relations, having no doubt myself as to the necessity and propriety of calling a State Convention, yet I respectfully recommend that you provide by law for submitting to the people of the State, the question of *Convention*, or *No Convention*, and also for the election of delegates by the people, in the ratio of legislative representation, to meet in State Convention, at the Capitol, at Nashville, at the earliest day practicable, to take into consideration our federal relations, and determine what action shall be taken by the State of Tennessee for the security of the rights and the peace of her citizens.

The question of *Convention* or *No Convention*, can and should be determined and the delegates chosen at the same election, which can be very easily accomplished by heading one set of tickets CONVENTION, and another set NO CONVENTION. If a majority of the people vote for Convention, then the persons receiving the largest number of votes in their respective counties and districts, to be commissioned as delegates.

This will place the whole matter in the hands of the people, for them, in their sovereignty, to determine how far their rights have been violated, the character of the redress or guaranty they will demand, or the action they will take for their present and future security.

If there be a remedy for the evils which afflict the country, consistent with the perpetuity of the Union, it will, in my opinion, be found in such constitutional amendments as will deprive the fanatical majorities of the North of the power to invade our rights or impair the security or value of our property.

Clear and well defined as our rights are, under the present Constitution, to participate equally with the citizens of all other States in the settlement of the common Territories, and to hold our slaves there until excluded by the formation of a State Constitution, yet every organized Territory will become a field of angry, if not bloody, strife between the Southern man and the Abolitionist, and we shall see the tragedies of Kansas re-enacted in each of them, as they approach the period of forming their State Constitutions.

Plain and unmistakable as is the duty of each State, to deliver up the fugitive slave to his owner, yet the attempt to reclaim, is at the peril of the master's life.

These evils can be obviated to a great extent, if not entirely, by the following amendments to the Constitution:

1st. Establish a line upon the Northern boundary of the present Slave States, and extend it through the Territories to the Pacific Ocean, upon such parallel of latitude as will divide them equitably between the North and South, expressly providing that all the territory now owned or that may be hereafter acquired North of that line, shall be forever free, and all South of it, *forever* slave. This will remove the question of existence or non-existence of slavery in our States and Territories entirely and forever from the arena of politics. The question being settled by the Constitution, is no longer open for the politician to ride into position by appealing to fanatical prejudices, or assailing the rights of his neighbors.

2d. In addition to the fugitive slave clause provide, that when a slave has been demanded of the Executive authority of the State to which he has fled, if he is not delivered, and the owner permitted to carry him out of the State in peace, that the State so failing to deliver, shall pay to the owner double the value of such slave, and secure his right of action in the Supreme Court of the United States. This will secure the return of the slave to his owner, or his value, with a sufficient sum to indemnify him for the expenses necessarily incident to the recovery.

3d. Provide for the protection of the owner in the peaceable possession of his slave while in transit, or temporarily sojourning in any of the States of the Confederacy; and in the event of the slave's escape or being taken from the owner, require the State to return, or account for him as in case of the fugitive.

4th. Expressly prohibit Congress from abolishing slavery in the

District of Columbia, in any dock yard, navy yard, arsenal, or district of any character whatever, within the limits of any slave State.

5th. That these provisions shall never be changed, except by the consent of all the slave States.

With these amendments to the Constitution, I should feel that our rights were reasonably secure, not only in theory, but in fact, and should indulge the hope of living in the Union in peace. Without these, or some other amendments, which promise an equal amount and certainty of security, there is no hope of peace or security in the government.

If the non-slaveholding States refuse to comply with a demand, so just and reasonable; refuse to abandon at once and forever their unjust war upon us, our institutions and our rights; refuse, as they have heretofore done, to perform, in good faith, the obligations of the compact of union, much as we may appreciate the power, prosperity, greatness, and glory of this government; deeply as we deplore the existence of causes which have already driven one State from the Union; much as we may regret the imperative necessity which they have wantonly and wickedly forced upon us, every consideration of self-preservation and self-respect require that we should assert and maintain our "equality in the Union, or independence out of it."

In my opinion, the only mode left us of perpetuating the Union upon the principles of justice and equality, upon which it was originally established, is by the Southern States, identified as they are, in interest, sentiment and feeling, and must, in the natural course of events, share a common destiny, uniting in the expression of a fixed and unalterable resolve, that the rights guaranteed by the Constitution must be *respected*, and *fully* and *perfectly* secured in the present Government, or asserted and maintained in the homogenous Confederacy of Southern States.

Mere questions of policy may be very often properly compromised, but there can be no compromise of cardinal and vital principles; no compromise between *right* and *wrong*. Principle must be vindicated, and right triumphant, be the consequences what they may. To compromise the one, or abandon the other, is not only unmanly and humiliating in the extreme, but always disastrous in its final results.

The South has no power to re-unite the scattered fragments of a violated Constitution and a once glorious government. She is acting on the defensive. She has been driven to the wall, and can submit to no further aggression. The North, however, *can* restore the Constitutional Union of our fathers, by undoing their work of alienation and hate, engendering thirty years of constant aggression, and by unlearning the lessons of malignant hostility to the South, and her institutions, with which their press, pulpit and schools have persistently infected the public mind.

Let them do this, and peace will again establish her court in the midst of this once happy country, and the union of these States be restored to that spirit of fraternity, equality and justice, which gave it birth.

Let them do this, and the vitality which has been crushed out of the Constitution may be restored, giving renewed strength and vigor to the body politic.

But can we hope for such results? Two months have already passed, since the development of facts which make the perpetuity of the Union depend, *alone*, upon their giving to the South satisfactory guarantees for her chartered rights. Yet, there has been no proposition at all satisfactory, made by any member of the dominant and aggressive party of that section. So far from it, their Senators and Representatives in Congress, have voted down and spurned every proposition that looked to the accomplishment of this object, no matter whence emanating; and the fact, that their constituencies have, in no authoritative manner, issued words of rebuke or warning to them, must be taken as conclusive proof of their acquiescence in the policy.

In view of those facts, I cannot close my eyes to the conclusion, that Tennessee will be powerless in any efforts she may make to quell the storm that pervades the country. The work of alienation and disruption has gone so far, that it will be extremely difficult, if not impossible, to arrest it; and before your adjournment, in all human probability, the only practical question for the State to determine, will be whether she will unite her fortunes with a Northern or Southern Confederacy; upon which question, when presented, I am certain there can be little or no division in sentiment, identified as we are in every respect with the South.

If this calamity shall befall the country, the South will have the consolation of knowing that she is in no manner responsible for the disaster. The responsibility rests alone upon the Northern people, who have willfully broken the bond of Union, repudiated the obligations and duties which it imposes, and only cling to its benefits. Yet even in this dark hour of responsibility and peril let no man countenance the idea for a moment, that the dissolution of the Federal Union reduces the country to anarchy, or proves the theory of self-government to be a failure. Such conclusions would be not only erroneous but unworthy of ourselves and our revolutionary ancestry while our State governments exist possessing all the machinery, perfect and complete, which is necessary to the purposes of civil government, just as they existed before the Union was formed.

The sages and patriots of the revolution, when in the act of severing their connection with the mother country, and establishing the great cardinal principles of free government, solemnly declared that governments were instituted among men to secure their rights "to life, liberty, and the pursuit of happiness; deriving their just powers from the consent of the governed; that whenever any form of government becomes destructive of these ends, it is the right of the people to alter or abolish it, and to institute new government, laying its foundation on such principles, and organizing its powers in such form, as to them shall seem most likely to effect their safety and happiness. * * * * But when a long train of abuses and usurpations, pursuing invariably the same object, evinces a design to reduce them under absolute despotism, it is their right, it is their duty, to throw off such government, and to provide new guards for their future security."

Recognizing these great principles, the people of Tennessee incorporated in their declaration of rights, as a fundamental article of the Constitution of the State, "That government being instituted for the common benefit, the doctrine of non-resistance against arbitrary power and oppression is absurd, slavish, and destructive of the good and happiness of mankind."

Whatever line of policy may be adopted by the people of Tennessee, with regard to the present Federal relations of the State, I am sure that the swords of her brave and gallant men will never be drawn for the purpose of coercing, subjugating, or holding as a conquered province, any one of her sister States, whose *people* may declare their independence of the Federal Government, for the purpose of being relieved from "a long train of abuses and usurpations." To admit the right or policy of coercion, would be untrue to the example of our fathers and the glorious memories of the past, destructive of those great and fundamental principles of civil liberty, purchased with their blood; destructive of State sovereignty and equality; tending to centralization, and thus subject the rights of the minority to the despotism of an unrestrained majority.

Widely as we may differ with some of our sister Southern States as to the wisdom of their policy; desirous as we may be that whatever action taken in this emergency, should be taken by the South as a unit; hopeful as we may be of finding some remedy for our grievances consistent with the perpetuity of the present Confederacy, the question, at last, is one which each member of that Confederacy must determine for itself, and any attempt upon the part of the others to hold, by means of a military force, an unwilling sovereignty as a member of a common Union, must inevitably lead to the worst form of internecine war, and if successful, result in the establishment of a new and totally different Government from the one established by the Constitution— the Constitutional Union being a Union of *consent* and not of *force*, of *peace*, and not of *blood*—composed of sovereignties, free, and politically equal. But the new and coercive Government, while it would "derive its powers" to govern a portion of the States "*from the consent of the governed*," would derive the power by which it governed the remainder, from the *cannon and the sword*, and not from their *consent*—a Union, not of equals, but of the victors and the vanquished, pinned together by the bayonet and congealed in blood.

I devoutly trust that a merciful Providence may avert such a calamity, and believe that there is no respectable portion of our people, whatever may be their differences of opinion upon other questions, who are so blind to reason, or so lost to patriotism and every sentiment of civil liberty, as to give countenance to a policy so fatal in its results, and so revolting to every sentiment of humanity.

While I sincerely trust that Tennessee may never be driven to the desperate alternative of appealing to arms in defence of the rights of her people, I nevertheless deem it proper, in view of the present excited state of the public mind and unsettled condition of the country, to call your attention to the fact that, with the exception of a small number of volunteer companies, we have no military organization in the State, the militia have disorganized immediately after the repeal of the law which required drills and public parades. Independent of the impending crisis, I regard a thorough reorganization of the militia as imperatively demanded by every consideration of prudence and safety. I therefore submit the question to your consideration, with the earnest hope that you will adopt such plan of organization as will secure to the State at all times, and under all circumstances, an efficient and reliable military force.

I am unable, in the absence of full reports from the clerks of the several counties, to inform you as to the military strength of the State. Such reports as have been made to this department shall be laid before you. I do not doubt, however, that the military strength of the State may be safely estimated at one hundred and twenty thousand men.

It is proper, in this connection, that I call your attention to the report of John Heriges, Keeper of Public Arms, herewith transmitted, showing the number, character and condition of the public arms of the State, and respectfully recommend that you provide for the purchase of such number and character of arms, for the use of the State, as may be necessary to thoroughly arm an efficient military force.

{*Here Harris noted that because of crop failures, destruction of commercial confidence, general stagnation in the trade and financial areas, many banks had suspended specie payment. The governor did not offer a solution, but asked the legislature to consider a proper response.*}

I am aware that there are many questions of a general character with regard to which the constituents of many of you desire legislation, but having convened you in extraordinary session, upon what I conceived to be an extraordinary occasion in the history of the country, and feeling the necessity of prompt and immediate action upon the absorbing questions connected with the political crisis of the day, I have intentionally avoided submitting any others than those to which I have especially called attention, trusting that no material interest will suffer by being postponed until the next regular session of the General Assembly.

With the earnest hope that your session may be short and agreeable, and devoutly trusting that an All Wise Providence may watch over your deliberations and guide and direct you in the adoption of such measures as will redound to the general welfare, peace, prosperity, and glory of our State and country, the questions, fraught as they are with weighty responsibilities and fearfully important consequences, are respectfully committed to your hands.

Source: *Senate Journal of the Extra Session of the Thirty-Third General Assembly of the State of Tennessee, Which Convened at Nashville, on the First Monday in January, A. D. 1861* (Nashville: J. O. Griffith and Company, Public Printers, 1861), 6–19.

CHAPTER THREE

Tennessee General Assembly Resolutions

January 1861

Throughout the legislative session of the Thirty-Third General Assembly, numerous representatives and senators offered resolutions intended to guide the deliberations of the legislature. Some suggested that secession was not the correct response to the Republican position on slavery or to Lincoln's electoral victory. Others, envisioning a not-too-distant attack upon the institution of slavery by the victorious party, called for immediate secession based solely on the election of a Republican to the presidency. Representative John G. McCabe from Cannon County, for example, cautioned against a rush to separation arguing that our "complaint is not against the Federal Government, but against the nullifying [northern] States." At the other end of the spectrum sat Dr. James L. Thompson, representing Smith and Sumner Counties, who insisted that Lincoln's election was sufficient reason to secede based as it was (in his view) upon the Republican Party's objectives of "the ultimate extinction of African slavery, and the equality of the negro with the white man." The resolutions reproduced below constitute a representative sample of the different political views proposed during the session.

Representative George Vernon Hebb, Lincoln County Middle Tennessee (Democrat)

January 8, 1861

George V. Hebb (1823–1896) was a farmer from Mulberry, Lincoln County, who had served in the Mexican War. In 1849 he married Jane Rochester Yell, whose father had been the second governor of Arkansas, Archibald Yell. Hebb was elected to the Thirty-Third General Assembly as a Democrat; during the war he served in the Confederate Army.

Mr. Hebb introduced House Resolution, No. 4, as follows:

WHEREAS, The election of a sectional President of the United States, whose principles are avowed hostility to the institutions of the South, and whose associates have proclaimed that free and slave labor cannot exist under the same government, and that there always shall be an irrepressible conflict between the two; and that no more territory shall be admitted as a State that tolerates slavery, although the people may desire it, thereby debarring us of equal right in this Confederacy. It is with deep and solemn sorrow that these truths are no longer to be denied; therefore,

Be it resolved by the General Assembly of the State of Tennessee, That the following resolutions be recommended to the people of the State of Tennessee, and to our sister States in the South:

1. That the time has come when the South as one people, having one destiny and one interest, should come together, as a unit, for the purpose of making preparations to meet the crisis which may occur by depriving us of our rights.

2. That we recommend to all the Southern States, that there be a Southern Congress, which shall meet in Huntsville, Alabama, on the first Monday in March, 1861, and that each Congressional District be entitled to one member of Congress, and on the assembling of the same, they shall delegate some central place as a permanent seat of Government for the South. That the Constitution of the United States

shall be the basis upon which the Government shall be formed—with a Legislature and Senatorial branch—the Senators to be elected by the States for the term of four years; upon the assembling of a Congress, they shall elect a President and Vice-President, who shall retain their places as President and Vice-President until a regular election shall be held, which shall be designated by said Congress. The President and Vice President shall be elected for the term of four years, and shall be forever ineligible to hold office as President of the same.

3. That we recommend that each State pledge itself to abide by whatever act may be passed by the Congress, and that appropriation be made by each State to pay its proportional part of all appropriations made by the said Congress, in building a National State House, and any other buildings which may be needed.

4. That one of the objects of Congress shall be to raise an army and navy, such as may be deemed sufficient for the protection of said Southern States, and for the further purpose of erecting armories, foundries, magazines, and camp and garrison equippage, which may be needed for said army.

5. That the sum of $—— be appropriated to carry out any appropriations that may be made by said Congress; the Governor of the State is directed to draw on the Treasurer for the same, and that our members of Congress be allowed $8 per diem, with the same mileage that is now allowed members of the General Assembly of the State of Tennessee.

6. That the said Congress send Commissioners to Washington, to get an act passed by the Congress of the United States, to convey forever their proportional part of the territory to the said Southern States, to be completely under their control, the South obligating herself to convey the like amount of territory to be brought in as a State, whenever they have a population of 133,000, and conform in every other respect with the Constitution of the United States.

7. That the object of forming said Confederacy is not for the purpose of interfering with the laws of the General Government, as long as they keep within the limits of the Constitution of the United States, and not interfere with our rights.

8. That the Governor of Tennessee be directed to appoint immediately, one Commissioner to each Southern State, with the request that their proposition be laid before their Legislatures and Conventions, and that said Commissioner get an expression of the States they may be sent to, whether said Southern States will agree to said arrangement.

Source: *House Journal of the Extra Session of the Thirty-Third General Assembly of the State of Tennessee, Which Convened at Nashville on the First Monday in January, A. D. 1861* (Nashville: J. O. Griffith and Company, Public Printers, 1861), 24–25.

REPRESENTATIVE WILLIAM H. WISENER, BEDFORD COUNTY MIDDLE TENNESSEE (OPPOSITIONIST)
January 8, 1861

William H. Wisener (1812–1882) was a sometime editor of the Shelbyville Peoples Advocate, *an attorney, and farmer. He was elected to the Thirty-Third General Assembly as an Opposition Party candidate.*

Mr. Wisener introduced Resolutions, No. 6, 7 and 8, as follows:

WHEREAS, There are difficulties and dangers existing and impending which threaten the overthrow of the Government, and upon which it may be expected the Legislature of Tennessee should express an opinion; be it, therefore,

Resolved by the General Assembly of the State of Tennessee, That secession is unconstitutional, and a remedy for no existing evil.

Resolved further, That nullification is equally unconstitutional, and tends only to mischief and anarchy.

Resolved further, That the government of the United States is adequate to the protection of all our rights, when properly administered; it should, therefore, be maintained in all its vigor within its constitutional sphere.

Resolved further, That impeachment under the Constitution and the ballot-box are the proper and constitutional remedies against unfaithful or incompetent public officers.

No. 7, as follows:

Resolved, That it is inexpedient, at this time, calling a Convention of the State upon the plan proposed in the Governor's message, or upon any other plan, or for any purpose whatever,

No. 8, as follows:

Resolved, That it is inexpedient to pass any law at this time to organize or arm the militia of the State.

Source: *House Journal of the Extra Session of the Thirty-Third General Assembly of the State of Tennessee, Which Convened at Nashville on the First Monday in January, A. D. 1861* (Nashville: J. O. Griffith and Company, Public Printers, 1861), 25–26.

Representative Joseph J. Beaty,
Giles County
Middle Tennessee (Democrat)
January 8, 1861

Dr. Joseph J. Beaty (1820–1872) studied medicine at the University of Nashville and was elected to the Thirty-Third General Assembly as a Democrat. During the war he enlisted as a corporal in the Confederate Army.

Mr. Beaty introduced House Resolution No. 10, as follows:

WHEREAS the federal Constitution was adopted by the several States, in their separate and sovereign capacity, for the purposes of mutual advantage and protection, and the several States, in assenting to the same, delegated to the General Government certain specified powers, expressly reserving to the States all other powers not thus delegated to the Federal Government, and when the government thus formed shall cease to perform its functions, or fail to accomplish the end for which it was established, then it is the right, as well as the duty, of the several States, parties to the contract, to resume the powers thus delegated for their own mutual protection and safety.

Whereas the institution of African slavery existed prior to the adoption of the federal Constitution, and was expressly recognized in that instrument, and was so understood at the time of its adoption, and any act on the part of the General Government calculated to impair its efficacy, or destroy its validity, directly or indirectly, in any of the States where it does now or may hereafter exist, is a palpable infraction of the original compact, which should be met by a stern and unqualified resistence on the part of the Southern States.

Whereas the people of the non-slaveholding States have assumed a revolutionary position towards the people of the slave-holding States, in waging a relentless war against the institution of slavery, and the right of the master to property in his slave, for the last forty years:

They have set at defiance the provision of the Constitution which provides for the rendition of fugitive slaves escaping from one State into another:

They have enticed our slaves from us, and by State legislation and mob violence prevented their return:

They continue to agitate the question of slavery, with the view of depreciating the value of that species of property:

They have encouraged a hostile invasion of a sister State whereby her unoffending citizens have been murdered, and, to add insult to injury, they publicly proclaim the author of this atrocious deed a martyr in a just and holy cause:

They have encouraged secret emissaries to come among us with the view of enticing our slaves to rebellion, thus endangering both our lives and property; and last, but not least,

They elected a President upon purely sectional principles; in the language of Mr. Bell, "in utter disregard of consequences," whose only recommendation for this elevated position, according to Mr. Douglas, in his speech at Chicago, July 9th, 1858, consists of his "bold advocacy of a war of sections—a war of the North against the South, of Free

States against Slave States—a war of extermination, to be continued relentlessly until one or the other shall be subdued." Therefore, be it

Resolved 1. That we regard the election of A. Lincoln and Hannibal Hamlin, as President and Vice President of the United States, representing, as they do, the avowed policy of the Black Republican party, to prohibit the extension of slavery into any of the territories belonging to the government, thus circumscribing it to its present limits, thereby insuring its speedy and final extinction, as being utterly incompatible with the safety of the southern States in the Union, without additional guarantees.

2d. We hold that the territories acquired by the common blood and common treasure, are the common property of all the people of all the States of this Union, and that every citizen of the United States has a clear constitutional right to go into said territories, and carry with him any kind of property recognized by the Constitution, slaves included, and that it is the duty of the government to afford such protection for every species of property, during the territorial existence, as may be necessary for the enjoyment of the same; and that neither Congress nor the territorial Legislature have any power, under the Constitution, to impair the right of the owner to his property.

3d. That we have implicit confidence in the guarantees of the federal Constitution, when faithfully and fairly executed, and are willing to comply with all its requirements, still, we cannot bear its burdens, unless we can be the recipients of its bounty; and if the Black Republican party shall insist upon our unconditional submission to its unjust and aggressive demands, then it will become the imperative duty of Tennesseans to assert their rights in the Union if possible, but failing in this, they will not stop to count the cost, but will assert and maintain them at all hazards and to the last extremity, even though it should result in a disruption of the Federal Union.

4. That several of the non-slaveholding States, with the view of obstructing the operation of the fugitive slave law, have passed so called personal liberty laws, which are in palpable violation of that clause of the Constitution, which provides for the rendition of fugitive slaves,

and as a matter of constitutional right, we demand their unconditional repeal.

5. We respectfully suggest, that the people of the slaveholding States, through their appointed representatives, meet in general conference as soon as practicable, and present to the people of the northern States a clear and concise statement of the questions in issue, and if the latter shall refuse to concede us our constitutional rights, then we can consistently take leave of a Union "known to us only by the insults it has sanctioned, and the wrongs it has legalized."

6. That in recommending a conference of all the southern States, we do not regard such a cause as indispensably necessary, for we recognize the right of the several States, in the language of the Kentucky Resolutions of 1798–99, "to judge for themselves of the infractions of the compact, as well as the mode and manner of redress."

7. That while we regret the hasty action on the part of the people of South Carolina, in separating from her sister States in this critical juncture of affairs, still, we will resist, to the last extremity, any action on the part of the federal government, tending to use force or violence to bring them into subjugation.

8. We have read with profound regret, the late speech of the Hon. Andrew Johnson, delivered in the Senate of the United States, in which he not only denies the right of a State peacefully to secede from the Union, but invokes the powers of the federal government to coerce the people of South Carolina into submission.[1] Believing as we do, that such sentiments will find no response among the majority of the people of Tennessee, and feeling the necessity of having representatives in the counsels of the nation who will reflect the will of the people, in this, our day of trial, we, the representatives of the people of the State of Tennessee, in their General Assembly, do respectfully request the Hon. Andrew Johnson to resign his seat in the United States Senate, in order that his place may be filled by one who knows our rights, and will dare defend them;

Which resolutions, under the rule, lie over one day.

Source: *House Journal of the Extra Session of the Thirty-Third General Assembly of the State of Tennessee, Which Convened at Nashville on the First Monday in January, A. D. 1861* (Nashville: J. O. Griffith and Company, Public Printers, 1861), 27–29.

REPRESENTATIVE JOHN G. MCCABE,
CANNON COUNTY
MIDDLE TENNESSEE (DEMOCRAT)
January 11, 1861

John G. McCabe (1828–?) was born in Cannon County, engaged in farming, and served only one term in the general assembly. He enlisted in Company A, 18th Tennessee Infantry (Confederate), elected captain in 1862, and was wounded near Murfreesboro on January 2, 1863.

Mr. McCabe offered House Resolution No. 27, as follows:

Resolved by the House of Representatives in Extraordinary Convention convened, That the Constitution and the laws passed in pursuance thereof is the supreme law of the land, the enactment of any State notwithstanding.

2. *Resolved*, That our attachment to the Federal Government is deep and abiding, and that the Government of the United States has established justice to all concerned, and that the enforcement of its constitutional laws will promote the welfare and restore peace and tranquility, and continue the blessings of liberty.

3. *Resolved*, That we do not recognize the right of any one member of this confederacy to withdraw upon its own volition without consent of the other States.

4. *Resolved*, That while we deprecate the passage of laws in some of the States, intended to obstruct the execution of the fugitive slave law, we would not be justified in an attack upon the Federal Government. Our complaint is not against the Federal Government, but against the nullifying States.

5. *Resolved,* That it is the duty of the Federal Government to return all fugitives to their owners, or pay such owners the loss sustained.

6. *Resolved,* That it is the duty of the Federal Government to collect and pay into the treasury of the United States the revenue from all the ports within her border, and that no nominal act of secession by any State should prevent the Federal Government from discharging this duty.

7. *Resolved,* That we deeply deplore the precipitate and intemperate action of some of the States of this Confederacy, in their attempt to dismember and destroy the union of the States, and that we regret the attempt to deprive the border slave States of the advantage of the fugitive slave law and the Constitution, under which now they can get their rights in the Union, and placing them on the border of a foreign country, with a perfect certainty of abolitionizing them, as unjust, and deserving from Tennessee an early condemnation.

8. *Resolved,* That while we condemn the fanatical action of some of the Northern States, that have attempted to nullify the laws of the Federal Government, by their State legislative enactments, we do not find fault with, or in any manner implicate, those other Northern States that have not passed such unconstitutional laws, and that it is our highest duty to strengthen the bond of the Union, between the conservative States North and South.

9. *Resolved,* That we do not regard secession of {*sic*} disunion as an adequate remedy for existing evils, but that such could only tend to aggravate them.

10. *Resolved further,* That with a view to establish a permanent peace, and fraternal regard among all the States of this Confederacy, and with a view of forever settling the vexed question between the States, we propose a Convention or Conference of the border States, both North and South.

11. *Resolved,* That said Convention meet at as early day as possible, and that each State have a delegation equal to her representatives in Congress and the Senate of the U.S., to be chosen by the people.

12. *Resolved,* That no delegate be admitted to a seat in said Con-

vention from any State that has actually seceded from the Union, or having laws on her statute book nullifying the fugitive slave law.

13. *Resolved*, That Tennessee will abide the decision of said Conference or Convention.

Which resolutions lie over under the rule.

Source: *House Journal of the Extra Session of the Thirty-Third General Assembly of the State of Tennessee, Which Convened at Nashville on the First Monday in January, A. D. 1861* (Nashville: J. O. Griffith and Company, Public Printers, 1861), 47–48.

Representative William Edwin Ball Jones, Overton County
Middle Tennessee (Democrat)
January 12, 1861

William E. B. Jones (1828–1888) was an attorney from Livingston, Overton County. Following secession, he served one year in the Confederate Army.

Mr. Jones offered House Resolution No. 33, as follows:

Resolved, That while we do not believe such objects in the aggregate are now entertained by a great body of the members of that party, yet, that ambitious demagogues, unprincipled leaders, and deluded fanatics do entertain and avow them; and that whatever of conservatism the party may possess will be overpowered by the latter, unless an adjustment and understanding be had *now*, and the questions growing out of slavery be *now finally* and *forever* settled between the North and the South.

Resolved, That the lasting gratitude of patriots is due to those gallant men of the North who have stood by the Federal Constitution and our rights in every peril, and that the recent developments of public opinion among the *people* of the North induce us to indulge a hope (feeble we acknowledge it to be) that a reaction in public sentiment may occur, when our constitutional demands will be gratified—at least we are opposed to leaving the experiment untried.

Resolved, That, in our opinion, the Federal Constitution is sufficient for the protection and maintenance of all our rights properly construed and honestly enforced; but that, as the Republican party, soon to be inaugurated into power, denies such a construction and enforcement, the dangers to us, present and future, threatened and impending, demand a final settlement by constitutional amendments or otherwise, as may be deemed best.

Resolved, That we profess an unfaltering devotion to the Federal Constitution, as our fathers made it, and to the Union as the result of that Constitution; and that we are unwilling to sever the ties that bind these States together until every honorable and just means shall have been exhausted to obtain our rights within the Federal Union.

Resolved, That, in our opinion, the destinies and interests of the slaveholding States are deeply interlinked and blended; that we favor wise, calm, and deliberate counsels in every State; that we would have preferred, and do now prefer, the joint and united action of those States to attain our common rights in the Union, and that when the last effort honor dictates shall have been unavailingly exerted by this State, and those that may co-operate with us, through a Southern Convention or otherwise, for that purpose, in the Union, then by virtue of that right *canonized* in our hearts and sanctioned by the blood of the American revolution, we advocate the joint and United action of such States in going out of the Union, or rather in repairing the Federal Government which then will have been virtually dissolved by our brethren of the North.

Resolved, That we, irrespective of our past political and party associations, *concur* in the opinion that the troubled and threatened condition of the country, awakening as it does the most serious apprehensions for its peace, as well as for the integrity of our present system of Federal Government, not only justified, but demanded the convening of the Legislature of the State with a view to such legislation in the present emergency as patriotism and enlightened conservative deliberations may require.

Resolved, That among such measures as ought, in our opinion, to be brought before the Legislature by the Governor, in his message, we embrace, the arming, equipping, and thorough re-organization of the militia of the State, having due regard to economy; and for the purpose alone of our own protection as a State against external violence, and internal and servile insurrections; we would oppose such measures for other objects at the *present* juncture of our affairs.

Resolved, That we deem the success of the Republican party in the late Presidential election, a breach of the *spirit*, while it is in consonance with the *form*, of the Federal Constitution; and for these, among other reasons, it avows the determination to prohibit slavery, a "relic of barbarism"[2] in all the Territories now belonging to the United States, in open violation of the power of Congress, as determined by the Supreme Court of the United States; it looks to the abolition of slavery in the District of Columbia, in the navy yards and arsenals of the United States; it intends the non-execution of the slave law by the Federal Government, judging from its obstruction and nullification by personal liberty bills and armed mobs in several of the Northern States; it means the non-admission of any other slave State into the Union, and the overthrow thereby of the power of the slave States in the Federal Government; it intends the prohibition of the inter-slave trade between the several States; and when, by the increase of federal representation, it attains the power, a reorganization of the Federal Judiciary, so as to abolitionize the Supreme Court of the United States; and finally, by a series of measures, such as have been indicated, or by constitutional amendments, to extinguish the branded barbarism from the soil of the United States, and if need be bring forward to the accomplishment of that object an "irrepressible conflict."[3] These purposes, so far as not openly declared as the principles of that party, we apprehend to be its ulterior designs.

Resolved, That we believe the institution of slavery promotive of the happiness of all classes of the people in those States where it exists, the rich and the poor, the master and the slave; and that history and experience teach us that our own prosperity, in every department of social and national greatness, is too intimately dependent thereon to yield it, against our own consent, without an irrepressible conflict, and, if need be, a deadly conflict.

Resolved, That we deem this occasion not inappropriate to the expression of our unqualified opposition to the re-opening of the African slave trade.

Resolved, That we are opposed, in the present crisis, to the coercion, by the Federal Government, of any Southern State or its citizens, for the reason, among others, that such coercion would inevitably lead to a general civil war.

Resolved, That we are in favor of calling a convention of delegates, in our State, to consider the present condition of affairs, and to demand of the Federal Government, the protection of our rights; but if said convention be called, and should an ordinance of secession be passed by them, it should be submitted to and ratified by a majority of the qualified voters in the State before it takes effect.

Which resolutions lie over under the rule.

Source: *House Journal of the Extra Session of the Thirty-Third General Assembly of the State of Tennessee, Which Convened at Nashville on the First Monday in January, A. D. 1861* (Nashville: J. O. Griffith and Company, Public Printers, 1861), 55–57.

SENATOR JAMES L. THOMPSON,
SMITH AND SUMNER COUNTIES
MIDDLE TENNESSEE (DEMOCRAT)
January 16, 1861
Senate Resolution No. 17

Dr. James L. Thompson (1821–?) studied medicine at Transylvania University in Lexington, Kentucky, and received his MD degree from Philadelphia Medical College. During the war he served as a surgeon in the Confederate Army.

WHEREAS, The election of Mr. Lincoln to the office of President and of Mr. Hamlin to the office of Vice-President of the United

States, by a party entirely sectional in its organization, and based upon principles hostile to the interest, honor, and prosperity of the South; and whereas, the increasing strength of this sectional party in the Northern States since 1856, having inspired its leaders and their fanatical followers with almost an insane determination of purpose to accomplish the great objects of its organization, viz: the ultimate extinction of African slavery, and the equality of the negro with the white man, by an open violation of every principle as set forth in the preamble to the Constitution, and, also, in violation of the provisions of that instrument; and whereas, the General Government was created and formed by a compact of the States, and all its powers being derived therefrom, possessing only such powers as were conceded by the States having retained all the powers to themselves that were not ceded to the General Government, and the power to coerce, or govern a State without its consent, being nowhere to be found in the enumeration of delegated powers to the Government; and whereas, it was never contemplated by the framers of our Constitution that sectional parties, with sectional principles, should ever control the destinies of this country, therefore,

Resolved by the General Assembly of the State of Tennessee, That the election of Mr. Lincoln is an evidence of the overpowering strength of a sectional party, with the avowed declaration of hostility to the institution of African slavery as it exists in the South, and the fact of its overshadowing influence upon our entire country, and the previous wrongs and aggressions of that party, is a sufficient cause for Tennessee to sever her connection with the Union, and to re-assume to herself all the powers ceded to the General Government, and to assume an independent sovereignty. Her honor, interest, and future welfare impels her to this course.

Resolved, That the glorious example of South Carolina, Alabama, Florida, and Mississippi, and the other Cotton States, are worthy of emulation by Tennessee; and we anxiously await the time when she will, like them, throw off the shackles of bondage which the approaching Black Republican despotism will so grievously oppress her, and take her proud position with them as an independent sovereignty.

Resolved, That when Tennessee, in connection with other Southern States, shall have declared their separate independence, that we earnestly desire a United Southern Confederacy, based upon the Constitution of our fathers.

Resolved, That any attempt on the part of the General Government to coerce the seceding States, will be an assumption of power it does not legitimately possess, and our Representatives in Congress are hereby requested, and our Senators instructed to use every means within their power to prevent the same; failing in which, they are hereby requested and instructed to return home to their constituents.

Source: *Senate Journal of the Extra Session of the Thirty-Third General Assembly of the State of Tennessee, Which Convened at Nashville, on the First Monday in January, A. D. 1861* (Nashville: J. O. Griffith and Company, Public Printers, 1861), 52–54.

CHAPTER FOUR

US House of Representatives
January, February, March 1861

*Tennessee's ten delegates to the United States House of Rep-
resentatives were typical of the political diversity of Tennessee's
population. With three being Democrats and seven aligned with
the Opposition Party, their speeches presented below provide arguments across the political spectrum. While Emerson Etheridge
and Reese Brabson made persuasive pleas for Union, James
Thomas and William Avery presented equally adamant appeals
in favor of secession. Thomas A. R. Nelson, William Stokes, James
Quarles, Robert Hatton, and Horace Maynard offered a middle
ground advocating compromise. John Vines Wright, a Democrat
representing Tennessee's Seventh Congressional District, did
not address the secession crisis during the second secession of the
Thirty-Sixth Congress.*

*By January 17, when Representative James Thomas offered
his remarks, four states (South Carolina, Mississippi, Florida,
and Alabama) had declared their separation from the United
States. Over the next six weeks, three more states (Georgia,
Louisiana, and Texas) followed suit. As those states proclaimed
their independence and then became the Confederate States of
America, they captured and occupied federal property including
forts, navy yards, and arsenals. Only four southern forts remained under United States control throughout the war: Fort
Pickens in Pensacola, Florida; Fort Taylor at the extreme end of
the Florida Keys; Fort Jefferson in the Dry Tortugas, and Fort
Monroe, Virginia.*

James Houston Thomas,
6th District
Middle Tennessee (Democrat)
January 17, 1861

James H. Thomas (1808–1876) graduated from Jackson College in Columbia, Tennessee, and started his law practice there in 1830. He served as attorney general of the state from 1836 to 1842, as a US representative from 1847 to 1851, and again from 1859 to 1861 before resuming his law practice in Columbia.

In this speech, Representative Thomas, while not being a supporter of secession, understood that the Deep South's need to leave the Union resulted from northern hostility to slavery. Lincoln was elected not because he "either favored or was opposed to a protective tariff," or, he argued, for any other reason "disconnected to slavery." The people of the North would have been willing to grant southerners their constitutional rights if only they had not been misled, "grossly misled," on the subject of slavery.

Mr. THOMAS. The object of our discussion in the House should be to promote the general welfare of the country. To effect that object, a harmonious feeling should predominate, if possible; but I must say that the character of the debate which has preceded has not been to my taste. Yet, sir, we must conform ourselves to the circumstances by which we are surrounded; and, with a view of discharging my duty, I desire to submit some remarks to the consideration of the committee, upon the subject which now so seriously engrosses public attention.

The question of slavery has ever been troublesome to this country. Yet our fathers were enabled to dispose of it, and to dispose of it in such a way as to secure, not only our liberties, but the establishment of a Government which has led to a happiness and prosperity of our people unexampled in the history of the human family. When the Declaration of Independence was framed, every State of this Union was a slaveholding State. They went through that war, and this troublesome question troubled not the council, the camp, or the battle-field. We conducted that war to a successful termination, and to the establishment of our independence. In process of time, when our convention assembled to establish a constitution, we had twelve slave States and but one free State. There was then in the northern mind a hostility to slavery.

{*Representative Thomas here explains that while there existed in the North a "hostility" to slavery, the Founding Fathers, nevertheless, were able to accommodate the slave trade, the return of fugitive slaves, the admission of slave states into the Union, and the purchase of Louisiana "with its slave property," without upsetting the equilibrium of the country. But, he continued, "a sensitiveness" toward the subject of slavery gradually "got into the school-houses, into the school-books, into the pulpit, and into all the various modes of education, and into all the means used in the formation of the moral sentiments of the people."*}

And what is the result? It has formed political associations, and a political party which now proposes to take control of the Government of the country, and to do it upon the one single, isolated idea of hostility to southern institutions. In 1856, this party first assumed a prominent and threatening attitude toward the South. And what do we find them declaring upon that occasion? When they formed the Republican party, in 1856, they formed it without regard to past political differences and divisions. When they came to lay down their principles, they announced that as their cardinal doctrine. In that body we find men who had been Whigs, Democrats, and Americans; men who had belonged to all the political parties of the country; but all their past party predilections were to be lain aside, and the new party, without regard to them, was to be formed. It was so formed, and their declaration was:

Resolved, That the Constitution confers upon Congress sovereign power over the Territories of the United States for their government, and in the exercise of that power, it is both the right and the duty of Congress to prohibit in all the Territories the twin relics of barbarism—polygamy and slavery.

In 1860 the same party again laid down their platform; which was as follows:

8. That the normal condition of all the territory of the United States is that of freedom. That as our republican fathers, when they had abolished slavery in all our national territory, ordained that 'no person should be deprived of life, liberty, or property, without due process of law.' It becomes our duty, by legislation, whenever such legislation is necessary, to maintain this provision of the Constitution against all attempts to violate it; and we deny the authority of Congress, of a Territorial Legislature, or of any individuals, to give legal existence to slavery in any Territory of the United States.

When that party, in 1860, in convention, came to look out for a representative of the principles which they intended to inaugurate in the Government, provided they succeeded, it looked all over the country for such an individual. The two most prominent and eminent men who presented themselves for that nomination were Hon. Mr. Seward, of New York, and Mr. Lincoln, of the State of Illinois. Upon the first ballot Mr. Seward received a large plurality of the votes. But he was not nominated; and Mr. Lincoln was finally unanimously nominated and elected by that party; and it is now openly declared to the country that the former gentleman, Mr. Seward, is to be the prime minister of Mr. Lincoln, the successful candidate of the Republican party for President. The gentlemen owe their elevation to office to their opposition to southern institutions. They were selected and voted for, not for personal predilections, but for their devotion to the doctrines which they were known to have advocated, and for opinions they were known to entertain.

Now, I call the attention of the committee and of the country to what, in brief, these opinions were. Mr. Seward declares:

Slavery can be limited to the present bounds; it can be amelio-rated; it can be, and it must be abolished, and you and I can and must do it. The task is as simple and easy as its consummation will be beneficial, and its rewards glowing. It only requires to follow this simple rule of action: to do everywhere and on every occasion what we can, and not to neglect or refuse to do what we can, at any time, because at that precise time, and on that particular occasion, we cannot do more. Circumstances determine possibilities. * * * * Extend a cordial welcome to the fugitive who lays his weary limbs at your door, and defend him as you would your paternal gods.

Correct your own error that slavery has any constitutional guarantees which may not be released, and ought not to be relin-quished. * * * * You will soon bring the parties of the country into an effective aggression upon slavery.

Again, he declares:

What a commentary upon the history of man is the fact, that eighteen years after the death of John Quincy Adams, the peo-ple have for their standard-bearer Abraham Lincoln confessing the obligations of the higher law, which the sage of Quincy pro-claimed, and contending, for weal or woe, for life or death, in the irrepressible conflict between freedom and slavery.[1] I desire only to say that we are in the last stage of the conflict, before the great triumphal inauguration of this policy into the Government of the United States.

Now, sir, Mr. Seward was the highest candidate on the first ballot, and is to be the prime minister of the incoming Administration. We now come to the declaration of the candidate who was ultimately nominated unanimously by that convention. What does Mr. Lincoln declare? And it is such declarations as these that have given him his present high position in the country. He says: "What I do say is, that no man is good enough to govern another man *without the other man's consent*. I say this is the leading principle, the SHEET ANCHOR of *American Republicanism*."

Again, in Chicago, on the 10th of July, 1858, he said:

> I should like to know if, taking the old Declaration of Independence, which declares that all men are equal upon principle, and making exceptions to it, where will it stop? If one man says it does not mean a negro, why not another say it does not mean some other man? If that declaration is not the truth, let us get the statute-book in which we find it, and tear it out. Who is so bold as to do it? If it is not true, let us tear it out. [Cries of 'No!' 'No!'] Let us stick to it; let us stand firmly by it, then. * * * * Let us discard all this quibbling about this man and the other man—this race and that race and the other race being inferior, and therefore they must be placed in an inferior position—discarding the standard that we have left us. Let us discard all these things, and unite as one people throughout this land until we shall once more stand up declaring that all men are created equal. * * * * I leave you, hoping that the lamp of liberty will burn in your bosom until there shall no longer be a doubt that all men are created free and equal.[2]

Now, sir, here we have placed before us the ground on which this candidate was presented for election. And what is it? It is not that he either favored or was opposed to a protective tariff; not that he was for one policy or the other, disconnected with slavery. I ask you whether, if there had been no slaves in the United States, and if he had entertained similar opinions about slavery in Cuba or Brazil, would such opinions have been considered when the nomination came to be made? No, sir, that nomination was made solely, mainly, and particularly, on the ground of hostility to slavery. It is one of his open declarations that he hates slavery as bad as any Abolitionist. It was that very hatred which gave him the confidence of the party that has elected him to power.

Then, how do we stand? Here is a party composed of men of the northern States alone, of whom not a single individual owns a slave; and probably not one twentieth of those who voted for Mr. Lincoln ever saw a slave. They have none of the evils or advantages of that institution among them. And yet they chose Mr. Lincoln for his opinions in regard to an institution with which they have no connection, and in which they have no practical interest. He was selected because of his hatred to slavery. In other words, he was selected, not for any particular views of policy that he has in regard to northern institutions or northern interests, but because of the views which he entertains in regard to southern interests. He was elected, not to govern the North, but to govern the South; to govern a portion of the Union in which he has no party, and where there is no respectable portion of citizens who, for a moment, tolerate his election to office on such principles. So far as the South is concerned, we of the South have had no more to do in the election of Mr. Lincoln than we have to do with the election of the Emperor of France. He is to us a foreign ruler. He is elected by men who have no sympathy with us, who are hostile to our great interests.

I submit to the consideration of every candid mind, if any court on earth would appoint a guardian over a property where the application was made for the sole purpose of destroying the estate; where the applicant was hostile to the interest of which he desired to have the control, and, only sought the trust for its destruction; is there a court on earth, claiming to know what equity and justice is, who would for a moment think of appointing him? And yet you are determined to place the guardianship of the rights of the South on the slavery question, in the hands of men who come here declaring their hostility to slavery, and claiming the right to take charge of that institution to which they are hostile, and on the destruction of which they are determined. I submit to the consideration of this committee,[3] and of the country, whether it is an American principle, that the party who has no interest in the subject-matter should select a guardian for it, and choose him from among those hostile to it.

But it may be said our Government is one of majorities. True: in one sense it is a Government of majorities. But Mr. Lincoln has only a bare majority of the electoral vote; and when you come to examine the record of the great popular voice of the people of the United States, you will find that he is nearly a million in the minority. Thus, by nearly a million minority of votes, has Mr. Lincoln been elected to the office of President of the United States.

Again, sir, this idea of majorities governing ought to be limited to the people who are interested in the subject. The people of Massachusetts or the people of Virginia might well submit a subject to the will of their respective States, and be governed by the majority; but the principle does not hold good where the question is submitted to those who have no interest whatever in it.

Upon the subject of slavery, or any local interest of the South, I maintain that if majorities in the North, or if every man in the North, were in favor of hostile legislation, it would be anti-American, and contrary to all the principles of our Government for them to assume to govern such local institution, and especially to govern it in such a way as to bring about its destruction. Why is it that the northern people have felt it incumbent on them to join in a crusade against this institution? We are often told that the slave power has had control of the Government; but I maintain that the Government has not been controlled with a view to promote slavery, or in opposition to slavery; and that is the view in which the South has ever maintained the Government should be controlled. But slavery is a living, existing interest in the country, and should share the common weal or common woe of the country, like other great interests.

{*Here Representative Thomas reviewed the territorial expansion of the United States since 1783 and the relationship between lands slave and free. He concluded: "The South has increased her limits about 33 per cent., while the North has extended near 1,000 per cent. In 1,217,160 square miles of the territory thus acquired by the North, slavery existed by law, but is now abolished. Of the small amount acquired by the South, it was all slave territory when acquired and so remains."*}

That is the history of the progress of the two sections. Where, then, is there the slightest pretext of our northern friends for one moment entertaining the belief that slavery is to be spread all over the country. This idea that the South, or the Democratic party, or any other party at the South, are slavery propagandists, by and through the Federal Government, is a mistake, and northern politicians have misled the public mind of the North when they have attempted to promulge such an idea. The only position taken by any party in the South is, that we of the South are equals in this Union, and that when Territories are acquired our citizens have the right, under our Constitution, to go there, and that no power short of the people of the Territories themselves can at any time exclude them from this right. There is some division among us as to when the people of a Territory should act—whether they should do it while in a territorial capacity, or whether they should wait until they form a State constitution; but all agree that there is no power which can exclude the South from her rights in a Territory but the people who settle that Territory. We are in favor of the largest liberty to the people to go to the Territories that are acquired by the common blood and the common treasure of all the States and of all the citizens of all the States, and to stand upon a perfect equality in relation to their rights in those Territories.

What objection can the North have to that? It is not that slavery will go up North. Every man who knows the character of the northern people, knows that they look well to their own interests, and they have abolished slavery in the northern States; and in doing that, they have shown by their example that there is no fear that slavery will ever go where it is unprofitable. This being so, why is it that there is this hostility in the public mind at the North against this institution of slavery? Sir, they have got ingrafted on their minds an idea that slavery is sinful, and that this Government is responsible for the sin of slavery, if it be tolerated. Doubtless a large majority of the people of the North are devoted to the Constitution of this country, and are willing to give us our constitutional rights, if they were not misled upon this subject. In my humble judgment they have been, whether intentionally or not, grossly misled. They have been taught that the Constitution of the country does not recognize the right of property in man, and that if slavery is permitted to go into any of the Territories it will make them accessory to this great sin of slavery. Why, sir, we must look to the circumstances that attended our Declaration of Independence, and the formation of this Constitution. The ships of the North and of the South were then engaged in the African slave trade. They were going to Africa, and there buying or kindnapping {*sic*} negroes, and bringing them to the United States, and selling them to the citizens of the Union as slaves. A proposition was made to abolish that trade, or to give Congress the power to abolish it; but the North, the States of Massachusetts, Connecticut, and New Hampshire, said that they wanted the trade extended, at least until 1808; thus giving them twenty years more to bring this species of property to the United States, sell it, and pocket the profits of the sale. It was the idea entertained then, universally. Nobody thought of any thing else than that they were legally bought and sold as property.

> {*Representative Thomas briefly spoke here about the constitutional right of property in slaves being recognized by the courts and Congress, and in the right of having fugitive slaves being returned to the owner. "And so" he observed, "in respect to all the difficulties which our friends of the North find growing out of the recognition of the right of property in slaves. There are no difficulties which did not exist in the minds of our fathers who framed the Constitution, and which were not fully met by them in the instrument framed by them, with the intention of compromising and settling them upon principles having respect to the rights of all the States of the Union."*}

Now, sir, when we look at the history of this country and see its progress; when we see the difficulties which have from time to time come up and been settled by the wisdom of our fathers, is it not strange that our friends in the North should unite in such numbers upon an issue that has so little in it, affecting not only their own welfare, but the welfare of the whole country? Why, sir, if we are permitted to take our slaves into the common Territories of the country, it does not add a single one to the number; it does not bring another slave within the limits of the United States. It only authorizes the master to change his location; it does not bring him nearer to you. Most likely it will have the effect of removing him further from those gentlemen from the North who represent that section upon this floor. But gentlemen tell us they want these Territories for free labor. Mr. Chairman {Cadwallader Colden Washburn (1818–1882), from Wisconsin}, I submit that there is much in the conduct of this party at the North calculated to break up and forever destroy that feeling of friendship which once existed, and must again exist before we can sustain a united Government. The Territories of the Government are the common property of all the States. No man will say that the South has failed to contribute her share in their acquisition, whether it be in cash or blood. No man can say it.

Then why should we not have a common right to that territory? What are you gentlemen of the North indicating by your policy in this House? It is not to secure territory for your own children. You do not expect to populate it by your own offspring; certainly not in the present day. You have, during the present session, passed a bill giving an inheritance in that territory not only to your children, but to the children of every man in the world who chooses to go there, to the children even of the Hessian,[4] who, for a price, fought against our fathers in the war of the Revolution; while you refuse to permit the descendants of General Green {sic},[5] or of any of the heroes of the Revolution in the South, to go there and take their property with them.

Call you this fair dealing? Is this loyalty to us or to the memories of the Revolution? Is it that spirit that actuated the framers of the Constitution, when they, compromising all the difficulties before them, framed the Government under which we have grown up and existed as a nation so long and so prosperously?

Sir, these difficulties are continually thrown in our way. A determined disposition is manifested to take that territory from us, to circumscribe us within our present limits; while they will permit homesteads to be granted to the descendants of our former enemies, and will populate it with men who cannot even speak our language, and to whom they should be bound by no stronger ties of affection than they should be to the men of the South, who shared in all the dangers and hardships of its acquisition.

I have no hostility to foreigners; but, sir, when I see the legislative bodies of my country, legislating with a view to give them precedence over the descendants of the revolutionary sires of the South, I feel that it is time for us to speak out—to demand at least the rights of the people of the South. There can be nothing wrong in that. We do not claim any exclusive right in any of the Territories. We only claim the same right in those Territories that are secured to the people of the North. We demand nothing more; we can submit, sir, to nothing less. We do not ask to exclude one of the northern people, or any species of property possessed by the northern people. But you propose to exclude us, unless we divest ourselves of our household servants—a property which is endeared to us from our earliest recollections, and for which we have higher regard than for any other species of our property. The relations which exist between the master and servant create a sympathy unlike that which you feel for your homestead and your farm horses and wagons. It is a kind of friendship. It is a devotion of fellow-feeling characteristic of that institution, which never has been, and which I fear never will be, justly appreciated by the North. They are a part of us. They sympathize with us, and we sympathize with them. Our rights are their rights; and when we prosper, they prosper. If we can go to a country where we can do better than where we are, the slaves that go with us are bettered in an equal proportion with ourselves. Hence, sir, it is that we claim all the rights of equality in this Union.

{*Here Representative Thomas proclaimed that "the South feels her rights are no longer safe in this Government without some new guarantees for their protection." Secession is a reality, he stated, and the government cannot prevent states from leaving. If the attempt is made, "every State from this to the Rio Grande will unite as a band of brothers, and as a band of brothers will resist to the last; resist any and every blow struck against a seceding State to compel her to remain in the Union."*}

Mr. Chairman, we regard the Constitution of the United States as the casket[6] in which our forefathers deposited the jewels of justice;

of the insurance of domestic tranquility; of provision for the common defense; the promotion of the general welfare, and the security of the blessings of liberty to ourselves and our posterity. Those were the jewels deposited in the casket. When you rifle it of these treasures, do you suppose that eulogies upon the glorious Union will attach the people and the States of the South to it? No, sir; they will dash it from them as an unholy thing. It is the treasure that gives it value, and not that in which the treasure is contained.

But I have heard the idea frequently thrown out that you do not mean to make war upon the seceding States; that all you mean to do is, to let them do without the United States courts and post offices. It is declared that this Government will let the seceding States do without the advantages of this Union, while they will be compelled to pay their share of the revenue. That is the sort of coercion which George III attempted to put in force against the revolted American colonies. He made war upon them for no other purpose but to compel them to pay the tea tax and the stamp duty. Is such a war consistent with the principles of American freedom? If so, then you can prosecute your war for the purpose of collecting the revenue, and yet use no coercion. Suppose the Constitution of the United States made it the especial duty of the Government to coerce every State that was not willingly subject to its control; what would you do? You would only enforce the law; the very thing, sir, you now claim that you will do, and yet you will not coerce.

Mr. Chairman, let this thing be attended to; not that I invite it, but let it be attended to; or who can imagine the terrible consequences that must result? Is it not known that one, five, or fifteen States cannot be conquered and held in subjection? It cannot be done; nor do I claim that we can conquer the North. What did it cost this Government to get fifteen hundred Seminole warriors out of the Everglades of Florida? We expended more than thirty million dollars out of the public Treasury in that little war; and now, when you talk of conquering States, the whole arithmetic fails in figures to count the cost that will follow the attempt. I submit this, not as a threat, but as the plain consequences of an act of this character. If such policy as this is to result in no good to any portion of the Union, but in interminable evil, I submit, why is it necessary or expedient? And let me say, here, that all that is said or done upon this subject of conquering, or using force, or coercion, but adds fuel to the flame through the whole South. If this Government had manifested a more peaceable disposition, and had, from the commencement of this excitement, proclaimed through Congress that no force would be used, I believe that not more than one State would have been out of the Union at this time. We should have had more time for a settlement of these difficulties.

The remedy, if remedy there be, is in conciliation. Read, if you please, your writers upon the subject of national law, and they universally concur in the idea that the true and proper mode of putting down civil war is to grant to the people what they ask. And what has the South asked which should not be granted? She has never come into the Congress of the United States and asked for the passage of a law favoring and establishing slavery upon any portion of the continent. She has only asked that all the rights we have shall be protected by the Government. We do not get rights from this Government. We have them over and above the Government. The Government does not create rights, but only protects them. Governments are established to protect rights; and we only ask that Congress shall pass laws to protect rights which we already possess.

If this matter is to be settled—and possibly it yet may be—it must be done by a concession. And what do you yield? What do our northern friends yield? Nothing; absolutely nothing. They will have the same rights in the Territories which we will have. The feeling all over the South is, "equality in the Union, or independence out of it." That is the watchword. That is the feeling of our people of all sections, so far as my information extends.

My constituents have not been, nor have I been, for secession. We have hoped for safety in the Union; and have desired that all means to effect that end shall be exhausted before a resort is had to disunion. But while we waited for your returning sense of justice towards us, disunion has overtaken us; four, and perhaps five, States have seceded;

and the forts and arsenals, from North Carolina to the Rio Grande, are nearly all in possession of the seceding States. We can be content with no adjustment that will not unite the South with us. The southern States have a common interest and a common destiny.

You censure the southern States for their precipitancy. Upon this subject we of the border slave States have more reason to complain than you. They and we have told you for years, in the most solemn manner, that we could not submit to your aggressions, and entreated you to forbear; yet you have not heeded, but have insulted us and told us that it was with us mere boastfulness.

You complain that the seceding States have seized the forts and other public property. These forts were permitted to be erected in these States for their defense, and the arms that have been taken were placed there for the same purpose. The Federal Government has no right to use this property for any other purpose. And whenever the people who had granted the sites of the forts for their defense discovered that they were to be used for the opposite purpose—of an attack upon them—it was not only just, but wise, for them to see that they were used for their defense, the legitimate purpose for which they were erected.

You complain that Florida and other States were purchased and paid for, and that they cannot, therefore, secede. Gentlemen are surely {not} for reviving the doctrines of the dark ages of the common law, by which they would make the inhabitants of the purchased territory *villains in gross*,[7] attached to the freehold, and bought and sold with it. Florida cost $5,000,000. Every State of the old thirteen was purchased. They cost the blood of the Revolution—a price greatly above that paid for our subsequent acquisitions. In all the treaties, acquiring territory, we have stipulated for their admission as States upon terms of equality with the original States. This fact at once answers this objection. The States, new and old, are equal in rights in every particular.

You could have quieted the country, and restored peace and prosperity, at no sacrifice but the yielding of your prejudice. We cannot, without ruin and dishonor. In the language of a distinguished southerner:

We may for a generation enjoy comparative ease, gather up our feet in our beds, and die in peace; but our children will go forth beggared from the homes of their fathers. Fishermen will cast their nets where your proud commercial navy now rides at anchor, and dry them upon the shore now covered with your bales of merchandise. Sapped, circumvented, undermined, the institutions of your soil will be overthrown; and within five and twenty years the history of St. Domingo will be the record of the South. If dead men's bones can tremble, ours will move under the muttered curses of sons and daughters, denouncing the blindness and love of ease which left them an inheritance of woe.[8]

This calamity we will aver; peaceably if we can, forcibly if we must. [Here the hammer fell.]

Source: *Congressional Globe*, 36th Cong. 2nd Sess., 435–38.

Emerson Etheridge, 9th District West Tennessee (Oppositionist)
January 23, 1861

Emerson Etheridge (1819–1902) studied for the law and began his practice in Dresden, Weakley County, in 1840. He served in the state legislature from 1845 to 1847 before being elected as a Whig to the Thirty-Third Congress (1853–1855) and as an American Party candidate to the Thirty-Fourth Congress (1855–1857). Failing in his reelection bid, he was then elected in 1858 as an Opposition Party candidate to the Thirty-Sixth Congress.

Representative Etheridge began his address by reminding his colleagues that the federal government and the Constitution contained methods for solving "emergencies as we are now compelled to meet." The federal government, he argued, had passed no law regarding slavery that had not been "dictated or controlled by

the statesmen of the South," or which had not been "demanded by
the public opinion of the South. . . . " Secession would only "aggra-
vate" sectional differences and "prove no remedy for anything."

Sir, this revolution which threatens speedily to involve us all, and which is suggestive of so terrible a future, is the most extraordinary, unpardonable, and indefensible the world has ever looked upon; and public men all over the country, of whom better things were expected— men who, a few months ago, were indignant at the bare suspicion of their sympathy or complicity with those who were then plotting revolution—are now counseling armed rebellion, and playing with the worst passions of mankind, as though nothing serious were involved in the result.

I propose to meet fairly the dread alternative presented by these precipitators; to meet them in a candid spirit, and to array in opposition to their real and pretended grievances, some of the manifold blessings which all sections of the country have derived from the Government—a Government which smiles even yet benignantly upon its misguided children. And may I not ask, what utter madness and folly must there be in subverting the Government for the purpose of securing *out of the Union* rights or privileges which may not be secured or vindicated by candid appeals to our kindred and friends, who salute the same flag, and acknowledge a common ancestry.

It is a remarkable and most significant fact, that this revolution is not justified or carried on with reference so much to anything which *has* been done by Congress, or any political party, as because of dangers which, it is alleged, are to be apprehended *in the future.* The only thing charged to have been already done or performed, as was said by my friend from Virginia, [Mr. Millson,][9] two days ago, is the passage, by the Legislatures of some of the free States, of the so-called personal liberty bills. If I had the time—I have not—I believe precipitation reigns here, and each moment, as it "rides upon the dial's point," (pointing to the clock,) admonishes me that I, too, must be precipitate. If I had time I could show—and I challenge contradiction from any disunionist, if such there be here—that you will be infinitely more the victims of the unfriendly legislation of the free States, when the Government has been destroyed, than you are now, or ever can be, while the Constitution endures and the Union is maintained. This—the passage of the personal liberty bills—I repeat, is the only thing now actually done or performed, by any department of Government, State, or Federal, of which even disunionists can complain. I will endeavor, then, to state the dangers you profess to fear in the future.

1. You say the people of the North are opposed to the execution of the fugitive slave law.

2. That the Republican party, when they obtain control of both branches of Congress, intend to exclude slavery from all the Territories by act of Congress.

3. That the people of the North refuse to grant congressional protection to slave property in the free Territories.

4. That they intend, finally, to change the Federal Constitution, thereby to enable them to abolish slavery in the States.

5. That the people of the free States are opposed to slavery.

6. That the people of the respective sections are not homogeneous; that they hate each other.

7. That some of the people of the free States favor the social and political equality of the negro.

8. That the South is in danger of invasions, similar to John Brown's raid into Virginia.

I think I have fairly stated the various charges which the disunionists have embodied into this indictment against the Government they seek to overthrow, and the people they would treat as enemies. Now, sir, I frankly confess that the personal liberty bills do exist in some of the free States. They are, whenever designed to evade the Constitution or the laws passed under it, without extenuation or excuse. But it is gratifying to perceive, if the signs of the times are worth anything, that all these personal liberty bills, which in any manner conflict with the Constitution, are soon to be swept from the statute-books of the free States. And if this were not so, it should not be forgotten that these laws have existed during the whole of the last eight years of Democratic rule, and without so much as a threat of revolution for such a cause; nor should it be overlooked, that if they are *unconstitutional* they are simply void; and if they are passed without a violation of the Constitution, as States-rights men you have less reason to complain. I repeat, they will soon be repealed. Nothing retards it now, in my opinion, but that general repugnance which all men feel in doing anything seemingly "upon compulsion." I repeat, this is the only act that has been done, by State or Federal authority, upon which disunion is justified by its advocates; and, as I before said, the other grounds of complaint are in reference to things you profess to believe will *hereafter* occur; things which never have happened, and which never could transpire if the seceding States had continued in the Union, and your Representatives had remained at their posts. I might further remark, in regard to these personal liberty bills, that they do not, as I am assured, exist in the border free States, the States which immediately adjoin the slave States—Iowa, Illinois, Indiana, Ohio, Pennsylvania, and New Jersey. Where, then, do they exist? They are found on the statute-books only of such far-off States as Vermont; a State in which, I am assured, there has not been a fugitive slave for forty years; a State as inaccessible to a slave's approach as his escape is impossible from South Carolina.

But you say that slaves escape from the southern States, and are permitted to pass *through* the free States and take refuge in Canada. I grant this to be true; and they will, in all time to come, occasionally escape from their owners. No system of laws can guard against it. In some negroes a disposition to run away is inherent. It must be endured, unless, perchance, you can invent some peculiar ligament to restrain the elasticity of their legs. [Laughter.] I reside within a day's ride of the free States, yet I have never known more than one slave to make his escape from my own neighborhood into the free States. He passed through that part of Kentucky now represented by my friend, [Mr. BURNETT,][10] and took refuge in Illinois. He was arrested by some of the citizens of that State, and taken back to his owner. Now, I will not blame my friend from Kentucky for permitting this fugitive to pass through his district, nor will I counsel disunion because his constituents did not arrest him on his way. Fugitive slaves do pass through the free States, and find freedom in Canada; but have you any means of reclaiming them now in the British dominions; and will not a disruption of the Union, in effect, bring the Canada line down to the banks of the Ohio?

But what appeals have the southern States made to the free States to repeal these statutes? Is not their existence rather an imaginary than a real grievance? For I am informed that under them no fugitive slave has ever been liberated; nor has there been, at any time, a prosecution of fine, forfeiture or conviction, for any alleged violation of their provisions. Instead of seeking relief in that spirit which would have given dignity and effect to the appeal, the whole matter has been left to the party newspapers and politicians.

But the precipitators complain, as I have stated, that many of the people of the free States are hostile to the execution of the fugitive slave law. Doubtless this is so to a great extent; but this is not the fault of the Federal Government, nor of the law. Mr. Buchanan, in his late annual message to Congress, used this very language: "The fugitive slave law has been carried into execution in every contested case since the commencement of the present Administration."

And it is a matter of history, that not a dozen slaves have been rescued within the last forty years from the custody of the officers of the United States, while acting under the authority of that law. You know the statement I make is true, although the people of the South are made to believe that it is impossible to recapture a runaway slave without his being in almost every instance rescued from the custody of the officers of the law. And while every rescue is made a matter of public notoriety, mention is rarely, if ever made, of the instances in which the law is enforced. We all know that fugitive slaves are almost constantly being captured in the free States and carried back to their owners; but information of cases of this kind rarely find their way into the party newspapers—certainly not in those which advocate disunion. But a mob or a riot, originating in matters of this kind, is the food upon which secession leaders wax wroth and grow fat. If the fugitive slave law is not *now* well executed, will it be more faithfully enforced if you dissolve the Union? Will you then have any fugitive slave law whatever? It cannot exist for a moment beyond the life of that Constitution which secession seeks to destroy.[11]

{*Representative Etheridge continued to find fault with seces-sionists observing that the "seceding States are now no sufferers from the evils of which they complain." Focusing on the 1850 Fugitive Slave Act, he insisted that northern reluctance to fully enforce the law was "not the fault of the Federal Government." Secession, he argued, would do nothing to improve the return of fugitive slaves.*}

The precipitators assign, as another cause for their attempt to overthrow the Government, that the people of the free States intend to abolish slavery in the States where it exists. Now, sir, I do not believe there is one word of truth in this allegation, and those who make it ought to know better; and if such were their desire, we all know they have no such power. The whole Republican party denounce this charge as false. I am here in the presence of the members of this House, and I aver that there is not a man in this Congress, of any party, from any quarter of the country, who claims the power or avows the purpose to interfere with slavery in the States where it exists. [Cries of "Not one!" from the Republican side of the House.] If there is one, I wish to know it, [A voice, "There are none!"], because he will receive the rebuke, not only of his colleagues, but of every man who wishes to live up to the Constitution. But, sir, this purpose is imputed to the people of the free States by the disunionists and their allies, in the teeth of the most solemn assurance which a political party can make to the world; and I hesitate not to say that this assurance has been, in many instances, purposely withheld from the people of the slave States, so that this misrepresentation might produce its baleful effects upon the popular mind. I remember that, during the last summer, some of the newspapers in my own State affected to be horrified because I read the following resolution from the Republican platform: "That the maintenance inviolate of the rights of the States, and especially the right of each State to order and control its own domestic institutions, according to its own judgment exclusively, is essential to that balance of power on which the perfection and endurance of our potential fabric depends; and we denounce the lawless invasion by armed force of the soil of any State or Territory, no matter under what pretext, as among the gravest of crimes."

And I do not hesitate now, in this presence, to assert, that no political party that ever assembled in convention in this country, has given stronger guarantees against any desire or any power to interfere with slavery in the States of this Union. They did more than this—that which no other political party in this country has ever done; apprehending the possibility of invasions similar to that of John Brown, they denounce, in express terms, all such raids "as among the gravest of crimes." Common fairness requires that we take gentlemen at their word; but if more were wanting in this regard, they are now willing, to appease your apprehensions—if any such you have—to vote for an amendment to the Constitution, declaring, in express terms, that Congress shall never have power or authority to legislate in regard to slavery in the States where it may exist.[12] Such a provision would be, in fact, no amendment at all, but a declaration of what the Constitution already is; for no intelligent lawyer, no man of sense, believes that the Constitution now confers upon Congress any such power.

{*Etheridge here implored his colleagues to focus on their similarities rather than their differences. The people of the North and South, he reasoned, "do not hate each other one particle more than did the embittered lenders of the old Whig and Democratic parties at the close of those sanguinary political conflicts which marked our history a few brief years ago."*}

It is alleged that a portion of the people of the free States favor the social equality of the negro. Well, if this be so to any considerable extent, I am very sorry for it, and wish it were otherwise. To say the least, it exhibits, in my judgment, a very bad taste; but I do not believe it is so to any considerable extent. But if it were, would separation change their taste or make them repudiate such social equality. I will not make any special allusion, or recur particularly to a chapter in our past party warfare. Were I to do so, I might show how an alleged predilection for the social equality of the negro was once charged upon a gallant soldier and veteran statesman, who, during an eventful life, was a specific favorite of the people, North and South.[13] But this I will say, that scandal is the poisonous weapon of all political parties in truly exciting times. It is often invoked, and but rarely in vain. I may say that the political equality of the negro was not wholly unknown to the people of some of the slave States thirty years ago. Half a century elapsed, in some of the southern States, before the right of suffrage was denied to the free negro population. I live in a State whose public men have not been wholly unknown to fame. We yet preserve recollections of Jackson and Polk. The first constitution of Tennessee was made in 1796. It remained unchanged until the year of grace 1835, and one of the peculiar features of that constitution was, that it sanctioned and approved the political equality of the negro to the extent of allowing the right of suffrage; and if he owned a sufficient amount of property, he was given a preference over the white man who had none.[14] Andrew Jackson was a member of the convention that ordained that constitution. His signature is attached to it to-day; and twice, before it was changed, he was made President of the United States. In the State of New York, but two months ago, a proposition to give political equality to the negro, to the extent of universal suffrage, was voted down by more than ten to one. It did not receive the vote of any considerable minority in a single county in the State. I repeat, that the political equality of the negro, to the extent I have named—and it is, I believe, the extent to which it prevails in any of the free States—has existed heretofore in many of the southern States. It formerly prevailed in my native State—North Carolina—where, until within the last thirty years, free negroes were allowed the right of suffrage. May we not exercise a little charity and forbearance upon this matter, especially as we set the example, and have no rightful power to prevent its exercise in other States. Most of the free States never have, and do not now permit negro suffrage, while social equality is a thing almost wholly unknown, even in the most radical of the anti-slavery States. The people of Tennessee advanced somewhat slowly, as is shown by their allowing negro suffrage from 1796 until 1835; and as these Republicans are somewhat progressive, perhaps they, too, after a while, may change their policy.

{*Here Representative Etheridge turned to John Brown's raid and questioned whether secession would provide better protection from invasion than presently existed. He also reminded the House that Pennsylvania, instead of preparing to invade the South, assisted in the arrest of two of Brown's men who had escaped there; the men were quickly "tried, convicted, and executed."*}

Sir, the great evil of the times is, that the people of all the different sections have listened so much to persistent misrepresentations, that they actually know less of each other's true purposes and feelings to-day than they did thirty years ago. The policy of the radical Abolitionists is to intensify the opposition to slavery which has always existed in the northern mind. To do this, they publish every libel that fanaticism can invent, and apply it to the great body of the people of the South. And the purpose of the disunionists of the South has been, and now is, to give notoriety to every extreme opinion of northern ultraists as the prevailing sentiment of the great body of the people of the free States. In each section, the most intemperate expressions and conduct of the other are represented as the rule instead of the exception. Thus, misrepresentation, perversion, and falsehood, have done their work, and we are now reaping the bitter fruits. Last year Texas was represented as in flames; peaceful villages and habitations were said to be consumed by the torch of northern abolition incendiaries. The public mind was frenzied; and no doubt the innocent were often made victims to that wide-spread alarm which time and reflection will prove to have been unfounded. But, were these exaggerations all stern realities, would separation or disunion increase the power of the people there to protect themselves from the dagger or the torch? Will that State have greater facilities for punishing inciters of insurrection when *out* of the Union, than are now found *within it?* Reason and common sense answer, no. A northern Abolitionist, or other person, who goes to Texas to tamper with slaves or promote rebellion, deserves a permanent lodgment in an asylum for the insane. Of all the places in the world, Texas is the last to welcome or appreciate his presence. As well might the most devoutly pious seek happiness by folding his Christian mantle around him, and plunging into the gulf which separates Lazarus from the rich man in hell. [Laughter.] So much then for the various allegations which the seceders have preferred against the Federal Government.

I have, for the sake of the argument, accepted all your charges as true, and allowed you to present them in their most aggravated form; and were they all really true to the extent that partisan coloring has painted them, still, so well satisfied am I that disunion would aggravate them all, and prove no remedy for anything, that I would endure all these evils for years to come, before I would overthrow my country, and entail upon its kindred people the inevitable horrors of fraternal war. Sir, I go further. I so love my country that I would add to all things a continuance of the unfortunate reign of James Buchanan and his late advisers for eight years more. I would repeat the sad experiment of the "old public functionary" for a dozen years, before I would consent to murder my country and extinguish the patriot's last and dearest hopes.

In regard to the pending question, and others of a kindred nature, I have only time to say, that I am ready to vote for the proposition originally submitted to the Senate, and commonly called the Crittenden amendments. I will vote, of course, for the proposition which I had the honor to submit to the House a few days ago; and, failing in this, I will support, in good faith, the measures reported by the gentleman from Ohio [Mr. Corwin][15] from the committee of thirty-three. I will support any one of these, preferring, of course, my own. And should each and all of these measures fail; should all other pending propositions be voted down, I will not then abandon the Union of these States, and the untold blessings it lavishes upon the votaries of civil liberty throughout the world. Failing in each and all of these measures, I will return home, and link my destinies with those who are ready to confront disunion. If needs be, I will meet it with a torch in one hand

and a sword in the other; and so help me God, so long as the stars and stripes wave over my State, or any part of it, I will never bow the knee to the storm of disunion. [Great applause in the galleries.]

Mr. Speaker, let us look impartially for a moment at some of the leading political events of the past. They will justify the assertion that, from the time the Constitution was ordained down to this hour, no act has been passed by Congress in regard to slavery anywhere, in the States or Territories, which was not dictated or controlled by the statesmen of the South, demanded by the public opinion of the South, or which has not received the sanction and approval of the leading statesmen of that section of country. The whole policy of the Federal Government in regard to the government of the Territories, and the slavery question in all its bearings, is just such as Mr. Lincoln will be compelled, by the Constitution and his oath of office, to enforce. More, sir: it is the policy which has been initiated and carried into effect by the Democratic or dominant party of the South. It has been enforced upon the country by them, and has heretofore met their cordial approval.

{*Etheridge here spoke of the expansion of the country and that southern demands for more land were always met. Detailing the acquisition of Louisiana, Florida, and Texas, he lectured, "Whatever territory the men of the South have asked Congress to acquire, the same has been acquired." He then turned to policies desired by the South and conceded by the North: fugitive slave laws of 1793 and 1850, and territorial concessions in 1850. "It is worthy of observation, Mr. Speaker," he noted, "that every argument of a disunionist may be successfully met and refuted by the complaints of another."*}

Mr. Speaker, I shall attempt no apology for the position of the Republican platform which declares it to be the right and duty of Congress to prohibit slavery in the Territories. I do not hesitate here, as I have done elsewhere, to pronounce this feature of their party creed to be wrong, if for no other reason, because the extension or restriction of slavery, as they well know, depends now on causes which are more controlling than any mere act of Congress. It has proved a most unwise and unnecessary feature in their political creed. It was inserted, I apprehend, for a reason similar to that which has caused a certain dominant party in the South, for years past, to make the negro issue paramount to all others—*to carry an election.* And at last our southern friends have found, to their sorrow, that this Sambo game is one that two can play at. I hope, as they have lost the stakes, they will resort to no other means than the ballot-box to regain their party power. I implore you to avoid the dire alternative to disunion; trust to that reaction in public opinion which is sure to come in every case where wrong and error exists, and reason is left free to combat it. And it is because I have faith in the sober second thought of the people everywhere, that I propose to appeal from this Congress to them. If, sir, you have grievances, are you disposed to break up the Government rather than ask the people of the free States, your brethren and kindred, to consider them? No; let us adjourn this unhappy quarrel to the people, the real people, to whom the Government belongs. It is but eighteen months until this whole dispute will be transferred by the Constitution to the whole people of the United States; but I implore you to transfer it to them now; and I apprehend those who persist in refusing so reasonable a demand will be consigned to retirement and obscurity. I am not afraid to trust the people, and I shall be content to abide by their deliberate decision upon all these questions when made.

I ask, again, why destroy our country because this Congress may fail to agree upon specific legislative measures or constitutional amendments, which have been before the country but a few weeks, and upon which the people of the States, North and South, have had no means of passing a final judgment? I protest against it.

{*Here Etheridge attempted to dampen southern fears of the incoming Republican administration arguing that the slave states will be more secure in the Union than without. After mentioning that the Senate would hold a majority of Democrats for the next four years, he added: "The next House of Representatives, if the*

seceding States are represented, will be also largely opposed to the Republican party; while the Supreme Court, heretofore claimed as the sheet-anchor of those who are now disunionists, is composed almost entirely of the political opponents of Mr. Lincoln."
Then Ohio Democrat Clement Vallandigham inquired whether there was any part of the Crittenden Amendment that would remove the "delusion" from which southern men were accused of suffering?}

I will answer that question frankly. There is: I tell the gentleman from Ohio, the true Union men of the South are standing to-day struggling with all their powers to preserve the Government; fighting, as they believe, for the cause of religion, humanity, civilization, and progress; and all these things are involved in the peace of the country. And that peace may depend upon the adoption of these propositions. They are surrounded by a tempestuous despotism—everywhere confronting a panic which is made to feed itself. It is all-devouring. Why, sir, it is well known to every gentleman who reads the newspapers, that wherever this disunion sentiment predominates, it is simply a reign of terror.

Go to the cities of South Carolina, and what do you see? Men frantic and in arms. Go to Charleston, to Tallahassee, to Montgomery, to Jackson—to any place where those conventions were assembled, and you see the military in full control of everything. These conventions deliberated three or four hours only over the fate of an empire.[16] Everything that might have invoked calmness or deliberation had disappeared, and martial music and warlike demonstrations attested the fallacy of a peaceful disruption of the States.

Mr. LEAKE.[17] Will the gentleman allow me to ask him a question?

Mr. ETHERIDGE. Certainly.

Mr. LEAKE. I merely wish to know whether the gentleman is speaking on the side of the North or the South?

Mr. ETHERIDGE. I am speaking on a side that has few Representatives upon this floor. I am speaking on the side of my country. [Great applause in the galleries.]

Why, sir, as I was proceeding to say, what is the state of affairs now in all the villages and cities of the Gulf States? Sir, bold men, educated men, ambitious men, men of chivalry and daring, are heading the military forces. Men, women, and children are excited, just as the pomp and circumstance of war will excite everybody. Thousands believe honestly that Lincoln and his cohorts are coming down to apply the torch and the knife to the dwellings and the people of the South. [Here the hammer fell.]

{*Following the end of Etheridge's allotted time, there ensued much discussion of whether he should be allowed to continue. The Speaker ultimately decided that he could "proceed for five minutes."*}

I will not, after what has just occurred, detain the House but a moment. I will conclude by saying, that I shall vote for the propositions of the venerable Senator from Kentucky, [Mr. CRITTENDEN;] I shall, as I have before said, vote for the proposition submitted by myself, and if these fail, I shall sustain the measures reported by the gentleman from Ohio, [Mr. CORWIN.] Sir, I will vote for anything which will relieve the public mind from the painful apprehensions under which it now labors. If anything of this kind can pass this Congress—and I do not despair—it will do my heart good to know that the tide of revolution has been thereby stayed. But, as I have already stated, if nothing is finally done, I will go home to my people; I will throw myself in "the imminent deadly breach," and resist the storm of disunion to the last; and, sir, if the worst must come to the worst, if I am to be dragged to the fearful precipice and made the reluctant victim or the unwilling observer of my country's ruin, I now, in advance, wash my hands of the shame and the crime which will attach to those who would overthrow the public liberty to erect a despotism upon its ruins. Sir, where the flag of my country floats, there I will go. I will cling to it in this dark hour of its peril, with that sacred trust and confidence a saint must feel in clinging to God. [Great applause in the galleries.]

Source: *Congressional Globe*, 36th Cong. 2nd Sess., Appendix, 111–16.

Thomas Amos Rogers Nelson,
1st District
East Tennessee (Oppositionist)
January 25, 1861

Thomas A. R. Nelson (1812–1873) was born in Kingston, Roane County, Tennessee, graduated from East Tennessee College in 1828, and commenced his law practice in Washington County. He served two terms as attorney general of the first judicial circuit before being appointed commissioner to China by President Millard Fillmore in 1851. He ran as an Opposition Party candidate in his successful bid for a House seat in the Thirty-Sixth Congress, and was elected president of the 1861 East Tennessee Convention. In 1868, Nelson defended President Andrew Johnson in his impeachment trial.

Representative Nelson began his speech by recalling that early in the session he had proposed three amendments to the Constitution that he believed "would form a proper basis for a compromise." His amendments would have 1) extended the Missouri Compromise line through the territories ceded by Mexico, prohibiting slavery to the north and preserving it to the south, 2) strengthened the Fugitive Slave Law of 1850, and 3) provided that future presidential ballots must contain a nominee from north of the 36°30' line and another from south of said line. Nelson believed "those resolutions would give peace to our country."

It is not my purpose to argue those resolutions at length; but I may say, in regard to them, that the most important of them—one which it was hoped would be promptly accepted by all parties—is that which proposed a restoration, in principle, of the Missouri compromise line. It was hoped, at the time that line was offered to the Republican party, that they would rally to its support, because the repeal of the Missouri compromise line was the origin of the party. It was feared that members from the South belonging to the Democratic party would not agree to the adoption of that line, because they contend that, under the decision of the Supreme Court, in the Dred Scott case, we have an equal right to go with our slaves to all the Territories of the United States; and as the line of 36°30' gives up our claim to establish slavery north of it, and the Crittenden resolutions only demand protection south of it, there was a reasonable probability that it would meet with strong opposition from the South. I was pleased and gratified in the committee to see southern gentlemen, holding extreme opinions, rallying to the support of that line; and I believe, this day, if the two Houses of Congress will adopt the Crittenden resolutions, or some resolutions of a similar character, it will give peace and repose to our country.

Those resolutions, would, in my humble judgment, be satisfactory to a large majority of the southern States, perhaps to all of them but one. And cannot they be voted for without any sacrifice of honor and principle upon the part of northern gentlemen? Northern gentlemen say they cannot support the line of 36°30', because they say it is a concession of slavery south of that line. How is it a concession to slavery south of that line? Does not slavery exist there already, by the laws of New Mexico?[18] And when we ask you to rally to the support of that line, do we ask you to relinquish one jot or tittle of your principles? We ask you to do nothing more than to recognize what already exists south of that line, without your procurement and independent of your action—to acknowledge the fact that slavery is there, and to say that you will not interfere with it. What do we give you as compensation for that? We offer you that slavery shall be forever prohibited north of that line; and if there is any concession in this manner, I maintain that it is a concession from the South, to the North. It is an abandonment of the Dred Scott decision, so far as slavery is concerned, north of the line of 36°30'. I repeat, it is only asking the Republican party not to pledge themselves to establish slavery, but simply to recognize a fact which exists without their agency, and for which they are in no conceivable form responsible: the one fact that the people of that country have recognized and established slavery themselves. Sir, what concession is there in this? Does the word concession grate harshly upon the Republican ear? I have been pained to hear gentlemen of that party announce on this floor their utter repugnance to concession and compromise. I will not, I cannot, believe this sentiment is common to a majority of the members of that party. Remember, gentlemen, that our Government was formed in a spirit of compromise. It has been preserved in the same spirit. Nothing will save it now but a manifestation of the same spirit. No compromise! No concession! Why, sir, we act upon this principle every day of our lives, and in all our social and business intercourse; and had not our Creator compromised with his own law and with fallen man, by sending his Son to save us, we would have no hope in this world, or in the world to come.

Mr. Speaker, many southern gentlemen regard it as humiliating, degrading, to treat the Republican party with any sort of deference or respect. Sir, I regard nothing as humiliating when the weal of my country is at stake; and I entreat, I implore, the members of that party to consider well before they reject the proposition for a compromise line; not because it emanated from me; not because it was proposed also by other gentlemen whose opinions are entitled to high respect; but because a large portion of the country has expressed itself for it, and because, preeminent among those who have recommended it, stands the great name of the distinguished Senator from Kentucky.[19] Ah, sir, it would not merely electrify the whole country, if this measure should be adopted, but in the sere and yellow leaf of age, a patriot, a statesman, an honest and honorable man, an "old man eloquent," a man of sterling worth, one who

> Never bent the pregnant hinges of the knee,
> Where thrift might follow fawning,[20]

would be delighted and rejoiced, in winding up his splendid and noble career as a statesman, by doing one great and final act for the preservation of our institutions. Yes, sir, if that old man, who seems, to mortal eyes, to be trembling upon the verge of the grave, and who, in a few short years at most, must depart from us, but whose life, I trust, will be long spared—I say if he were honored by the adoption of his plan of settlement; if he could feel that the last act of his public life had saved his country, I can almost fancy that when he passes to

That undiscovered country, from whose bourn

No traveler returns,[21]

the first welcome he will receive to the brighter sphere that awaits him, will be from the genial spirit of the noble-hearted Clay,[22] and that upon the green bank beyond the dark river of death, they will shake hands upon the deliverance, the redemption of their beloved country. [Great applause in the galleries.]

I shall not discuss this question any further, because within the time by which I am limited by the rules of the House I shall not be able to say one half of what I desire to say to the House and the country. I must notice these things hastily and imperfectly.

I hope, Mr. Speaker, that gentlemen of the Republican party will forgive me when I say that we of the South think we have just cause of fear and apprehension of the North. I do not say this to you, or to your party, in any spirit of bravado or unkindness. We have had too much of that already; and would to God that feelings of hatred and revenge, which are too often manifested, were banished from our Halls, and that, as brethren, having a common love for our common country, we could come together upon some honorable terms of adjustment, that would be satisfactory to the consciences of us all.

Now, Mr. Speaker, why do I say we have just cause of fear? I have not the time to print them out, except only in a general way. We have cause of fear in the abolition publications of books, sermons, and speeches, which have been so much circulated in the North, and in which we of the South have been so grossly and unjustly abused. We have cause of fear in the personal liberty bills which have been passed by northern Legislatures, and which have been sanctioned by northern conventions. It gives me pleasure to say, however, that the present indications are that most, or all, of these will be repealed. We have had just cause of fear in the facts that men have violated the Constitution of the United States, which secures the right of arresting fugitives from service or labor, and have resisted lawful efforts to apprehend our slaves when they have run away from us; and men, who have endeavored to enforce the constitutional right which belongs to us, have been murdered in cold blood upon northern soil, as Kennedy and Gorsuch were murdered, a few years ago, in Pennsylvania.[23] We have had wicked and unlawful assaults made upon our peace by such men as John Brown and his associates; and incendiary documents have, time and again, been thrown into our midst to kindle the flames of insurrection in the South.

We have, Mr. Speaker, a greater cause of fear, if possible, in the fact that prominent members of the Republican party have announced the doctrine upon the floor of the House of Representatives that the Supreme Court, as now constituted, is a partisan tribunal, and are doing all they can to sap the public confidence of the greatest judicial tribunal upon earth. And here let me say, that if there is any one thing in this country which, above all others, gives to the people security in their civil and religious liberties, it is the independence and faithfulness of judicial tribunals. We may talk as much as we please about our equality; but the impartial administration of justice, more than all other causes, secures and enforces it. There is one place yet where all men are equal in our country; and that, sir, is in a court of justice. There the poor and the rich stand upon the same footing; and there the judge, with the impartial balance in his hand, weighs the rights of either. There the man who has been oppressed and injured by his neighbor can go; and there he can feel that his rights will be asserted and maintained. The only national liberty we enjoy is that which is guarded by our laws, and enforced by an independent judiciary. The great element of its success is public confidence; but let the assaults which have been made by the Republicans upon the highest tribunal in the world be repeated through the land, and let the respect of our people for our Supreme Court, and other courts, be destroyed, and I tell you, Mr. Speaker, that we may bid "farewell, a long farewell, to all our greatness" as a nation.

{*Representative Nelson then referred to an amendment proposed earlier by Republican Charles Francis Adams of Massachusetts that would have prevented slavery from being abolished in any slave state without the consent of all the states of the Union. Nelson stated that that amendment along with one reinstating* the Missouri Compromise line would "give quiet and peace to the South, and save our country from the horrors of civil war."}

I hope, Mr. Speaker, that there are enough gentlemen on that side of the House who will offer us even that. If they do, let us take it into consideration; and let us consider it not as partisans, but as patriots. Let us endeavor to meet them in the same spirit in which they come to us. If we do that, we can soon settle and adjust the difficulties that now exist in the country. I trust that gentlemen of the Republican party will not consider that I am asking too much when I ask this. Intelligent as they are, they know but little of the true state of feeling in the South. I have here, and wish I had time to comment upon it, the message recently sent by the Governor of the State of Tennessee to the Legislature.[24] It is a sort of bill of indictment against the Republican party of the North. Among other things, it charges you with a design to abolish slavery in the District of Columbia; charges you with a design to interfere with the inter-State slave trade, although your platform contains nothing on the subject of slavery in this District, and has a distinct disavowal of any intention to interfere with our domestic institution in the States where it exists. It contains numerous other charges of that character; and I regret that I have not time to notice them all, for I could furnish arguments and reasons why gentlemen of the Republican party should be willing to meet us in a spirit of conciliation.

As I have been asked again, I may say that so far as I am personally concerned, I would be willing to receive the Missouri compromise line as it originally was. I doubt, however, whether that would be satisfactory to the entire South, and I do not undertake to speak for other gentlemen in regard to it. I would be willing to assent to almost anything rather than see this land drenched in blood; rather than see brother arrayed against brother, and friend against friend, in the horrible strife which will soon exist if we do not do something to quiet this spirit of disunion which prevails.

Mr. MORSE.[25] Will the gentleman allow me to ask him a question? The gentleman said a moment ago that the Governor of his State had brought two charges against the Republican party—that that party intended to abolish slavery in the District of Columbia and to prohibit the slave trade between the States. I want to answer those charges, and I do so by saying that since the organization of the Republican party, no man, North or South, ever heard a Republican take any such ground. It is not in any Republican platform nor in any Republican speech. Republicans do not want to do any such thing.

Mr. NELSON. I am glad to hear the gentleman thus express himself. I wish to let members of the Republican party know the state of sentiment entertained and uttered by high public functionaries in my State, and in other places of the South. It is charged here that the Republican party has justified and exalted to the highest honors of admiration, the horrid murders and arsons of the John Brown raid, and has canonized the felons as saints and martyrs. I say, not to the Republican party, but because it is due to the cause of truth, that if you judge of the party by its platform, it distinctly denounced the raid of John Brown, and declared that the party would never interfere with slavery in the States. I speak this not for the ear of the House, but for the people of the State of Tennessee. "Let justice be done, though the heavens fall." [26] [Cries of "Good!"]

In order to let gentlemen know why we beg and implore them to rally around some just standard of compromise, I have referred to the manner in which they are represented by a high public functionary. They are charged with having burned towns, poisoned wells, and conspired with slaves to depopulate northern Texas; although one gentleman from Texas declared in committee, as I hope he will do in the House, that there was little or no foundation for it. [27]

It is said in the message of the governor of Tennessee, that in the presidential election the Republican party asserted the equality of the black with the white race. How that fact is, I am uninformed; but we all know that Mr. Lincoln, when he was interrogated on that very subject by Judge Douglas in the contest of 1858, distinctly disavowed any such doctrine as being held by him.

Now, Mr. Speaker, I have endeavored to do justice to the Republicans, both in the charges which I have made against them, and in those from which I have defended them. I deem it proper to say this, because a convention has been called in my State, because propositions are made to arm the State, and because the storm of secession is sweeping over the State to-day; and it is almost impossible to resist it, unless gentlemen come up and meet us in the spirit of compromise of which I have so often spoken.

> {*Some general conversations ensued here regarding the Republican Party's intentions toward emancipation.*}

Mr. Speaker, an argument, which I omitted to mention, in regard to the Missouri compromise line, is one which I have no doubt will suggest itself to every gentleman; but at the same time, it should not be omitted. What is that? It is, that it will give peace and repose to the larger portion of the South—perhaps to all; perhaps to every southern State. I cannot undertake to speak for South Carolina, because the spirit of disunion has been rampant there for many years, and because they desire to destroy the Union for other reasons not connected with the question of slavery. But the adoption of the Missouri compromise line would settle this question. I will not say that, if the Republicans refuse to give us anything more than they have given us in the report of the committee,[28] I will advise the people of Tennessee to secede from the Union, and encounter all the horrors of civil war. I will not undertake to say that if they will go no further, I will advise resistance. But what I have to say is, that the argument I present to you to-day is addressed to your intelligence and patriotism, and not designed to operate upon the fears of gentlemen; not designed to prevent them from coming up to the requirements of the emergency in which they are placed; arguments fairly addressed to men who are my equals; men who have as much right to sit here as I have; men who have still the good of our common country at heart, and who, instead of using the power which they possess for the purpose of coercing the southern States into obedience by civil war, should exercise a generous magnanimity, and grant those just demands which cannot injure them, but, by restoring peace, will benefit the whole country.

Now, Mr. Speaker, as it is said that the cause of secession is gaining strength in Tennessee, I wish to say a few words—more, I confess, for the ear of the people of that State, than for this House. I wish to say to the people of Tennessee, that they, in the exercise of their rights as freemen, should survey the ground well, over which disunion asks them to tread. They should look at the origin of this movement, and to the instrumentality which has been used to bring it about. They should remember that in the cotton States—ay, sir, among Democrats who have rejoiced in all time past to magnify and glorify the power of the people—the men who have led this movement have not deigned to consult the people at all in regard to what they have done. They have not condescended to let them vote for secession or no secession. I have no doubt that if the great heart of the southern people could be exhibited here to-day, the result would show that there are hundreds and thousands of men even in South Carolina who, if they could be permitted to speak, would say they were against civil war, and against disunion. I doubt not that such is the fact in every southern State. But the tyranny of a despotic majority is there—tyranny more to be dreaded than musketry or batteries. Freemen are so situated that they dare not speak their true thoughts. I would invoke the people of Tennessee also to remember the prophetic language, as it turns out to be, of Mr. Yancey: *"We shall fire the southern heart, instruct the southern mind, give courage to each other; and, at the proper moment, by one organized, concerted action, we can precipitate the cotton States into a revolution."*[29] Not three years have elapsed since Mr. Yancey thus wrote. How wondrously has the southern heart been fired! How rapidly have seceding States given courage to each other. With no time for popular deliberation, the concerted movement long mediated has precipitated, hurried them headlong into revolution; and now they groan under taxation and prostrate credit, and hear "the thunder of the captains and the shouting."[30]

If the people of Tennessee will look well into the manifesto of South Carolina, in which she declares her independence, they will see to what straits those who prepared that document were reduced, in order to find any plausible ground on which to place the disunion of the State. It is not alone upon the slavery question. There are other and older issues with which the other southern States can have but little sympathy. Let the people of Tennessee, before they join the secession movement, direct their attention further to the fact that Governor Gist,[31] in one of his messages to the Legislature of South Carolina, assumed the duty of alluding, in a manner which, when carefully considered, is exceedingly offensive, to what he is pleased to call "the border States." I will not undertake to quote his language literally; but I remember he said in substance, in that message, that he desired them to enact a law to prevent the introduction of slaves into their State from any border State, and that one effect of such legislation will be, that the border States will be forced to join the secession movement, or to emancipate their slaves, or that our "confederates," as he chooses to call them, will do it for us. What is this but an attempt to force the border States, against their will, into the revolution?

This movement has been carried on to completion in South Carolina, without consultation with the border States as to her secession and hostile acts. She first put herself in the attitude of rebellion against the Government; the other cotton States have followed in their turn; and now, whether right or wrong, willing or unwilling, they desire to drag us into the whirlpool of disunion. As a Tennessean, I desire to raise my voice against being driven into civil war. I protest against tyranny from any quarter whatever—against the tyranny that is attempted to be practiced upon us in the North, when they would force opinions upon us contrary to our will, and against this fiercer tyranny of the South, that proclaims fidelity to the Union treason, and would drag every southern State into the vortex of civil war.

{*After being interrupted by Representative Francis Burton Craige (1811–1875) of North Carolina, Nelson continued to argue against being forced into secession by the cotton states. "I say to the people of Tennessee that they should resist this attempt to coerce them to do what they are otherwise unwilling to do; resist it, if need be, with arms, and unto the death. It is an insult that freemen ought not submit to."*}

But, Mr. Speaker, I was going on to say, when interrupted, that the secession movement does not commend itself to the people of the State of Tennessee, either in the manner or the circumstances under which it was gotten up, or in the arguments by which it has been supported, or in that last argument of arms by which it is attempted to be carried through. It has other objections that our people in Tennessee will soon feel if they fall into the movement. What are they? From the accounts which we get from South Carolina, the people of that State are already groaning under taxation—a heavy, intolerable burden; and if the people of the State of Tennessee are seduced into this rebellion, they will soon find that the tax gatherers will be at every door. If his visits are not agreeable now, when we are taxed less heavily than any other people, what will they be when he comes, as it were, with a whip of scorpions in his hand? Let the border South rush to war to avoid anticipated evils which may never come, and we will not only suffer in the matter of taxation, but in every other respect in which it is possible for a people to suffer.

I ask the people of Tennessee, when they see this secession movement organized and carried out by preconcert; when they remember that some of its advocates declared, openly, that they had meditated it for twenty years, and long before the Republican party was dreamed of; when they reflect that the slavery question has been seized hold of, not because of its intrinsic importance, but because it could be artfully used to favor disunion, long contemplated on other grounds; when they see that, notwithstanding all the wrong that has been done us by the North, there has been perversion and misrepresentation in the South in regard to the purposes of a great political party in the North; when they see all that, I ask them whether they are willing to submit to heavy taxation in order to build up the rich nabobs of the South, and, perchance, to establish a monarchy, with kings and lords and dukes and grandees to ride, booted and spurred, over their prostrate liberty? No, sir; if war is to come upon us, if civil discord is to reign where peace so sweetly smiled before, the men who will have to fight the battles will not be your partisan leaders, who desire to be colonels and captains, majors and generals, governors and ministers; but it will be the farmers, the mechanics, and the laboring men of the country. I ask them—and I would to God that my voice could echo and reecho from one end of my State to the other—are they willing to submit to this in order to build up a pampered aristocracy in the South? [Applause.] Are they willing to do it in order to establish a military despotism in the South? For, Mr. Speaker, not the least of all the evils which threaten us in the southern States, is the danger of military domination. Already we hear

> the trump and the drum,
> And the mournful sound of the barbarous horn,
> And the flap of the banners that flit as they're borne,
> And the neigh of the steed and the multitude's hum.[32]

The clash and the shouts are yet to come! Beware of polished blades and gilded epaulets. They may be used to crush yourselves. We have seen a great political movement, which gentlemen ludicrously call "peaceable secession," suddenly assume all the pomp and circumstance of glorious war, by arming and proposing to arm the whole of the southern States. How easy for ambition to turn this movement against the liberties of the people? Peaceable secession! and yet the whole of the southern States in arms. This is the manner in which they are attempting to carry out a long premeditated plot; and now, throughout the southern States, the despotism of military power is beginning to be felt. Cockades are in the ascendant, and the plowshares may rust. A reign of terror is already beginning to trammel free speech in the South; and I doubt not that in many places the iron heel of military power is felt, and men opposed to rashness and precipitancy dare not speak as freemen should speak, and as they would wish to speak, against secession. Let the people of Tennessee awake, arouse! Let them remember that "eternal vigilance is the price of liberty." Let them open their eyes and behold a danger at their doors more imminent, if possible, than that of Black Republicanism. Let them beware of military conquerors—and let the whole land beware of them; for, sir, if we shall overthrow the peaceful institutions which we have so long enjoyed; if we shall dissolve the Union of the American States, some Caesar or Napoleon will soon trample down the liberties of the people and destroy the last hope and the last vestige of freedom upon the earth.

{*Representative Nelson continued here to praise the Union and question the logic of secession. "Why should we destroy our Government," he asked. Invoking Washington, Jackson, and Clay, Nelson proclaimed he would never consent to the dissolution of the Union.*}

My countrymen, let us heed these warning voices. Let us settle all our controversies in the Union. Oh, trust not to that last delusive argument of the secessionists, that this Government, once dissolved, can be reconstructed. That will never be. The causes which destroy it will forever preclude a reunion. Hate will be intensified, and a war of extermination will ensue. It is in vain for either section to calculate upon the cowardice of the other. All are of the same race. All are alike brave; and a war once begun between us will have no parallel in the contests which history has described. May Almighty God avert it!

It has been said, "agree with thine adversary quickly whilst thou art in the way with him."[33] If we are governed by this salutary rule, all domestic difficulties will soon pass away from our country, peace will again smile in all our borders, and we will once more enjoy those privileges with which we have so long been blessed far above every other people.

Source: *Congressional Globe*, 36th Cong. 2nd Sess., Appendix, 106–11.

William Tecumseh Avery,
10th District
West Tennessee (Democrat)
January 31, 1861

William Tecumseh Avery (1819–1880) was born in Hardeman County, Tennessee, graduated from Jackson College in Maury

County, and began his law practice in Memphis in 1840. After serving in the state legislature (1843–1845), he was elected to the Thirty-Fifth and Thirty-Sixth Congresses (1857–1861). During the war he served as a lieutenant colonel in the Confederate Army.

Representative Avery presented an impassioned rebuttal to Emerson Etheridge's speech of a week earlier. Labeling it "extraordinary" and "unnatural," he refuted it point by point pronouncing that only by amending the Constitution can northerners prevent secession. Avery devoted a fair amount of time attacking the alleged Republican belief that there is "equality in the races." In a direct rebuttal to Etheridge's assertion that, "where the flag of my country floats, there I will go," Avery concluded: "My first and highest allegiance is to my State."

Mr. AVERY said:

Mr. SPEAKER, I had not intended to say one word during the whole course of this debate, conscious as I was, that the period for profitable discussion and argument on the part of the Representatives of the people of the South had passed, and the time for action had come; nor would I have violated that determination, did I not deem it a duty that I owe to myself, to my constituency, and to my State, to vindicate them from the false opinions that this House and the country might entertain concerning their position in the present crisis of the Union, judging from some of the speeches which have been made upon this floor by those who claim to represent the sentiments of that people and that State. I wish to set my State right in this perilous controversy; and in doing so, to reply to the extraordinary, and I may say, unnatural speech made the other day by my colleague from the ninth congressional district of Tennessee, [Mr. ETHERIDGE.][34] An official report of that speech having not yet appeared in the Globe, the official organ of this House, I am indebted to my colleague, to whom I applied this morning, for a copy in pamphlet form, at the same time stating to him that I expected to reply to it this evening, and desired his presence. I regret very much not to see him in his seat. The New

York Tribune, one of the 24th of January—the morning after my colleague's speech—contains the following complimentary notice of it: "The able and patriotic speech of Mr. ETHERIDGE, of Tennessee in the United States House of Representatives yesterday, was worthy of his high reputation, and cannot fail to command the general situation of the country. He presents a firm and inflexible front to treason in any shape, and is for the Union, first and last, and at all hazards."

I will also read from the Cincinnati Gazette, another Republican organ, a still more eulogistic notice:

> Hon. EMERSON ETHERIDGE, of Tennessee, made a speech in the House of Representatives yesterday, which, for boldness, for power, for patriotism, and for eloquence, has not been excelled. The position of this man of the South is in striking contrast with that of the driveling demagogues who pretended to represent the Democracy of Ohio in convention at Columbus yesterday. We rejoice that it is in our power to send out in the same paper a report of the speech of Mr. ETHERIDGE and the proceedings of the Democratic convention. The people will strike the difference and make up the verdict. From this time the name of Hon. EMERSON ETHERIDGE, of Tennessee, will be warmly and favorably canvassed in connection with Mr. Lincoln's Cabinet.

I have said, Mr. Speaker, the extraordinary and unnatural speech of my colleague; and I think that I am warranted in thus designating a speech made by a Representative of a southern constituency upon this floor, which is thus hailed and applauded by the chief organs of the Republican party. The gentleman began by saying that if he had a jury of good and lawful men, duly impaneled, sworn, and charged to try the issue joined between the North and the South, he would, before that impartial tribunal, submit this case without argument, confident in the assurance that he would receive a speedy and righteous verdict.

My colleague may have fancied that he was engaged in his old vocation, defending before a jury the offenders of the law—pleading the cause of criminals at the bar of public justice. The extract from the

Cincinnati Gazette, which I have just read, might suggest to a more uncharitable mind than mine that a contingent fee, in the shape of high place in the Cabinet councils of Mr. Lincoln, sharpened the intellect and quickened the powers of his defense. But I will not be thus uncharitable. I will say, however, that, in my judgment, a Representative of a southern constituency, born and nurtured upon southern soil, in a crisis like this, is far forgetful of his State, her rights, her interests, and her honor, when he unblushingly stands forth, cheered on by them, to champion the cause of the sworn enemies of his section.

The leading idea in my colleague's speech is, that the North has been guilty of no wrong to justify the "extraordinary, unpardonable, and indefensible" action on the part of the people of the South; that the southern mind is maddened and insane. And yet, he wants to adjourn the question over to this mad and insane populace. Who, but the people, in their sovereign capacity, have moved this mighty revolution, even to the dismemberment of the Confederacy? Is it possible that those States, having more than double the population of the original thirteen, and are all madly driven to desperation for nothing? Sir, I ask again, is it possible that the whole body of the South, the people of fifteen sovereign States, are madly bent, as my colleague says, "on believing a lie that they may be damned?" What thought Mr. Fillmore about this thing—my colleague's "model President?"[35] In replying to a large New York meeting, informing him that he had been appointed to proceed as ambassador to intercede with the South, he declined going, saying:

> What they want, [the southern people,] and what I want, is some assurance from the Republican party, now dominant at the North, that they, or at least the conservative portion of them, are ready and willing to come forward and repeal all unconstitutional slave laws, live up to the compromises of the Constitution, execute the laws of Congress honestly and faithfully, and treat our southern brethren as friends. When I can have any such reliable assurance as this to give, I will go most cheerfully and urge our southern brethren to follow our example, and restore harmony and fraternal affection between the North and the South.

At present, our labors should be here. Let us put ourselves right, and then we can, with more confidence and justice, appeal to them.

Why, sir, even my colleague from the first district [Mr. Nelson][36] enumerates a catalogue of causes of fear which we justly have from the Republican party; the greatest of which, to use his own language, "is in the fact that prominent members of the Republican party have announced the doctrine upon the floor of the House of Representatives that the Supreme Court, as now constituted, is a partisan tribunal, and are doing all they can to sap public confidence in the greatest judicial tribunal upon earth."

Sir, every single resolution which has been passed by the most conservative people of the South, in their primary assemblies, large and small, in their legislative bodies everywhere, proclaim that there have been aggressions; that there have been wrongs; and that those wrongs and aggressions must be righted, and that speedily, or they will declare themselves absolved from all allegiance to this Government. Is it to be expected that those to whom conservative men all over the land are appealing to come to the rescue of the country; they alone who have perpetrated the wrong; they who alone can remedy it—is it to be expected that they will come forward and remedy those wrongs, when a Representative of southern constituents tells them that there have been none? I say, that every solitary resolution passed by the people of the South—I mean the Union people; I mean the most conservative people; I do not mean the disunionists or the fire-eaters, but those who are considered of the most compromising school of southern rights—has declared that there are wrongs, and that those wrongs must be redressed. That, sir, is the sentiment of Tennessee.

I have here the resolutions recently passed by the Legislature of Tennessee by an unprecedented majority; passed with only six dis-senting votes in the House, and I believe five in the Senate. That body of one hundred members came fresh from their constituency. Let us see what the potential voice of Tennessee says in regard to the wrongs of the people of Tennessee; and what they say must be put into an amended Constitution, or they, too, will fasten upon themselves this "unpardonable" sin of disunion. Here it is:

A declaratory amendment that African slaves, as held under the institutions of the slaveholding States, shall be recognized as property, and entitled to the *status* of other property in the States where slavery exists; in all places within the exclusive jurisdiction of Congress within the slave States; in all the Territories south of 36°30'; in the District of Columbia; in transit and whilst temporarily sojourning with the owner in the non-slaveholding States and Territories north of 36°30'; and when fugitives from the owner in the several places above named, as well as in all places in the exclusive jurisdiction of Congress in the non-slaveholding States.

That in all the territory now owned, or which may be hereafter acquired by the United States south of the parallel 36°30', African slavery shall be recognized as existing, and be protected by all departments of the Federal and territorial governments; and in all north of that line, now owned or to be acquired, it shall not be recognized as existing; and whenever States formed out of any of said territory south of said line, having a population equal to that of a congressional district, shall apply for admission into the Union, the same shall be admitted as slave States; while States north of the line formed out of said territory, and having a population equal to a congressional district, shall be admitted without slavery; but the States formed out of said territory, north and south, having been admitted as members of the Union, shall have all the powers over the institutions of slavery possessed by other States of the Union.

That slave property shall be rendered secure in transit through, or while temporarily sojourning in, non-slaveholding States or Territories, or in the District of Columbia.

An amendment to the effect that all fugitives are to be deemed those offending the laws within the jurisdiction of the State, and who escape therefrom to other States; and that it is the duty of each State to suppress armed invasions of another State.[37]

These are the chief points contained in the resolutions of the Legislature of Tennessee, which they present as the ultimatum of that State. Do not these resolutions point to wrongs? and that these wrongs must be righted, and that speedily? They declare that the right of property in slaves must be recognized; that the right of transit into free States and Territories shall be admitted and protected; that the right of temporary residence and holding slaves in such States and Territories shall also be recognized by the Constitution, and protected; and that in all the territory of the United States south of 36°30', now held and hereafter to be acquired, slavery shall be acknowledged and protected by all departments of the Government.

But what do they go on further and say?

> 5. *Resolved*, That should a plan of adjustment satisfactory to the South not be acceded to by the requisite number of States to perfect amendments to the Constitution of the United States, it is the opinion of this General Assembly that the slaveholding States should adopt for themselves the Constitution of the United States, with such amendments as may be satisfactory to the slaveholding States; and that they should invite into a Union with them all States of the North which are willing to abide such amended Constitution and frame of Government; severing at once all connections with States refusing such reasonable guarantees to our future safety; such renewed conditions of Federal Union being first submitted for ratification to conventions of all the States respectively.

Not that this plan of adjustment must be satisfactory to one community; not to one State or any number of southern States; not alone to the Union men, but to the whole and entire South; and unless these "just and reasonable guarantees" are given, they are for disunion, and for forming a Union with no people or State that will not give them.

But what says the Nashville Banner, the home organ of Mr. Bell, and the leading paper of my colleague's party—if he has a party—in the State? This paper, in its issue of the 25th January, uses this significant language:

The resolutions adopted by the General Assembly, published in our paper a few days since, define the position of Tennessee satisfactorily, as we believe, to the great mass of the people. They substantially adopt the Crittenden compromise as a basis of adjustment of the pending issues between North and South; and Tennessee will say to the people of the North, not in a spirit of blustering defiance and braggadocio, but firmly and calmly, and with a sincere and honest desire that this adjustment may be accepted—we demand nothing more—*we will accept of nothing less.*

Here, sir, is what this newspaper, representing the most conservative element in Tennessee, says is the uncompromising position of that State with regard to these resolutions, that "she demands nothing more, and will accept nothing less."

{*Representative Avery was asked by Representative David Kilgore, a Republican from Indiana, to "specify wrongs" done to the South. He responded by listing and discussing the personal liberty laws of the North and reluctance there to enforce the fugitive slave law, the belief that "the people of the free States intend to abolish slavery where it exists in the States," and the charge that Republicans favored "the equality of the races."*}

These are the sentiments of the master spirits of the Republican party—their President, their first and their second Cabinet officer {William H. Seward and Salmon P. Chase}; and yet we are told no such sentiments belong to the party.

My colleague, in this connection, referred to the past history of Tennessee, and declared that, from 1796 to 1835, that State has sanctioned and deliberately approved the principle of negro equality; that Jackson had sanctioned and approved it.

Mr. Speaker, it is true that, in the formation of the constitution of the State of Tennessee, in 1796, in defining what should be the qualifications of voters, it confined this qualification to "all free male citizens over the age of twenty-one years;" but no man, I presume, then thought of negro equality or negro suffrage. The word "white" was left out in the formation of this constitution. Advantage, however, is taken of this omission to make the charge that negro equality once was the doctrine of the State. Sir, no man there ever thought of approving the infamous doctrine of negro equality. I repudiate and spurn it as the sentiment of that State now or ever. Does any man believe that Andrew Jackson was an advocate of negro equality? And such a charge, too, to come from a Representative from Tennessee. It is true, they found that defect in the constitution of 1796; but when, in 1835, an opportunity was afforded for amendment, the word "white" was instantly substituted; and from that time it has been provided that the qualification of voters shall be confined to all free white male citizens over the age of twenty-one.

My colleague went on to argue that every single, solitary foot of southern territory had been acquired by northern treasure and northern votes; that they had willingly—yes, willingly—yielded to the South every demand that had been made. What are the facts in regard to this question of the acquisition of territory and of the admission of slave States into the Union? Let the record speak. It shows that every foot of slave territory has been acquired with the aid of a few northern Democrats, who have stood by us ever in the hour of our peril, but against the great majority of northern votes. It shows that every slave State that has ever been admitted into the Union has been admitted against the great majority of northern votes, against, the efforts of the Republican party now in power, who assume to take possession of purse and sword and administer the Government. My colleague says that the South got the Missouri compromise, and they repealed it. How did they get the Missouri compromise? Why, sir, it was taken as a poor boon to the South to prevent the North from saying that Missouri should only be admitted with slavery forever excluded from her territory, against the will of that people, as expressed in their con- stitution; and when they refused faithfully even to carry out that, it was repealed. The record shows that after the Missouri compromise was adopted, the very next session, when she presented herself with a slave constitution at the door of Congress for admission, sixty-one northern Representatives in the House voted for the repeal of that compromise, and for a proviso declaring that no slave should exist within the limits of the State of Missouri.

And so it has been with regard to every slave State—Florida, Arkansas, and Texas. My colleague says that we are indebted to northern Republicans for the acquisition of all these Territories, and he refers particularly to the Territory of Louisiana. Does he not know that the greatest portion of that territory, slave territory as it all was when we acquired it, is to-day free, and in the hands of the Republicans?—this party planted upon the declaration, too, that not another foot of slave territory we shall ever have; upon the declaration, in defiance of the Supreme Court, that we cannot carry our property into this common territory; with a President who declared in a speech at Chicago, July 10, 1858: "If I were in Congress and a vote should come up on a question whether slavery should be prohibited in a new Territory, in spite of the Dred Scott decision, I would vote that it should."

Sir, I was asked just now to specify some of the charges against the Republican party. Allow me to make some slight specification by substituting a short extract from a most eloquent and powerful speech of a southern Senator the other day on parting forever from that once August body.[38] In speaking of this fanatic spirit of the North, which is the very breath of this Republican party, he said:

> It denied us Christian communion, because it could not endure what it styles the moral leprosy of slaveholding; it refused us permission to sojourn, or even to pass through the North, with our property; it claimed freedom for the slave if brought by his master into a northern State; it violated the Constitution and treaties and laws of Congress, because designed to protect that property; it refused us any share of the lands acquired mainly by our diplomacy and blood and treasure; it refused our property any shelter or security beneath the flag of a common Government; it robbed us of our property, and refused to restore it; it refused to deliver criminals against our laws, who fled to the North with our property or our blood upon their hands; it threatened us, by solemn legislative acts, with ignominious punishment if we pursued our

property into a northern State; it murdered southern men when seeking the recovery of their property on northern soil; it invaded the borders of southern States, poisoned their wells, burnt their dwellings, and murdered their people; it denounced us by deliberate resolves of popular meetings, of party conventions, and of religious and even legislative assemblies, as habitual violators of the laws of God and the rights of humanity; it exerted all the moral and physical agencies that human ingenuity can devise or diabolical malice can employ to heap odium and infamy upon us, and to make us a by-word of hissing and of scorn throughout the civilized world.

The gentleman says, "with sword in one hand and torch in the other, he will go home and fight disunion." The question of Union or disunion is not now for Tennessee to settle. Six States, making a mighty empire, stretching from the Atlantic to the Mississippi, are already out of the Union; before another week to be followed by one more, with a domain almost as large as all the rest. The only question which will be left for Tennessee is, will she join these, her southern glorious sisters, or will she link her fortunes with the Republican North?

What does the gentleman mean by his torch and sword, and following the flag of his country wherever it floats? Does he mean, sir, if that flag floated over hostile armies marching into the borders of Tennessee to subjugate the people of that or a sister State, that he would be found fighting under it? Sir, if this be his meaning, let me point him to the following resolutions, passed almost unanimously by his own State:

> *Resolved by the General Assembly of the State of Tennessee*, That this General Assembly has heard with profound regret of the resolutions recently adopted by the State of New York, tendering men and money to the President of the United States, to be used in coercing certain sovereign States of the South into obedience to the Federal Government.
>
> *Resolved*, That this General Assembly receives the action of

the Legislature of New York as the indication of a purpose upon the part of the people of that State to further complicate existing difficulties, by forcing the people of the South to the extremity of submission or resistance; and so regarding it, the Governor of the State of Tennessee is hereby requested to inform the Executive of the State of New York, that it is the opinion of this General Assembly that whenever the authorities of that State shall send armed forces to the South for the purpose indicated in said resolutions, the people of Tennessee, uniting with their brethren of the South, will, as one man, resist such invasion of the soil of the South at all hazards, and to the last extremity.

This, sir, is the spontaneous and patriotic voice of the proud freemen of Tennessee. Let me tell the gentleman, too, that the author of these resolutions is his own constituent and a member of his own party. Can it be possible that, should the flag of his country be prostituted to the base and despotic purpose of subjugating sovereign States, he would still be there? That under it he would lift a fratricidal hand with "torch and sword?" My first and highest allegiance is to my State; and I pledge now, that when this ensanguined war shall come, (which may God in His providence avert!) the brave men of Tennessee will rally to the standard of their State, and resist unto the death any invasion of the soil of the South, it matters not under whatsoever banner the invading foe may come.

Source: *Congressional Globe*, 36th Cong 2nd Sess., Appendix, 121–24.

WILLIAM BRICKLY STOKES, 4TH DISTRICT MIDDLE TENNESSEE (OPPOSITIONIST)
February 1, 1861

William B. Stokes (1814–1897) served in the Tennessee House of Representatives (1849–1852) and then in the Tennessee Senate

(1855–1856) before being elected to the Thirty-Sixth Congress as
an Opposition Party candidate. During the war he joined the
United States Army as a major and was subsequently brevetted
a major general in the Tennessee Volunteers.

In this speech, Representative Stokes argued dramatically
against secession calling it "a monstrous paradox," "a wild cru-
sade," and "a wild, revolutionary scheme." He carefully listed
the grievances of the cotton states and lectured that none of them
warranted secession. It was well known to the country, he opined,
that had the South's departed senators and representatives "re-
mained in their seats, and stood to their posts like men and pa-
triots, not one dollar could the Administration of Mr. Lincoln
get out of the Treasury, unless by the consent of an opposition
House and a Democratic Senate." Like numerous other southern
moderates, Stokes argued that destroying the Union "because of
the existence of African slavery . . . will result in abolishing it
finally and forever."

The House having under consideration the report from the select
committee of thirty-three—

Mr. STOKES said:

Mr. SPEAKER: I feel that there is less necessity for me to address the House on the pending propositions since I have heard the
eloquent, unanswerable speech just made by the honorable gentleman
from Texas, [Mr. HAMILTON;][39] but as a Union man, as a lover of
my whole country, I deem it my imperative duty to my immediate
constituents and to the people of Tennessee to speak out frankly and
fearlessly the earnest convictions of my heart, and to warn them of
the dangers which lie before them. It is not my purpose to reply particularly to any of the various gentlemen who have preceded me in
debate. I will seek no issues with any member. My desire is to do and
contribute whatever I may toward the adjustment of the unhappy
differences that afflict the country; to allay as far as possible the storm
that howls about us; and to restore, as best we may, peace and harmony
to the American people. I shall treat the questions at issue honestly,

fairly, truthfully. I shall endeavor to speak the truth; yes, sir, the whole truth will I speak, although the heavens fall. Gentlemen who have preceded me have indulged freely in crimination and recrimination. Each party has endeavored to affix all blame and responsibility on the other. Such a course I will not attempt to imitate. I propose to consider the alleged causes for the agitation and excitement under which this Union totters to its fall; for the country is shaken and convulsed as it never was before. A little more than a year ago, it reposed in peace and prosperity. What has since occurred to distract and drive it to the verge of revolution and ruin? What are the causes of all this wild commotion and wide-spread alarm?

It is said, sir, that the Republican party is opposed to the further extension of slavery into the free Territories of the United States. This is true; and if I had the time, I could read resolution after resolution adopted by the Democratic party of the northern States, in conventions and Legislatures, in which they, too, declared it to be the duty of the Government to oppose the extension of slavery. Some Democratic conventions and Legislatures went so far as to declare it to be their ultimate design to *eradicate* slavery from the States where it now exists, by restricting its further extension, and such other lawful means as might finally lead to its *extinction*. If opposition to the further spread of slavery is *now* a cause for overthrowing the Government, was it not sufficient cause *then*, when the Democratic party had control of it? But at that time our southern brethren, who have since seceded, stood shoulder to shoulder, cheek by jowl, with those very northern men, announcing that the northern Democracy were the only men in that section who were faithful to the rights of the South. I opposed these men then, as now. I fought them with all my power. If, however, the refusal to permit the extension of slavery into the free Territories *then* was not a cause for breaking up this Union, certainly it ought not to be so regarded now.

{*Here Representative Stokes quoted from two dozen Democratic gatherings or dominated legislatures to make his point. Typical is a resolution from an 1848 convention in Ohio:* "Resolved, *That*

the people of Ohio now, as they have always done, look upon the
institution of slavery as an evil, unfavorable to the full develop-
ment of our institutions; and that, entertaining these sentiments
they will feel it to be their duty to use all the powers consistent
with the national compact to prevent its increase, to mitigate,
and finally eradicate *it.*"}

Mr. Speaker, the southern States which have seceded declare that they are separate and distinct sovereignties, because of their alleged withdrawal from this Union. Sir, the right of secession I will not discuss at this time, for I have already placed myself on record in regard to it in some remarks I made during the last session.[40] Now, I need only say that if a State has any right to withdraw from the Union, it is the right, not of secession, but of revolution. A constitutional right of secession is a monstrous paradox. Every State, however, that has suffered oppression or tyranny until it is no longer tolerable, has the inalienable right to protect itself, and, if needs be, to resort in that remedy which is above all constitutions—the right of revolution.

I shall not now further discuss the question of secession. I concur, in opinion, with the gentleman from Texas, [Mr. HAMILTON,] in the opinion just expressed by him, that no State can rightfully or constitutionally secede without the consent of the other States. I have been taught to believe that the doctrines and opinions of Washington, Madison, Jefferson, and Jackson, were right; and I find no sufficient reason for abandoning them now. On the contrary, I find in the events of the day much to cause me to adhere more closely to their teachings.

Mr. Speaker, six States have passed ordinances declaring themselves free and independent sovereignties; and what do we find to be the fruits of this "peaceable" right of secession? Forts, arsenals, dockyards, arms, and munitions of war, public moneys, and property of various descriptions belonging to the United States have been seized by lawless mobs and bands of armed men. Not only that. The flag— the flag of Tennessee as well as of Pennsylvania; the flag of all the States—has been grossly insulted and fired upon as it waved over an unarmed ship,[41] bearing provisions to our own soldiers, in the service of the Government, while occupying and defending the property of the United States. In doing this, these seceding States, or the armed bodies of men who perpetrated these outrages, have been guilty of a violation of the laws of the land, and have made open war against the United States, as I will show. And they have violated and defied the plainest provisions of the Constitution.

I will read a few clauses from the Constitution. Section ten, article one, of the Constitution, says: "No State shall enter into any treaty, alliance, or confederation. * * * * No State shall without the consent of Congress, lay any duty of tonnage, keep troops or ships of war in time of peace, enter into any agreement or compact with another State, or with a foreign Power."

Article six, section three, says: "The Senators and Representatives * * * * shall be bound by oath or affirmation to support this Constitution."

Which is elsewhere declared to be "the supreme law of the land."

{*Stokes here reaffirmed his support for the Constitution, and questioned Louisiana's pledge to "recognize the free navigation of the Mississippi river* and its tributaries *by* all friendly States bordering thereon."}

Those cotton States have gone out and severed their connection with the Federal Government, as they say, and for what? What are the grievances?

1. They allege that the North has passed personal liberty bills.

2. That the fugitive slave law has not been faithfully executed.

3. That the Republican party is opposed to the further extension of slavery into the free Territories.

4. That the Republican party intend to abolish slavery in the District of Columbia, and in the dock-yards, arsenals, and navy-yards, under the exclusive jurisdiction of the United States.

5. That they intend finally to abolish slavery in the States.

6. That the Republican party hates slavery; that Garrison, Phillips,[42] and others denounce slavery, and that we are in danger of invasions similar to that which John Brown made upon the soil of Virginia.

You are all familiar with the John Brown affair; but we know that no party in the North, unless it be the few radical Abolitionists, justifies the conduct of John Brown. Then there were the alleged burnings of habitations and villages in Texas during the last year. An intelligent gentleman, long a resident of Texas, a few days ago furnished me with a map and other particulars, concerning these fires in Texas. From him I learned that most of them occurred many miles apart, on the same day and about the same hour of the day, to wit: at two o'clock, p. m., on the 8th of August last, when the thermometer was standing at 113°. From information derived from him, I am satisfied that these fires were not the work of incendiaries; yet it is charged that the North are sending their missionaries out there to burn up and destroy the property and habitations of the people of that State.

Another grievance complained of is the election of Lincoln by a sectional party. He, it is said, has no sympathy with the South, and therefore we are justified in precipitating a dissolution of the Union. It is said that Lincoln will oppose the further extension of slavery into the Territories which are now free. Let me read an extract from a speech of Mr. Buchanan, now President of the United States, which he made upon the proposition for the admission of Texas. He said:

> In arriving at the conclusion to support this treaty, [the annexation of Texas,] I had to encounter but one serious obstacle, and this was the question of slavery. While I ever maintained, and ever shall maintain, in their full force and vigor, the constitutional rights of the southern States over their slave property, I yet feel a strong repugnance by any act of mine to extend the present limits of the Union over a new slaveholding Territory. After mature reflection, however, I overcame these scruples, and now believe that the acquisition of Texas will be the means of limiting the domain of slavery. * * * * That the acquisition of Texas would, ere long, convert Maryland, Virginia, Kentucky, and Missouri, and

possibly others of the more northern slave States into free States, I entertain not a doubt.

I ask, then, if opposition to the extension of slavery is a cause for a dissolution of the Union, why it was not done when Mr. Buchanan was elected? for this extract proves him to have been as much opposed to the extension of slavery as it was possible for him to be. I say it was no sufficient cause when Mr. Buchanan was elected, and it furnishes only a pretext now.

Six States have already seceded, and one member from another State [Mr. Reagan][43] has gone home to the State of Texas. Thirty-one southern members of the House have retired from this Hall, and twelve Senators have vacated their seats in the Senate. They have left us their southern brethren, to fight the battle alone. Now, although Mr. Lincoln is elected, it is well known to this House, and to the country, that, had those gentlemen remained in their seats, and stood to their posts like men and patriots, not one dollar could the Administration of Mr. Lincoln get out of the Treasury, unless by the consent of an opposition House, and a Democratic Senate. He could not have formed his Cabinet, or even appointed a minister or a consul, without the consent of the Democratic Senate. Suppose, then, that they had stood their ground, and remained like men, as I think they ought to have done: what would have been the effect of it? Why, sir, if we had exercised our constitutional power in stopping supplies, and in refusing to confirm presidential appointments, we could have prevented any unconstitutional interference with our rights, had such interference been attempted by the incoming Administration. And with this power in our hands, it might have been used not only to prevent usurpation, but so as to have secured unequivocal acknowledgment of all our just rights under the Constitution. To this we might have compelled Republicans to accede, had our Representatives remained in their places. We could have decided to present to the people of the North and the South such amendments to the Constitution, or other guarantees, as we thought proper. We could have asked that these propositions be referred to the people of all the States, in the mode prescribed by the Constitution. We could thus have invoked the action of the people, in whose willingness to do right I have every confidence; and if the Republican party had refused to transfer the whole matter to the States and the people, or to come to some such reasonable terms of adjustment, we might have exercised the power of stopping the supplies; have refused to vote one dollar for carrying on this Government. But now, instead of having such power, we are left in the minority by the withdrawal of thirty-one members from the House and twelve from the Senate. And it now is in the power of the Republican party to refuse us whatever they choose, and yield us only whatever they are willing to accord.

Sir, a convention is to be held soon in Tennessee, in which the State—which I in part represent—is to decide whether she will go out of the Union. We are invited by the disunionists to follow them into this southern confederacy. I, for one, enter my solemn protest against any such suicidal conduct. I will never agree to any such an act of folly. What, sir; go into a southern confederacy; ally ourselves with the cotton States, after they have abandoned us here, after they have been faithless to us here; when, had they remained, we had the power of self-defense in our hands! If they would not stand by us under existing circumstances, can we rely upon them when we shall have joined ourselves to their southern confederacy? We cannot. Faithless now, faithless they would be then. Should they see any cause to be hereafter dissatisfied, they would doubtless come forward with another secession ordinance, and withdraw from the southern confederacy. And where would we then stand?

{*Representative Stokes here questioned the timing of secession following Lincoln's election quoting several members of the South Carolina secession convention who announced that they had been contemplating secession for many years.*}

Are these causes, I again ask, sufficient for the dissolution of the Union? If they are, then they exist outside of the election of Mr. Lincoln to the Presidency. And if they exist outside of Mr. Lincoln's election—and I have showed you they have existed for years—then Mr. Douglas,

Mr. Bell, or Mr. Breckinridge, could no more have kept the Union together than Mr. Lincoln can. But, if this movement goes merely upon the election of Mr. Lincoln, then, I say, it is too ridiculous to talk about. The present leading disunionists in my State, last summer, all promptly and earnestly insisted that the election of Mr. Lincoln was no cause for destroying the Federal Government.

These grievances, if grievances there be, existed for years past; and it was in the power of this Democratic party to have remedied them if they chose. They had majorities in both Houses last Congress.[44] All the territorial laws are to-day precisely as they were then, and as they passed them. If objectionable, why were they not changed when the Democratic party had control of both Houses of Congress, the Executive, and the judiciary? Why did not some gentleman propose to remedy them? Show me the motion on the Journal of this House, or any proposition that any southern man brought before Congress, to change our present territorial policy in regard to the slavery question. It cannot be done. The slavery question in the States and Territories is precisely where the Democratic party placed it, and where they have the power to maintain it. To do this, they have only to remain in their places, and the Republican party are powerless in both Houses of Congress.

Mr. Speaker, we have grievances to complain of; and I intend to show my Republican friends that we have just cause to complain of them for some of their acts; and I trust and hope that they will see the necessity of taking such action here and in the northern States as may allay the public excitement and tranquilize the popular mind.

I was speaking of the election of Lincoln. Sir, there were various causes why he was elected. There were several candidates. Millions were supporting Mr. Douglas for his devotion to the doctrine of non-intervention; others supported Mr. Breckinridge, and subscribed to the new code of protection to slavery in the Territories; while the Union party rallied under the leadership of Mr. Bell, pledged to "the Union, the Constitution, and *the enforcement of the laws.*" What else? One of the most powerful causes of all was the extravagance, the waste, the profligacy, and, I think I can safely say, the corruptions of the present

Administration. These things alone caused thousands of the people of the country to record their votes for Mr. Lincoln for the Presidency, who would not otherwise have voted for him.

I contend, sir, that the election of Mr. Lincoln, under these circumstances, is no reason for a dissolution of the Union. I think disunion can be fairly traced to the purposes and plans of the southern league, which was concocted and deliberately agreed upon over two years ago, by the leaders of the Democratic party in the cotton States, that they would go to Charleston and make certain demands on the northern Democrats; and, if refused, that they would set up a candidate of their own, and when defeated, as they expected and desired to be, then to strike for a southern confederacy. They have publicly declared that their purpose was ultimately to build up a southern confederacy upon the ruins of the present Union; to reopen the slave trade, conquer Mexico, and annex Cuba, if in their power to do so. They expect or desire to accomplish all this; and as it could not be attempted within the Union, secession became necessary before they could attempt this long cherished purpose. They expect the border States, with Tennessee and North Carolina, to follow them in this wild crusade. Their purpose is to commit the whole South to this wild, revolutionary scheme; and so they have declared over and over again.

Mr. Speaker, I cannot, I will not, consent to become a blind follower of those who boast that for years they have had no other or higher aim than the destruction of my country; and I make the assertion here in my place, without fear of being contradicted, that there is not one grievance complained of that cannot be remedied *in the Union*; nor is there one which can be remedied *out of it*. I desire my constituents to know that their best interests are in imminent peril, and that their peace and safety depend on standing by that Union which has blessed them, and avoiding secession and disunion as the grave of their happiness and prosperity. The idea that a few conspiring madmen, ambitious, disappointed politicians, men who are seeking for power, can band themselves together and say this Union must be destroyed at their bidding, is monstrous. So bold have become the advocates of this doctrine of secession, that if a gentleman now expresses himself in favor of the Union, and denies the wisdom or constitutional right of secession, he is denounced as a "submissionist." I am free to say, sir, that I had rather be called a "submissionist," a submissionist to the laws of my country, than act as others have done—play the part of a traitor, and become a rebel to a Government which never wronged me, and to which I owe my allegiance. *I am a submissionist.* I stand here in the presence of these Representatives of the people and proudly admit that I am a submissionist; I do submit—I have sworn to do so—to the Constitution and to the laws passed in pursuance thereof. I intend to submit to them. I intend to stand, in the future as in the past, on the Union platform adopted at Baltimore last summer—"the Union, the Constitution, and the enforcement of the laws." [Applause.]

But, say gentlemen, enforcement of the law is coercion; and the cry of coercion is got up in the South. They ask: "will you coerce a State?" No, sir; I am not for *coercing a State*. But I claim the right and power of the General Government to execute its laws whenever it is expedient to do it, or necessary for the safety, the protection, and the happiness of the people of all the States; in a word, when the public welfare requires it. I repeat, I am not for coercing a State; and at the same time I am not for allowing a State to coerce me. I do not recognize the right of the State of South Carolina to coerce the rest of the States. She has no right to do so, and I protest against it. I think, however, that moderation, prudence, and caution, ought to be used on the part of the President. Let us settle these difficulties peaceably, if we can. It can be done; and my opinion is, that it will be done, satisfactorily to reasonable men everywhere; at least satisfactorily to the border States, and Tennessee, and North Carolina. I have no idea of any settlement being made that will not satisfy the State of South Carolina. I do not look for that. I do not expect it; for Carolina has declared emphatically that she will accept no compromise, and will have none; that her separation is final and forever. But I do hope and believe that all difficulties will be settled so as to satisfy the people of the border States.

{Here Representative Stokes continued to speak out against the "deep-laid conspiracy" designed for the purpose of disunion. Admitting there were those in Tennessee who supported the "overthrow of the Government," he planted himself beside the "farmers, the mechanics, the merchants, and professional men, who are loyal to the Constitution and the Union, and who are now moving Heaven and earth to arrest the tide of disunion."}

Mr. Speaker, I speak what I am saying because it is my duty. I speak, as I said, for the farmer, for the old soldier; I speak for the mechanic, and for the child of toil; I speak, also for my wife and my children; I speak no less for my slaves, when I plead for the preservation of my country; for its destruction will involve all finally in one common ruin.

Gentlemen, I implore you, in the name of Heaven, to come to the rescue of our country. Forget your party prejudices while you do something that will strengthen the hands of the Union-loving men every where—something which, without injustice to any one, will enable us to beat back the armies of disunion, and to reunite the bonds which have so long held us together a happy and united people. For I believe that nothing less than the preservation of the Union can avert the ultimate horrors of a civil war, and the consequent destruction of all that is most dear to those who have homes and families to cherish and defend.

Mr. Speaker, it has been sometimes said that I am not a friend to the South. Why? I suppose it is because I will not agree to go with South Carolina in her mad career of destruction. Sir, I have spoken here to-day because I feel that I love my native South. I love the land of my birth, and the abode of my kindred. I love my people; and, in my judgment, the only way to preserve and protect their property, and to preserve the peace and happiness of all, is to keep this Union together, and live united like brethren.

Whenever you dissolve the Union, you bring, as a necessary result, the Canada line down to our borders, and you thereby increase the facilities for the escape of our slaves. And when they reach an independent, and perhaps a hostile country, how will you reclaim them? With the distance that there is now intervening, they sometimes escape, and they will continue to do so in all coming time. But, sir, I repeat, that when you dissolve the Union, you establish a hostile border three thousand miles in length, touching the boundaries of Maryland, of Virginia, of Kentucky, of Delaware, of Missouri, and even of Texas.

But, again: I say to the southern people, that we now have millions of friends at the North who are loyal to the Constitution, and the laws, and who have, through weal and through woe, stood up for our rights—friends outside the Republican party, and friends within that party; friends who are willing to live up to the requirements of the Constitution, and who, if we will be but patient, can and will effectually aid us in securing all our just rights and reasonable demands. Then, I want my constituents to know, that when they break up this Government, they not only aggravate every real or imaginary grievance, but we are necessarily alienated and estranged from our friends and kindred in the North, who are willing now and at all times, if needs be, to rush to our defense; but we shall have then made them our enemies. I implore gentlemen, then, to heal and harmonize these difficulties now, while we may, while we are here together as friends and as brothers, and while each and all of us have still an interest in this glorious Union. If we cannot do it *now*, tell me how it can be done after the Government shall have been destroyed, when we are without the Constitution and without that unity of interest and feeling which still make us one people?

Sir, I have no hesitation in saying that if the Union of these States is to be finally destroyed, *because of the existence of African slavery*, it will sooner or later result in the final destruction of slavery. I repeat, it will result in abolishing it finally and forever.

I do not for a moment doubt that the personal liberty laws will be repealed, or properly modified, within a few months—at all events, so soon as the people shall pass their judgment at the polls. I see that Rhode Island has taken the lead, and already repealed hers, and that steps have been taken in other States to accomplish a like result. It affords me pleasure to state that the Republican and Democratic parties in the free States are ready and willing so to amend the Constitution as to render it impossible for any one to believe that the people of the North desire to interfere with slavery in the States. This will do much good, and will greatly tend to the restoration of peace between the sections.

The Constitution declares that you shall surrender such persons as have escaped from service or labor from one State to another. We can alter and change the present fugitive slave law so as to make it, if possible, more effective, and at the same time to render it less offensive to the people of the free States.

We are told in the South that it is the intention of the Republican party to abolish slavery in the States where it now exists, and that therefore protection to our property, to our families, requires us to resist that party to the extent of overthrowing the Government! Our people are made to believe this charge. You can allay that fear, you can remedy this cause of complaint, without the sacrifice of principle or consistency. You have it now in your power to do it, and I appeal to you with the utmost confidence to give us an amendment to the Constitution to meet this cause of complaint. You declare the complaint unfounded, and insist that the Constitution is sufficient as it is. Then justice to yourselves requires that you should not hesitate in giving us this amendment, which we all admit is only rendering the present Constitution more specific and plain. By so doing you will put this branch of the controversy forever at rest. Do this, and adjust the territorial question, and you will not only restore peace to the country, but you will, as was said by my friend from North Carolina, [Mr. GILMER,][45] furnish a political winding-sheet for disunionists, fanatics, and traitors, North and South.

There are various ways of adjusting the vexed, yet abstract, question of slavery in the Territories. It matters but little how it is settled so far as the extension of slavery is concerned. Yet the principle involved has been the cause of much of our present trouble. I have always believed that it mattered not so much *how* you settled the question if you would adhere to the adjustment after it was made.

My honorable friend from North Carolina [Mr. GILMER] gave you a few days ago an illustration of this territorial question, which, for fairness, was, in my judgment, unanswerable. Suppose, said he, there was on one side of a certain line eighteen farmers, and on the other side fifteen, and not having land sufficient to carry on their farming operations, they should purchase another tract of land with their common money: would it be right for either party in such a case to deny participation in the cultivation of that land to the other? Certainly not. Why not, then, since the Territories of the United States belong alike to the people of the North and the people of the South, grant that there shall be a line run like that of the Missouri compromise of 36°30' north latitude—such a plan as is proposed in the original Crittenden resolutions? I speak particularly of the Crittenden resolutions, because they have apparently aroused more public attention than any other pending plan of adjustment. They have been read and considered by the people, North, South, East, and West. The general impression seems to be that they will satisfy reasonable men everywhere. I can vouch for the fact that this plan will satisfy the border States, Tennessee and North Carolina, in which the decisive battle for the Union is now being fought. Why not, then, adopt this plan of settlement?

{*Representative Stokes began winding up his speech by again urging his colleagues to "settle the slavery question." If they would not approve the Crittenden plan, then "adopt the propositions submitted by my colleague, [Mr. ETHERIDGE,] which are substantially the border State propositions."*}

In conclusion, I appeal to my Republican friends to do their duty, under a sense of their great responsibilities, and according to the dictates of a generous magnanimity. They have the power to restore peace to our unhappy country, and I confidently believe you will show your willingness to do so. I implore you, in behalf of our common country, that you will not stand hesitating, in such an hour as this, upon mere abstract and impracticable issues. When you follow the Constitution you surrender no principle, nor are you false to any platform of your party. Let us, Mr. Speaker, pass the Crittenden resolutions, or any other proposition which will conciliate our divided people, and attach them once more to this Union, as with hooks of steel. Let us do our whole duty in this dread emergency, and joy and gladness will once more pervade the limits of our whole country. Your noble conduct will then be hailed with shouts by a rejoicing people, who will attest their gratitude by the ringing of bells, the booming of cannon, the flying of canvas, and every token that a grateful people can manifest to the benefactors of mankind.

Let us not deceive ourselves with any such delusion as a reconstruction of the Government, in the event of a separation of the North and the South. Dismemberment will not be followed by a reunion of these States. Disunion means war—civil war—and fraternal blood cannot reunite us in the bonds of Union and brotherly love. Sir, these disunion, seceding Democrats broke up their party at Charleston. They cannot now reconstruct a political organization. The very spirit of disunion forbids it; and how can we expect the wanton destroyers of our present Union to reconstruct it when it has been torn to pieces. The idea is ridiculous. No man should permit himself to be thus deceived. I warn the honest masses of the country against this attempt to mislead them.

Mr. Speaker, I never have, nor I never will, utter one word designed to alienate one portion of our country from the other. Should I ever so far forget myself as to attempt writing or speaking a line or a word against the Union of these States, or in behalf of those who now seek the overthrow of the Government, I trust my tongue and arm may become palsied and motionless. Let me die, as I have lived, a citizen of the *free* United States of America.

Source: *Congressional Globe*, 36th Cong. 2nd Sess., Appendix, 133–38.

James Minor Quarles,
8th District
West Tennessee (Oppositionist)
February 1, 1861

James M. Quarles (1823–1901) was admitted to the bar in 1845 and began his law practice in Clarksville, Tennessee. He served as attorney general for the tenth judicial circuit from 1853 until 1859 when he was elected as an Opposition Party candidate to the Thirty-Sixth Congress. During the war, he served in the Confederate brigade commanded by his brother, William Andrew Quarles (1825–1893).

Representative Quarles was no fan of secession, but he believed that slavery was threatened by an "overshadowing and dominant party" in the free states whose guiding principle was "hostility to slavery." Slavery, he argued, is "misunderstood and misrepresented at the North." "It is not the harsh, barbarous thing it has been represented to you to be." Slaves, he continued, "are the happiest, best clothed and cared for laborers that the sun of heaven shines upon." The solution to the crisis, Quarles believed, could be found in the compromise amendment proposed by Kentucky senator John J. Crittenden which "disposes of the [slavery] question justly, fairly, and honorably to both sections. . . ." Tennessee, he concluded, should exhaust "every honorable means of compromise" before considering leaving the Union.

Mr. QUARLES said:

Mr. SPEAKER: I have not sought the floor in the vain belief that any feeble utterances of mine can stay the tide of events which is, I fear, bearing us with irresistible force into the maelstrom of anarchy and civil war; but in the hope that I may possibly induce gentlemen on both sides of the House to pause and reflect before they plunge our common country irrevocably into revolution and fraternal strife. Sir, I should be recreant to the high trusts which a generous and patriotic constituency have confided in me, if I did not exert my every energy to allay the excitement which now unhappily pervades every section of our country, and do every act which patriotism can prompt to give pause to our distracted land. This is not the time for disquisitions upon the theory of our Constitution, or for refined and critical distinctions between the rights of the Federal Government and those reserved to the States. Revolution actually exists, and we must deal with stern and unyielding facts. Six of our sister States have shot madly and hurriedly from their accustomed orbits, and no longer revolve around our Federal governmental center. The "sweet wreath of our Union has been unbound," universal distrust and wide-spread pecuniary disaster pervades every circle of society and all the avocations of life; and it is the first and highest duty of a patriot and Representative to address himself to the task of composing the differences which have produced these baneful consequences.

Mr. Speaker, there is no man who has less sympathy with the hasty and reckless course of our sister States of the South, in their wild scheme of disunion, than myself. They have been rash and precipitate in their action, and have refused even to advise and consult with us of the border slave States, whose interests were to be so materially affected by their action; but, in a delirium of excitement, which seems to have overborne their reason, they have rushed madly on, reckless of consequences to themselves or others. And without stopping to refute the political heresy of secession, under cover of which they seek shelter themselves, I content myself with the declaration that I believe it has no warrant in the Constitution of the United States. I think, sir, that when our forefathers adopted our present form of Government, they intended that it should be enduring, and were not guilty of the folly of leaving a reserved right in any one of the States to destroy the very Government they ordained, and consequently every right which was expressly delegated to it. I do believe, however, in the sacred right of revolution; and whenever any Government becomes oppressive to its citizens it is as well their right as it is their solemn duty to throw it off, and establish such a form of government as is consonant with their honor, liberty, and interests. This is the right our fathers exercised when they threw off the yoke of British domination and tyranny; and this is the word they used to describe it. It is the bolder and manlier word, and savors of the spirit of 1776. I deny the constitutional right of any State to secede from the Union, but affirm the inalienable, inherent right of every free man in it to revolutionize his Government whenever it becomes oppressive and destructive of the ends for which it was formed.

But, sir, in order to get at the true cause of the revolution now in progress in the Gulf States, it is necessary to revert to the initial point. Why this dissatisfaction among whole communities in the South? Is there no cause for it, or does it exist alone in the distempered imaginings of southern gentlemen? Let us arrive at a correct diagnosis of this political disease; and, if possible, eradicate it. Northern gentlemen ask for a specification of southern wrongs and grievances, and declare readiness to consider them. The differences which exist between the two sections, in my judgment, sir, consists, not so much in any particular acts of the northern States, although I could enumerate many which are violative both of the Constitution of the United States and the rights of property of citizens of the southern States, but in the fact that an overshadowing and dominant party has arisen in the free States of this Union, the leading, vital, and controlling principle of which is hostility to slavery, with the avowed and openly declared policy that the paramount domestic institution of the southern States shall be forever excluded from the common Territories; and declares, in the most deliberate and well-considered resolves of both conventions and Legislatures, that slavery is a great moral and political evil, and, as such, should be abolished wherever the Federal Government has the power, under the Constitution, to do so; and, with this one idea of anti-slavery, as a common party vinculum, have nominated and elected as President and Vice President of the United States, both residing in free States; and have succeeded in consolidating the entire North in their support.

The free States, with a system of labor dissimilar to that of the slave States, have a large majority in every department of the Government; and the Republican party now controls every free State in the Union—the free States being nineteen, while the slave States are but fifteen. This is a new phase in the politics of the country; and the slave States, being the weaker, are at the mercy of the dominant section.

This, sir, is the true source of uneasiness and distrust on the part of the South. They know their weakness and your power; and it is from the avowed hostility of the dominant section to one of the most cherished institutions of the weaker section that this apprehension and anxiety springs. And it is for this reason you see southern men asking further constitutional guarantees and a more explicit recognition of their peculiar institution—slavery—in the organic law of our Government.

And this brings me, sir, to the consideration of the several propositions now before the House; and I shall discuss them in the order in which they stand for our action. First, the proposed amendments to the Constitution, offered by Mr. CRITTENDEN in the Senate, and moved in this House by Mr. CLEMENS,[46] of Virginia, as an amendment to the propositions of the committee of thirty-three; which provides as follows:

{*Kentucky senator John J. Crittenden's six-part constitutional amendment protecting slavery in different ways was included here.*}

The first and most important of these proposed amendments to the Constitution establishes the old Missouri compromise line by constitutional amendment—the Supreme Court having decided that it could not be done by congressional enactment. Mr. Speaker, in order that we may properly understand and appreciate the present *status* of the slavery question, as connected with the Territories, it is necessary that we shall take a hurried glance at our territorial policy since the formation of our Government, and see if we can deduce from it any principles of equitable compromise, on which we can all honorably and consistently act, and settle our present differences.

{*Here Representative Quarles summarized the acquisition of territory by the United States from the American Revolution to the 1848 Treaty of Guadalupe Hidalgo by which Mexico ceded its northern provinces. Quarles concluded by stating that land controlled by the North totaled 1,575,803 square miles, while that by the South amounted to 890,978 square miles.*}

In the seventy-seven years which have elapsed since our independence as a nation of the earth was acknowledged by Great Britain, the southern or slave States have gained, in territory, 252,962 square miles, while the North, or free States, have gained, since the same period, 1,406,141 square miles. The South has increased the area of slave territory about 33 per cent, while the North has increased the area of free territory over 1,000 per cent. In 1,217,160 square miles of the territory thus acquired by the North, slavery existed by law at the time of its acquisition by our Government, and from which it has been abolished. In the 252,962 square miles of territory acquired by the South, slavery existed at the time of the acquisition, and continues yet to exist. Now, sirs, with these facts before us—and they are reliable—how can gentlemen say that the powers of the Federal Government have been used to foster, protect, and extend slavery at the expense of the free States. The statement is wholly untrue, and cannot be sustained. Thus much I desired to say, sir, in defense of my section, which has been grossly misrepresented upon this subject.

The question now for our immediate action is, how shall we dispose of the four hundred and seventy-six thousand five hundred and five square miles of territory embraced in the Territories of Utah and New Mexico? I think, sir, the proposition of the distinguished Senator from Kentucky [Mr. CRITTENDEN] disposes of this question justly, fairly, and honorably to both sections, and should therefore be adopted. It protects the time-honored Missouri compromise line through the Territory of New Mexico; prohibiting slavery on the north of that line and protecting it on the south of the line, while it is a Territory; leaving the people on each side of this line of partition the option to have slavery or not, as they may choose, when they form a constitution, preparatory to admission into the Union. Does this not strike gentlemen of the North as equitable, as reasonable? You of the North will by this have the lion's share of that which remains. But I am answered by the gentlemen of the Republican party that this would be inconsistent with the platform of their party as pronounced at Chicago last June, and that they cannot consent to protect slavery anywhere. I would appeal to gentlemen of that party to sink the partisan in the patriot, to lift their heads above the murky atmosphere of party politics, and remember that they have a country to serve as well as a party to obey. In every compromise, each party and each section must yield some of its claims. It was in this spirit our fathers formed our Constitution and organized our present form of government.

Now, let us see what each will gain and lose by the adoption of this amendment. You of the Republican party claim that you have the constitutional right, and it is your duty, to exclude slavery from all the common Territories; and you say so in your platform, upon which you have elected Mr. Lincoln. This right is denied by all parties at the South, and by many at the North; but we are not left in doubt about it, for the Supreme Court of the United States has expressly decided that a citizen may go to any Territory of the United States and take with him his slave, and that the General Government is bound, under the Constitution, to protect him in his right of property in the slave so carried to the Territory, as long as its territorial condition remains.

Chief Justice Taney, in the case of Dred Scott *vs*. Sanford, thus decides: "Every citizen of the United States has a right to take with him into the Territory any article of property which the Constitution of the United States recognizes as property. The Constitution of the United States recognizes slaves as property, and pledges the Federal Government to protect it. And Congress cannot exercise any more authority over property of that description than it may, constitutionally, over property of any other kind."

Thus we see that a slave owner now has the right, under the Constitution, to go with his slave property to any part of our common territory and keep his slave there, and it is the duty of the Federal Government to protect him in the right of property in his slave so carried. Now, if the South give up this right north of this line, in more than half of the territory now under consideration, is it too much for us of the South to ask you of the North to agree and consent that this principle of constitutional law, as expounded by the highest tribunal known to our laws shall remain in force south of the line of partition? We ask for no new right south of this line; but yield to you our right, judicially established by the court of last resort, in more than half the territory, in consideration that you will not abolish our constitutional rights south of the line. Surely, a fair-minded man will accede to this proposition.

{*Representative Quarles then proceeded to explain to his colleagues that the New Mexico Territory already had slavery and read portions of the slave code adopted by the territorial legislature in 1859. In answer to the Republican hesitation to "admit the right of property in a human being," he cited several instances of New England colonies condoning slavery prior to the Revolution, and reminded the House that the peace treaty of 1783 with Great Britain—signed by John Adams, Benjamin Franklin, John Jay, and others—recognized the "right of property in slaves." Quarles argued: "I would ask gentlemen of the North if Franklin and Adams and Jay could admit, in the very treaty of our independence, that the right of property in slaves existed, in order to secure our liberties, if they, their descendants, cannot now recognize the same right in order to perpetuate them?" He also quoted, "as the last and crowning authority upon this point," Chief Justice Taney's declaration in the* Dred Scott *case that "the right of property in a slave is distinctly and expressly affirmed in the Constitution."*}

Mr. Speaker, we can never have peace between the North and the South, in my judgment, on this question of slavery, without a line of partition, on the north of which slavery shall be prohibited, and on the south of which it shall be allowed and sustained. Then the agitators in both sections would be silenced; for there would be no debatable ground; there could be no dispute. Our fathers seeing this radical difference of opinion between the North and the South, divided the original territory, at the close of our war of independence, or soon thereafter, giving to the North five States—Ohio, Indiana, Illinois, Michigan, and Wisconsin—and giving to the South four States—Kentucky, Tennessee, Alabama, and Mississippi. We have seen that they again partitioned the Louisiana purchase by this very line, in 1820, and again ran this line through Texas; and now it is proposed to run it through to California from the Rio Grande and thus forever settle this dispute. Neither party can say it has conquered in this unhappy strife; for you of the Republican party get the old Missouri line reaffirmed and reestablished, the repeal of which gave birth to your party; and the principles of the Chicago platform will be applied to all that portion of the common territories lying north of the line of 36°30' north latitude, while the South gets slavery protected in all of the Territory lying south of the line during its territorial existence.

Nor are those who advocated the doctrine of popular sovereignty, as applicable to the Territory, precluded from the support of this proposition because of the inconsistency with that doctrine. This proposition proposes to make an amendment of the Constitution, so as to make that constitutional in express terms which you have heretofore denied was warranted by that instrument; whilst we of the constitutional Union party get that which we have long and earnestly labored for—a final settlement of the slavery agitation upon terms fair and honorable to all sections. Then, sir, why can we not all, with one voice, sustain and support it as a fair adjustment and compromise? This, sir, will give quiet to a distracted and agitated land, and peace, like a Halcyon, will again sit on our waters.

The second, third, and fourth propositions merely forbid Congress to do that which the Republicans profess not to desire to do—to abolish slavery in the forts, arsenals, and dock-yards; to abolish slavery in the District of Columbia, and the inter-State slave trade; and this proposition is to place it out of your power, so as to relieve you of the temptation and us of the apprehension in regard to these matters.

Article five is to give to the owner pay for slaves forcibly or fraudulently taken from him by mobs; to which I hear no serious objection. These are the leading features of this proposition. It is not, sir, what each individual man would be willing to accept, that should engage our deliberations; but what propositions will heal the wounds that now affect our common country, call back our sisters who have, in a moment of anger, become estranged, and once more form the family circle around our national hearthstone. Sir, I am not wedded to any set phrases, or to any man's proposition. I am willing, ready, and eager to accept substantial justice at the hands of the North at any moment. I care not who makes the proposition; nor will I cavil about words; this I prefer to any which has yet been offered. It would be political empiricism in us to pass as a compromise that which would not reconstruct our shattered Union, and hush the wild storm which now sweeps over the land. And this proposition, or some proposition with this as a basis, must be passed to effect that desired object.

{*Representative Quarles continued here to voice his support for Senator Crittenden's amendment and against the proposals offered by the House Committee of Thirty-Three on the issues regarding federal interference with slavery in the states and the return of fugitive slaves.*}

Mr. Speaker, much of this unhappy disturbance grows out of the fact that slavery, as it exists at the South, is misunderstood and misrepresented at the North. You of the North are told, and some of you no doubt believe, that slaves at the South are held to be and treated as mere property—as brutes. This is a mistake; and I here challenge a comparison with you, as to the treatment of your laborers and ours. Sir, in Tennessee it is murder to kill a slave; it is a penitentiary offense to maim him. If tried for crime, he is entitled to as many peremptory challenges as a white man, and to counsel in his defense. His owner is indictable if he does not properly feed and clothe him. We have no paupers, whether from age or misfortune; the young and the old, the valuable as well as the worthless, are alike cared for and protected. How is it with you?

Mr. BINGHAM.[47] I desire to ask the gentleman from Tennessee a question: suppose a white man maim a slave in your State, is he allowed to be a witness against the person who has maimed him?

Mr. QUARLES. No, sir; a slave is not permitted to testify in any case in Tennessee against a white person.

Mr. BINGHAM. In Ohio any man who is maimed by another has the right to testify against him in court.

Mr. QUARLES. Well, sir, that only shows that you have a different rule in your State in regard to who shall be witnesses in court from that which we have in Tennessee. We seek not to disturb those rules, and will not in any way interfere with your State policy. That is a matter for each State to regulate for itself. But I would ask the gentleman who cares for your poor, unfortunate operatives, when sickness, old age, or physical misfortune overtakes them—the orphan and the widow—among your laboring class?

Mr. BINGHAM. I answer the gentleman, the whole community. We have infirmaries in every county.

Mr. QUARLES. So have we, sir; but there are no slaves in them. We have no pauper slaves. The owner is forced by law to give them everything that is necessary for their comfortable subsistence.

Mr. BOULIGNY.[48] With the permission of the gentleman from Tennessee, in connection with the remark he has just made, I will cite an example in my own State, Louisiana. While I was in New Orleans last November, a planter residing in my district was arrested, and brought before the court for the ill-treatment of slaves; and he could not find bail in the whole district, and was sent to prison; and was, after a time, admitted to bail in the sum of $1,000 to answer the charge.

Mr. QUARLES. Similar cases, I have no doubt, could be cited from every slave State. You misunderstand our system of labor; it is not the harsh, barbarous thing it has been represented to you to be. Sir, after the relationships of husband and wife, parent and child, guardian and ward, and the collateral relations growing out of the ties of consanguinity, the next nearest with us is that of master and slave. They are the happiest, best clothed and cared for laborers that the sun of heaven shines upon.

Mr. Speaker, in one hour I cannot discuss all the questions of high and vital interest presented in those reports and resolutions; but I cannot take my seat without making an earnest appeal to gentlemen of the Republican party to come forward like men capable of grappling with and controlling the events by which we are surrounded, and make an honorable adjustment of these matters.

Gentlemen say I will not grant any terms of compromise to South Carolina. Sirs, it is not South Carolina who asks it; I ask it in the name of Virginia, the mother of States and of statesmen, in whose sacred bosom lie entombed Washington, Jefferson, Madison, and Monroe; in the name of North Carolina, who even now, amid the excitement which rages on her southern border, sits firmly enthroned on her lofty conservatism, conscious of her own strength should occasion call for its exercise. I ask it in the name of Kentucky, who is ready, in defense of the Union, to rebaptize her soil with the name of the dark and bloody ground. I ask it in the name of my own noble and gallant State, every pulsation of whose great heart is for the Union.

Sirs, let us go back to the purer days of the Republic, and catch the spirit of our fathers. Let us remember that southern blood gushed in living streams down the slopes of Bunker Hill, and that the bones of northern patriots whiten the field of Yorktown; that hand in hand our fathers tracked the snows of the Delaware with the blood that trickled from their unshod feet. Let us recall the hallowed memories that hang around the heights of the Hudson and linger along the shores of the Schuylkill and the Brandywine. Let us forget this bitter feud that has grown up between our sections, and banish forever this apple of discord from our halls of legislation. Sir, can it be that our glorious Union is to be dissolved?

> Say, can the South sell out its share in Bunker's hoary height?
> Or can the North give up its boast of Yorktown's closing fight?
> Can ye divide with equal lands a heritage of graves?
> Or rend in twain the starry flag that o'er them proudly waves?

No, sir; no. May the God of our fathers forbid it! For when that direful event shall happen, the sun of our glory will have set, and it will set without a twilight. Pass these propositions of the distinguished Senator from Kentucky, [Mr. CRITTENDEN,] and you will send a thrill of joy through the national heart, from the "pearly strand of the

Atlantic to the golden lip of the Pacific;" and every heart will leap with gladness as the glorious old banner floats out to the free breezes of heaven with every star gleaming on it.

But I am asked, what will Tennessee do in this crisis? Sir, she will exhaust every honorable means of compromise; she will appeal to you, as she is now doing through her commissioners sent here to confer with those of other States; and if she finds you incapable of the sacrifice of your party prejudices to save our glorious Union, she will appeal to your constituents—"from Philip drunk to Philip sober;" her action will be deliberate, conservative, patriotic, and temperate. No State values more highly the inestimable blessings of the Union. She will do everything except tarnish her unsullied honor to preserve it. No rashness will mark her counsels; but she will be guided in all she may do by a high sense of duty to herself and a fervid and glowing love of her whole country. She will stand as the "day's man" between the fierce and contending extremes of North and South; and with the olive branch of compromise in each hand, she will say in accents of affection, "Let there be no strife between you."

But, sir, if, in an evil hour, led on by rash, inconsiderate, and extreme men, you should attempt, under any pretext, however plausible, to subjugate her, or one of her sister States of the South, by force of arms,

> At once there'll rise so fierce a yell,
> As all the fiends from Heaven that fell
> Had pealed the banner cry of hell.[49]

And she will stand the dread arbitrament of the sword. This, in my opinion, is her position; and in this position, I am proud to say, I concur, with my whole heart; but, sir, whatever may be her choice or her fate in this dark hour, I, as one of her sons, will abide it; and, in the language of Ruth to Naomi, say to her: "Whither thou goest I will go; where thou lodgest I will lodge; thy people shall be my people, and thy God my God."[50]

Source: *Congressional Globe*, 36th Cong. 2nd Sess., Appendix, 138–42.

Horace Maynard,
2nd District
East Tennessee (Oppositionist)
February 6, 1861

Born in Massachusetts, Horace Maynard (1814–1882) graduated from Amherst College in 1838 and taught at the University of East Tennessee from 1838 to 1844. He was admitted to the bar in 1844 and began his legal practice in Knoxville. He was elected as an American Party candidate to the Thirty-Fifth Congress, as an Opposition Party candidate to the Thirty-Sixth Congress, and as a Unionist to the Thirty-Seventh Congress serving from 1857 to 1863. He was attorney general of Tennessee from 1863 to 1865, and upon the readmission of Tennessee to representation Maynard was elected as an Unconditional Unionist to the Thirty-Ninth Congress and reelected as a Republican to the four succeeding Congresses serving from 1866 to 1875.

As a moderate, Maynard strongly pushed for the passage of the Crittenden amendment telling his Republican colleagues that it had gained the favor of much of the country. To his Democratic colleagues, he argued that the South feared the incoming Republican administration because only radical Republican and abolitionist "pronouncements" were circulated throughout the slave states; moderate speeches never received public notice. He concluded: "Give us pledges, assurances, guarantees" that the rights of southerners "will not be invaded, that slavery will be preserved, and "we will return your forts and arsenals, your ships and navy-yards, your mints and bullion."

Mr. MAYNARD said:

Mr. SPEAKER: I address the House under no ordinary sense of responsibility. During the long debate upon the report of the committee of thirty-three I have been pained at what has seemed to me to be an utter want of comprehension, on the part of many gentlemen, of the great events that daily astonish us. We are now passing through or into—

[At this point the House, on motion of Mr. HARRIS,[51] of Maryland, took a recess until seven o'clock; after which Mr. MAYNARD resumed.]

When the House took a recess, I was just observing that during the debate that has continued now, upon the report of the committee of thirty-three, for some two or three weeks, I had been painfully struck with what seemed to me an utter want of appreciation, upon the part of many gentlemen, of the condition of affairs now upon us. We are in the midst of events of more moment, of greater importance to the future history of the world, than any that have occurred in any previous epoch in its history, so far as I have studied the history of the world. And yet these events are treated fluently, not to say flippantly, by gentlemen, in the terms of "treason," "revolt," "rebellion," as though it were an ordinary case of a riot of a mob. Gentlemen seem wholly unable to apprehend the upheaval of a discontented, aggrieved people, numbering upon millions, including many separate and independent States.

I have, from the beginning of our troubles, been impressed, anxiously impressed, with the same want of appreciation upon the part of a large portion of the country. As I understand the philosophy of the times, the question for our decision is this: can these confederated States remain together in one common Union, part free and part slave? In fifteen of the thirty-four States slavery exists as an institution, which it is not likely, in our day at least, will be abolished, or even materially modified. It is a subject which, if the people do not understand, they think they do; their opinions are made up, and they will not easily change them. On the other hand, in the remaining nineteen States, slavery does not exist. It is there regarded, as we were told by the gentleman from New York, [Mr. CONKLING,][52] a moral, a social, and a political evil; and it is abhorred and denounced as such. Their opinions are, doubtless, equally made up; and it is not probable that any material modification of them will be made. These conflicting opinions I do not propose to discuss. I have never discussed them here, and seldom elsewhere. Their discussion I regard as exceedingly unprofitable. There has been far too much of it already.

Then, sir, with this ineradicable difference of opinion, with this antagonistic feeling upon this one subject, the question arises: can these States remain in the same Confederacy together, part free and part slave? In that question is the source of our present difficulties; and upon its satisfactory solution depends their peaceable adjustment. The distinguished gentleman who has just been elected as President of the United States is reported to have answered it, not very long ago, most emphatically in the negative, that these States cannot continue together part free and part slave.[53] Another distinguished gentleman, whom he is understood to have selected as his premier, to be the head of his Administration, is reported to have said, more recently, that there is an irrepressible conflict between these States; that it must go on until, throughout the entire country, one of the two forms of labor overcomes and supplants the other.[54]

I deny the proposition in either mode of statement; and it is my business here and now—I am sorry there are not more present to hear what I have to say—I say, it is my business on this occasion to show that there is no such irreconcilable hostility, no such "sacred animosity," no such "irrepressible conflict," between these two great classes of States, that they cannot go on together in peace, in harmony, and with mutual advantage, as they have gone on for the last three quarters of a century, always, as now, part slave and part free.

It is due, however, to both of these distinguished gentlemen to add, that when they uttered those opinions their minds were most likely directed rather to the latter part of the proposition than to the former part; that they were considering, not the contingency of a dissolution of the Union, but the question whether slavery would be abolished. The dissolution of the Union they doubtless thought impossible; the abolition of slavery very probable. Recent occurrences, however, have reversed the order of the proposition, and in that reverse order I propose to consider it. The States being part slave and part free, can they remain together, under a common Government, portions of a common Confederacy? In considering this question, there are certain complications which surround and embarrass it, and which increase, to a great extent, its own intrinsic difficulty.

In the first place, there are now in some of the southern States, and have been for many years, a number of men, not large, but men of talent, men of respectability, of private worth, who have believed that these two classes of States ought not to remain in the same Confederacy. They profess to believe it would be better for the southern States to be separate and apart from the northern States; at liberty to develop their peculiar civilization, and to make in the highest degree available their peculiar form of labor. They have been assiduous to accomplish that result, and to impress their views and convictions upon their own people. That they are sincere, I am bound to suppose; that they are honest, it does not become me to deny; especially as I have no confidence whatever in their theory, nor the slightest sympathy with their policy. They have, with great sagacity, seized upon the present popular discontent, and are now impressing upon the public mind of the South their long-cherished doctrines with increased vigor, and with much more marked success than ever before. They are disunionists for the sake of disunion.

That is one of the difficulties which complicates this question. Another grows out of the manifest disposition of foreign Governments to interfere with our affairs. I refer especially to England. Any one who has observed her relations with this country, for years past, cannot fail to have been impressed with the fact that she has sought to rend asunder this Confederacy of States by every art at her command, by all means in her power. Hers has been the old policy to foment our sectional dissensions; to divide, that she might conquer. At the North, for the last thirty years, she has urged on the abolition excitement by money, by emissaries, by her literature, by the fostering hand she has extended to the abolition agitators on this side of the water. On the other hand, she has held out to the people of the South the blessings of free trade and direct importation, and the advantages to be derived from an intercourse with her that they do not derive from their intercourse with the free States of the North. Do not you, gentlemen of the Republican party, deceive yourselves by supposing that England is going to take part with you, or with the North, in this unhappy controversy. She will do no such thing. If you have cherished such an impression, I ask you to refer to the recent speech by Lord Palmerston,[55] made at the Southampton banquet on the 8th of last month; and also to the recent articles in the British press, especially one in the London Times of the 18th of the same month, to which I call particular attention, because it is understood to have been prepared and published by authority. You will there readily discover the intimation of an intention on the part of the English Government to recognize the existence of a southern confederacy as soon as it shall be organized, or in their estimation become a government *de facto*.

The reception of Mr. Thouvenel, the French Minister of Foreign Affairs,[56] of the commissioners of South Carolina, is an indication of what you may expect from that Government. With France and England united in support of a southern confederacy—France and England united and interfering to prevent coercion by the Federal Government of the seceding States—you will find all the civilized world arrayed with them on the same side. More than that: you will find your own Government compelled to succumb before the array of opinion and influence that will be brought to bear upon it, and forced into a recognition of the seceding States, either as coordinate and co-equal members in the Confederacy, or as a separate and independent Government out of it. To this humiliating attitude may we never be reduced! But, as a divided people, can we escape it? Believe me, this great example of republican liberty does not stand in full view of the monarchs of Europe without exciting their jealousy, and arousing every disposition in their minds to overpower and annihilate it. It is certainly their interest to do so. Is their inclination, think you, at variance with their interest? Our present troubles afford too tempting an opportunity for them to neglect; they will not neglect it.

It is also unfortunate, in the present attitude of affairs, that it should be for the interest of your party, not only that these six States should have seceded, but that, having seceded, they should remain outside of the Union; that your President elect should be reported to have said, when first informed of their contemplated secession, "Why then, we shall be enabled the more easily to get our nominations through the Senate.[57] All that is unfortunate. It complicates still further the present question, and greatly embarrasses its consideration.

Peculiarly unfortunate in this juncture is it that we have an Administration[58] which enjoys neither the affection nor the respect of scarcely a man, woman, or child in the country. A President without a party, denounced all over the country as imbecile and corrupt, showing himself unequal to every emergency that has arisen, is a sorry dependence to guide the ship of State through the midnight tempests of revolution. And to make confusion worse confounded, all the misdoings and short-comings of the Administration have been charged indiscriminately upon the entire South. "It is a southern Administration;" "the President is sold to the slaveholders," has been the preposterous cry; until it has gained large credence, and, possibly, is almost believed by the malicious wags who first started it; when, if the South had been canvassed from the capes of Delaware to Corpus-Christi, it would long since have been difficult to find one hundred men who would publicly defend him, much less vindicate him privately. Why, in the six Democratic presidential conventions, held during the last year, and all of them upon southern soil, I do not remember that a single delegate ever proposed the usual courtesy to the retiring President of a complimentary resolution. Yet, throughout the North the people of the South are arraigned at the bar of public opinion, by the politicians, the press, and even the pulpit, and held to answer for the maladministration of Mr. Buchanan, in addition to all the enormities charged upon his Cabinet officers.

It does not relieve our present embarrassments that the President elect is, to say the least of it, a gentleman of whom but very little is known to the country. We are told that he is an honest man. That, indeed, is something; but I hope the period has not yet arrived in American history when honesty shall have become so very rare as to be a vaunted qualification for the Presidency. Still, it is a qualification quite primary and very indispensable; as much as that a clerk should be able to read and write. Born in the wilds of Kentucky, reared in the wilds of Illinois, his whole experience in public life confined to a single term of service in Congress—and what that is, we all very well know—he became prominent, I may say, altogether from having two years ago taken a hand with the Administration in the great game against the "Little Giant," for the senatorship of Illinois, and in this way was known over the country as the man Mr. DOUGLAS[59] had nominally beaten in his great triumph over the constituted leaders of his party. That is the man, these his antecedents, who is so soon to take charge of the Government and to control its public affairs. What can we reasonably expect from such a Chief Magistrate in a time like this? a mere wisp in the hands of those who shall succeed in getting around his person. Complaints are made very generally that he gives no intimation of his policy; that he does not speak, and let the country know what he is going to do. I imagine that he keeps silence for the very good and sufficient reason that he has nothing to say. But all this only serves to complicate still more the grave and difficult question that is upon us for our decision, and which still recurs: can these States remain confederated, partly slave and partly free?

You sometimes ask us why it is that the question comes up now? What has been done, you inquire, to give it such present emphasis? What wrongs has the South sustained; what grievances has she bourne? Have we not elected our President by constitutional majorities in a constitutional way? These queries are propounded with all the simplicity of an innocence wholly unconscious of guile. Allow me, Mr. Speaker, to touch at the causes by which this fearful issue has been precipitated upon the country now. I will not recount the occurrences of the last twenty-five or thirty years to show the rapid increase of the spirit of anti-slavery, abolitionism, free-soilism, or whatever term this popular delusion has from time to time assumed. I will not follow up its history; it is quite unnecessary. Suffice it that this movement of hostility to slavery, this anti-southern crusade, culminated on the 6th of November, in the election of gentlemen from the free States to the first offices in the Government by the vote of the entire free States, excepting a portion of New Jersey, through the organization of a party that holds no other doctrine in common than the one principle of antagonism to the South and to the institution of slavery. For, disguise it as we will, that is the only common ground upon which all the members of the dominant party can consistently stand. That is the logic of your position, as a sectional party. At least it is generally so regarded by the people of the South.

> {*Here Representative Maynard elaborated on the theme that the Republican Party was misunderstood by and misrepresented in the South. The pronouncements of radical Republicans on the subject of slavery are widely circulated by secessionists throughout the South, but centrist comments almost never. "While your ultra speeches go into the South, and are there read by hundreds and thousands, your more moderate ones never find their way there; and if they did, I do not see very clearly how that would remedy the evil."*}

You have, however, succeeded. The people of the South look with apprehension upon your success. Members of your party have, in various ways, sought to assail them, and they apprehend the attempt will be more vigorously renewed. They apprehend an ultimate purpose to interfere with slavery everywhere within the jurisdiction of the Government—in the District of Columbia, in the dock-yards, forts, and arsenals, and to interfere with the traffic in slaves from State to State; and those who look more to the effect of moral causes, also apprehend that you will use the influence of your Administration against the institution of slavery itself; that the fact of being a slaveholder shall make a man a pariah—an outcast in your Government; and as it already practically excludes him from the high offices of President and Vice President, so it shall exclude him from the Cabinet, from executive offices, from diplomatic service, from honorable rank in the Army and the Navy; exclude him wherever the Government has power to represent itself by appointment. This apprehension, quickened by the consciousness that the South is in a hopeless political minority in every branch of the Government, has precipitated upon the country the great issue of Union or disunion, of peace or war; you say, precipitated untimely and without cause. To the eye of the statesman no popular movement is without cause, or occurs before its time. I was glad to hear the gentleman from Massachusetts, [Mr. ADAMS,][60] the other day, admit that there were causes for the present discontents. He, with the gentleman behind me, from the Cincinnati district of Ohio, [Mr. PENDLETON,][61] are the only northern members, so far as I have observed, who have conceded that there were grievances stirring up the minds and hearts of ten million men, worthy of being respectfully considered and candidly treated.

The question then recurs: can these States remain together in one Confederacy, part slave and part free? They have done so, as I have stated, for the last three quarters of a century, honorably, prosperously, and for the most part happily. I believe they may yet do so. By the same profound policy which united them in the beginning, they may still be held together. When the Government was first established, it was not done by assimilating uncongenial institutions, nor by harmonizing conflicting opinions, incapable of being brought into harmony; it was by compromise, by mutual concession, each section conceding something to the other. And from that day to this, in every extremity of our peril, the same spirit has always been invoked, and never in vain. At a very early period of this session, when difficulty was apprehended—not perhaps in a form as extraordinary as it now assumes—a general recurrence was had to the old settlement of 1820, when a line was drawn through the territory we then claimed to own, dividing the northern and southern portions of the Confederacy. It was proposed to reestablish and restore that old compromise line, that we might again live together in peace as we had done under it before for upwards of thirty years. That idea suggested itself not to one alone, but to many simultaneously. More than one member from New York entertained it. My colleague, who sits before me, [Mr. NELSON,][62] as I happen to know, prepared a proposition, and had it ready to bring forward, when it was offered by the distinguished and venerable Senator from Kentucky, [Mr. CRITTENDEN.][63] I shall not discuss that proposition. It has already been ably discussed by two of my colleagues, [Messrs. Nelson and Quarles.] It is enough to say it is the old proposition, upon the abolition of which you profess to have formed your party.

Indulge me, I pray, in a single word of explanation and expostulation. You speak of this proposition as the offer of the South. It is not, believe me, the offer of the South. It is the offer of the Union men of the South—the men who are willing to go further in the work of conciliation than he who goes furthest. It is the offer made by those men of the South who were opposed originally to the repeal of the Missouri compromise line—men who thought it ought not to have been repealed. The offer comes from them. Why, have you forgotten, pray tell me, that when it was proposed to obliterate that line, a distinguished Senator from my State [Mr. BELL][64] used his utmost influence to prevent it, advanced its continuance and perpetuity, for which, when he returned home, he was supplanted and set aside? He made a sacrifice of himself, not to restore peace, but to prevent strife. Have you forgotten that? Ay, certainly you have forgotten it; for when that eminent statesman was presented to you last summer as a candidate for the office of President, he hardly received, at your hands, as many votes as are to be found upon the petition over which you were quarreling here the other day.

Again, sir, when these men—men who were opposed originally and always to the repeal of the Missouri compromise line—have come back, headed by the venerable Senator from Kentucky, and, as the only reparation in their power, have offered to restore it in order that we might live together in peace, as before, how are they met? How is he met, the eloquent old man? With taunt and reproach and derisive words, and sly insinuations either that he has fallen into his dotage, or has "sold himself out to the Democracy." Well might he say with him of Uz, "Now they that are younger than I have me in derision, whose fathers I would have disdained to have set with the dogs of my flock."[65] You sometimes complain of southern ingratitude towards northern friends. I admit that instances have occurred in which, I think, this complaint is well founded. But it surely does not lie in your mouths to make it. After having, in 1844, by your votes for Birney, in the State of New York, defeated the peerless statesman of the West; after having, in 1860 turned the cold shoulder upon Mr. Bell after having, in 1861, scouted and insulted the aged Senator who so recently led you to victory against what you decried as a foul conspiracy to destroy the liberties of an embryo State, but who now comes as an ambassador for the South, a herald of peace, with offerings of peace tendered in all the sincerity of a sad and patriotic heart, and imploring you to reciprocate, in behalf of his people, the kind offices you were so ready to accept from him in behalf of your own; you, at least, should never complain of ingratitude; never, never![66] I beg you to understand that I speak in no spirit of unkindness; I appreciate fully the difficulties of your position in being called upon, at this early day, to engage in the work of conciliation, of peace, and harmony. You who, through your orators and your presses, have derided and denounced "Union-saving," and "Union-savers," as beneath the contempt of respectable men, could hardly be expected to engage in the work of saving the Union yourselves. Having denounced all those who have shown favor and kindness toward the people of the South as "dough-faces," as "hunkers," and I know not what other terms of reproach besides, you could hardly be expected to expose yourselves to a retaliation of the same sort of epithets. When I heard a gentleman, the other day, denouncing, with so much vigor and energy, the idea of compromise and concession to southern "rebels" and "traitors" as unworthy of free-born sons of freedom, and derogatory in the highest degree to their vertebral rigidity, I confess it seemed quite unreasonable to expect him to do anything which would provoke the bitterest zealot in the land to brand him with the ominous word "doughface,"[67] and thus mar the beauty of his radiant visage. He would doubtless esteem it decorous and pleasant to die for his country; but not to make such an unheard of sacrifice for it as this. I do not expect—I do not ask you, yourselves, to come forward as conciliators; but I do ask you—and this much I think we have a right to ask—in the name and in behalf of the Union men of the South, to let us have an expression of the sentiments of your people; let us go to your ballot-boxes, and meet them there. Admit us to the presence of your masters. That poor boon you may grant. That you ought to grant. You can do it without any disparagement, without dishonor, without discredit, and without imperiling your own political security. If the people heed our entreaties, and vote for these propositions, why then your policy in referring the question to them is vindicated; if they vote against them, then you are justified in not having yourselves adopted them. So that, in either event, whether the people adopt this great measure of healing, or reject it, you are personally secure. You, at least, are in no peril; you incur not the slightest hazard. Surely, surely, this small favor you ought to concede, in a time like this, to the judgment of the Union men of the South, who come to you and tell you that unless you give them something in the way, not of concession, but of guarantee, of pledge, of assurance, with which they can go before the people, they can no longer fight the battles of the Union upon their own soil.

{*Here ensued an exchange among Representative Maynard, Sidney Edgerton (Republican representative from Ohio) and Robert Mallory (Opposition Party representative from Kentucky) regarding the safety of northerners promoting the Republican position in the South. Could it be guaranteed, asked Edgerton, that northern men had the "right to go into the Southern states and advocate our principles" without being harmed. Maynard responded that if northerners attempted "the exercise of what they call 'free speech,'" (abolitionist speech as Maynard understood it), the answer was, no. "No well-ordered community that I was ever acquainted with would allow the decencies of society and the feelings of its citizens to be outraged with impunity." Representative Mallory disagreed declaring that any "gentleman" from the North could travel south and "with perfect impunity, without the least hazard of danger to himself, discuss this whole question of slavery in the Territories which is involved here now in the Crittenden proposition."*}

It is a fact known to every gentleman familiar with that part of the country that this question has been discussed time and again before vast assemblages of every class of the community, of both sexes and both colors. I speak of the entire South.

But it is asked why we press especially the Crittenden proposition? I will tell you. In the first place, the name of Mr. CRITTENDEN has given it influence, power, and credit, with the whole people. The country has responded to it both from the North and from the South. Go to your Clerk's desk, and read the thousands and tens of thousands of petitions praying us to adopt it. The action of State Legislatures, the action of public meetings, the action of public men and of private citizens, all over the country, points to it as a mode of conciliation and adjustment that will be acceptable to the popular mind all over the country. With such indications of public sentiment, I think we ought not to put aside this proposition, and to treat it with disregard. It is not right. It is unjust to those gathering multitudes who have presented themselves before us as petitioners, asking us to settle our difficulties upon this old basis, the readoption of which will place us where we were prior to the unfortunate legislation of 1854.[68]

But it is said—and a grave argument is pressed upon the House and upon the country—that the provision of the Crittenden proposition for territory to be hereafter acquired is unwise and objectionable. It is understood that this was not a part of Mr. CRITTENDEN's original proposition, but an amendment made subsequently to its introduction; and I will say, very frankly, that for myself I attach no importance to it whatever.[69] I am willing to accept the Crittenden proposition either as it came from his hand unamended, or with this amendment. I may suggest, however, that this provision indicates a pretty strong self-consciousness on the part of those who have adopted it. I believe I have never read or heard of but one instance equal to it—one that occurred in the professional career of the celebrated Daniel O'Connell.[70] On one occasion, after he had succeeded, by a most brilliant forensic effort, in acquitting a very notorious horse thief, and the whole fraternity came flocking to greet him and shake hands over the result, one of them more enthusiastic than the rest exclaimed in the ecstacy of the moment, "Mr. O'Connell, I want you to defend me *the next time I steal a horse.*" That we—I mean the people of the United States; we that call ourselves Anglo-Saxons; the men that have subdued so large a portion of the North American continent—that we shall eventually subdue, overcome, conquer, or settle, or whatever term you please to employ, the rest of the continent, is, I think, beyond the doubt of any reasonable man; but I am perfectly willing to leave the mode of that acquisition, the time of it, and the disposition to be made of the territory after its acquisition, with the other events that lie before us in the teeming future, to the high arbitrament of destiny. Hence I am not anxious either to provide for the mode by which we shall acquire future territory, as is done by some of the propositions for settlement, or the disposition we shall make of it after we get it. We will wait till the favoring time comes, and acquire it as best we can; then we can dispose of it as we think right.

Mr. Speaker, before I conclude, indulge me in another word to my Republican friends, to whom, I find, I have addressed a large portion of my remarks. A series of measures has been introduced into this House looking to belligerent operations against the States that have already seceded. As a friend of the Union, I implore you to attempt no such policy. I submit that it will be ineffective; that it is unwise; and that it will be attended with evil, and only evil. You may wage war; but, believe me, the moment you wage war, you array the entire South, as one man, in behalf of the portion that is attacked. It is as when a brother is assailed, all his brethren rush to his rescue, not stopping to inquire whether, in the contest, he be right or wrong. I beg you will forego any such policy as that. Trust to us, the Union men of the South—I say the Union men, not the Union party men—trust to us, the Union men of the South. Give us pledges, assurances, guarantees, with which we can go before our people and satisfy them that their rights shall not be invaded; that their equality in the Union shall be maintained inviolate; that the privileges which they have hitherto enjoyed shall still be preserved; and I pledge you that we will return your forts and arsenals, your ships and navy-yards, your mints and bullion. We will do it without the firing of a gun; without the shedding of a drop of blood. We will do it through the peaceful remedy of the ballot-box. No honor shall be assailed; no self-respect shall be lost; but we will restore this Government on the high and palmy state in which it existed before these troubles broke out. Again, and again, I beg that you will trust us. I entreat you to believe us. We can do all this; you cannot; you never can. Then we will unite to aid you in administering the Government soon to be devolved upon you, as we have aided another Administration than which yours may possibly be better; it can hardly be worse. And for this, we expect no reward. We neither desire, nor will we accept, your high Cabinet places, your offices, your posts of honor and emolument. We want none of them. We are serving not you or your party; but the country. We are laboring to preserve it only; and when your four years have rolled round, as soon they must, then, by the blessing of God, and the good sense of the American people, we will relieve you of this tremendous responsibility, and place the Government in the hands of other men, good, national, and patriotic men, of a party that shall embrace within its organization every one of the thirty-four States. [Applause in the galleries.] I trust, then, that all these measures of coercion; that all this thought of bloodshed, of fleets and armies, of forts and garrisons, and military posts, will be abandoned; and that you will listen to men who, you ought to know, if you do not, are as patriotic as you are; that love the country as well as you love it; that have made sacrifices for it that you never have made. I trust that you will listen to them; that you will not spurn their counsels; that you will not turn a deaf ear to their entreaties; but that you will accept the offer which they have made to you—the offer of peace, of conciliation. Give us, for once, a generous confidence; and if you are patriots, as I hope you are, and as you profess to be, you shall never have occasion to regret—certainly the country shall have no occasion to regret; mankind shall have no occasion to regret—that the interests of the nation were, in this calamitous time, intrusted to our hands. Do not hope, by any mere administrative expedients, to calm the discontents of an aggrieved people. Neither the bestowal of patronage nor the exhibition of power will avail. Listen to their grievances; remove the causes of their discontent. Whole peoples are never consciously wrong, and must not be proceeded against as criminals. They are never corrupt, and cannot be purchased with bribes.

A great coördinate assemblage has convened at the metropolis, called together by this exigent crisis in public affairs.[71] Men all unused to the dust and strife of politics, men ermined and robed from the bench, men from the deep and retired seclusion of private life, have been sent here to consult on the great rights and great interests now at stake. I pray that they shall not be turned away unheeded. I beseech you that their importunities, their urgent appeals, shall not be disregarded by you; for, believe me, if they go back to their people with words of despair on their lips, with feelings of despair in their hearts, the effect will be most momentous and most disastrous. You will regret it in a day when regrets will be vain. I trust, therefore, that you will not so far forget the duties that you owe to your country in this dark hour, as to turn a deaf ear to men who can have no motive whatever to mislead you, who can have no possible inducement to give false counsel; men who have been always true to the country; men who have contented themselves to live all their lives in hopeless political minorities, because they would adhere to what they believed to be principle, rather then follow a successful party; who deemed it better to be right than to be in power. Such men I beg you will not disregard; but that you will heed their words of warning in your legislative action, with a sense of the high responsibility that rests upon you. For I concur most heartily with you, sir, in the opinion which you ventured to express the other day, in opposition to that of a colleague of mine, [Mr. ETHERIDGE,][72] that we are not here as three hundred hack-men, gathered from the streets of a great city; that we are not here even as the same number of any other American citizens, from whatever quarter assembled; that we have been selected to represent large, respectable, interested, anxious constituencies. They are looking, and they have a right to look, with painful solicitude to our deliberations. They will hold us responsible; and woe, woe, to him who, in the day of our accountability, shall be found wanting; woe, woe, to him who shall have done nothing, so less than to him who shall have done wrong! At such a juncture inaction is the action of all others the most fatal.

Mr. Speaker, I know not that any words of mine or of others will affect the result of these deliberations. I know that, in great crises, conclusions are very apt to be foregone. I know that men are at such times governed by considerations which cannot be reached by any words either of wisdom or of folly. I have availed myself of this present opportunity to leave on record to those who come after me, if they shall ever think it worth while to know, my views and opinions in the present state of affairs, unwilling, as I was, to preserve a sullen, unyielding silence in this time of the country's peril.

Source: *Congressional Globe*, 36th Cong., 2nd Sess., Appendix, 164–67.

ROBERT HOPKINS HATTON, 5TH DISTRICT MIDDLE TENNESSEE (OPPOSITIONIST)
February 8, 1861

A native of Ohio, Robert H. Hatton (1826–1862) graduated from Cumberland University in Lebanon, Tennessee, in 1847, where he taught before being admitted to the bar in 1850 and setting up his law practice in Lebanon. Hatton served as a state representative from 1855 to 1857, and was the American Party's gubernatorial candidate in 1857 before being elected as an Opposition Party candidate to the Thirty-Sixth Congress in 1858. During the war, he served as a colonel in the Seventh Regiment, Tennessee Volunteer Infantry (Confederate). A week after he was promoted to brigadier general, he was killed at the Battle of Seven Pines, near Richmond, Virginia, on May 31, 1862.[73]

Representative Hatton harbored a passionate antipathy toward secession. Calling the departure of South Carolina (the birth state of his father) an "example of weakness and wickedness," he methodically critiqued the complaints of the South and concluded that secession solved none of them. Severing ties to the Union would neither ensure the existence of slavery in the territories, nor assist in the return of fugitive slaves. The former would "surrender all the Territories to the North," while the latter would effectively convert the free states into a foreign country. None of the South's grievances, he lectured, had their origins "in the Constitution, in the Union, or in any law enacted by Congress." And all of them could be remedied more "effectually" inside the Union than out of it.

Given Hatton's logical and methodical demolition of arguments supporting secession, his decision to join the Confederate cause might seem contradictory. Assigning motivations to individuals in that tumultuous period is often difficult because of the social and political tugs they experienced. Perhaps Hatton's decision mirrored that of Robert Penn Warren's grandfather. An anti-slavery Unionist from southern Kentucky, Grandfather Penn fought for the Confederacy because, as he explained to his grandson, "You went with your people."[74]

The House having under consideration the report from the select committee of thirty-three—

Mr. HATTON said:

Mr. SPEAKER: The honorable gentleman from New York, [Mr. SEDGWICK,][75] who addressed the House last upon yesterday, prefaced his speech with the remark—which has constituted the opening of almost every other speech during this session—that "we are in the midst of revolution."

Six States, Mr. Speaker—among them two of the original thirteen—have, within the last forty days, violently torn themselves loose from the Federal Government, and proclaimed themselves separate and independent States. Others are preparing to follow their example. Our country, until recently so peaceful and quiet, is being rapidly changed into a great camp of armed men. War, civil war, with all its train of attendant furies, is *imminent*.

Can nothing be done to stay this revolution? If not, it will sweep us all to a common ruin. Can nothing be done to save the Government from utter destruction? I address this question especially to the Republican party. Your leader upon this floor, [Mr. SHERMAN,][76] in this debate remarked, a few days since, that if it was not done, and "this Republic fall, liberty would die." Cannot the curse of civil war be averted? If not, as that distinguished gentleman on the same occasion said, "the condition of our country North, South, East, and West, will be worse than that of Mexico;" our fair land scourged and blighted as by the hand of an angry God, will be divided into fragments, in which "military despotisms will be substituted for the will of the people."

{*Representative Hatton here appealed to House Republicans to "arrest this storm." The solution was in their hands. If they would give the border slave states "the weapons of conciliation and concession," a "certain and peaceful triumph" would result and even those states that had seceded "may return to the sister-hood of States."*}

But, Mr. Speaker, I am met here, by Republicans, with the oft-repeated question, "What do you want us to do?" I answer you, gentlemen of the North, we demand nothing that it is unfair to ask, that would be dishonorable in you to grant.

I desire, Mr. Speaker, at the outset of what I have to say in this connection, to express my sincere gratification at the movement already made in the Legislatures of a number of the northern States, to repeal what are called their personal liberty laws; laws which, without profit to the North, are offensive to the South, and are fruitful only of discord and alienation between the two sections.

Some of you have said,"would you have our people repeal those laws under threats?" I say, no, gentlemen; I would not have you do anything under threats. I would, however, have you repeal them under your own sense of what is right; under your own sense of the sacred-ness of compacts; under your own consciousness of the necessity of domestic peace and tranquility, which these laws are so well calibrated to disturb. Let these laws be speedily repealed, and it will go very far in allaying the excitement of the people. The adoption of the resolution upon this subject, recommended in the report under consideration, will facilitate this end.

There are other causes of disturbance between the North and South. It has been alleged by men high in position in the South, and by a large portion of the southern people it is believed—with what degree of reason I will not stop to inquire—that the ultimate purpose of the Republican party is, to destroy the institution of slavery in the States.

I am glad to know that it has been proposed by that party, that, by an amendment of the Constitution, this source of apprehension and irritation shall be put forever at rest. The proposition of the distinguished gentleman from Massachusetts, [Mr. ADAMS,][77] reported by the committee of thirty-three, would, if adopted effectually do this.

{*The* Congressional Globe *here inserted the following "joint resolution to amend the Constitution of the United States, reported by Mr. CORWIN (Thomas Corwin, Chairman of the Committee of Thirty-three), from the committee of thirty-three." It reads:*

Be it resolved by the Senate and House of Representatives of the United States of America in Congress assembled, (two thirds of both Houses concurring,) That the following article be proposed to the Legislatures of the several States as an amendment to the Constitution of the United States, which, when ratified by three fourths of said Legislatures, shall be valid, to all intents and purposes, as part of the said Constitution:

ARTICLE 12.{*sic*} No amendment of this Constitution having for its object any interference within the States with the relation between their citizens and those described in section second of the first article of the Constitution as "all other persons," shall originate within any State that does not recognize that relation within its own limits, or shall be valid without the assent of every one of the States composing the Union.}

It is not pretended that, under the Constitution, as it is, Congress has any right to disturb slavery in the States. The proposed amendment to the Constitution is simply to put it out of the power of the North ever to acquire such right, by an amendment by them of the Constitution.

The question of slavery in the District of Columbia, in the dock-yards and arsenals, and of the inter-State slave trade, have been subjects of much discussion. It is confidently asserted in the South that the Republican party, so soon as it shall have the power, will abolish slavery in this District, in the dock-yards and arsenals, and prohibit the inter-State slave trade. The exercise of such a power, if you had it, much more its usurpation, would be regarded by the whole South as a flagrant wrong on that section. You say you have no intention of exercising any such power, if you have it. In the debate last night, the gentleman from Pennsylvania [Mr. JUNKIN][78] disclaimed for his party any such intentions. This disclaimer has been often made during this debate. The committee of thirty-three say, in the report before us, that there is no proposition, from any quarter claiming or proposing the exercise of such a right. Still, gentlemen, if you have no such purpose, would it harm you to place in the Constitution an amendment that would free our people from any such apprehension? In doing it, you would surrender no right which, you say, you intend or desire to exercise.

But, Mr. Speaker, the most serious ground of difficulty, at least the one which seems to be the most difficult to adjust, is the subject of slavery in the Territories. Not that it is the most important. No, sir. *Practically*, so far as any Territory we now possess is concerned, there is *literally nothing in it*. But the politicians of both sections of the country have so long and so angrily quarreled over it, that the people have got it into their heads that there is something vitally concerning them in it. Hence, they are obdurately tenacious of their respective views.

Gentlemen of the Republican party have said to us: would you have us surrender our principles? I reply, must we abandon ours? You say you are right; may you not be in error? You say that we are wrong; may we not be in the right? Suppose, then, that this question as to the power and duty of Congress in the Territories was an open one: I ask you, ought you not to defer to some extent to our opinions? But we say it is not an open question. We say that it has been adjudicated by a competent tribunal, deciding that we are right and that you are in error.[79]

You say the opinion of the court to which I refer was a mere *obiter dictum*, and consequently has none of the weight of the judgment of a court. For the sake of argument let us grant it. Still you must confess that seven out of nine of the judges of the Supreme Court have, in elaborate opinions, declared that we were right and that you were wrong. This being the *status* of the legal argument between us, I submit to you, gentlemen, whether the proposition which we make to you is not a fair one: that we compromise our difficulties to the Constitution providing—what? That in all the territory of the United States north of 36°30' north latitude, your theory shall be recognized, and be put into practical operation, and that in all the territory south of that line, our theory shall practically prevail.

Certain gentlemen of the Republican party have said, in answer to this view of the subject, and by way of apology for their obstinate refusal to counsel concession and compromise, that they are but following in the footsteps of Washington and Jefferson and other distinguished men of the South, who, at an early day, expressed opinions unfavorable to the extension of slavery. Mr. Speaker, if this argument were not otherwise unsound, its fallacy would be made apparent by the fact that I might refer not only to what distinguished men of the North, at an early day, said, but what they *did*, to prove not only that African slavery was right, but that the foreign slave trade was a traffic to be fostered and protected. Your ancestors held slaves so long as they were profitable, and insisted on the right of carrying on the slave trade for twenty-one years after the adoption of the Constitution. The most rigorous fugitive slave law ever in existence on the American continent was enacted by the ancestry of the gentlemen of New England, by which fugitive slaves were captured and returned to their masters at the public expense, and with as little reference to the formalities of the law as are observed, to-day, in my State in the case of a horse posted as an estray.

Now, Mr. Speaker, with all deference and kindness to gentlemen, whether of the North or South—separating the arguments of gentlemen from the gentlemen themselves—I will be excused for saying that all such reasoning, as to what is now expedient and proper to be done, predicated on any such facts, is shallow and dangerous sophistry. If persisted in by gentlemen, and made the basis of their action, amidst the complications that surround us, all hope of restoring harmony and good fellowship between the sections, will prove illusory.

{*Representative Hatton paused in his recitation of grievances and solutions to remonstrate against the apathy of his colleagues. "I must be pardoned for saying," he lectured, "that I have been pained, from the first day of the session till the present time, at the seeming indifference of Representatives, from both North and South, in regard to propositions which vitally concern the very existence of the Government." Northerners held themselves blameless while southerners, "instead of being disposed to cast water upon the fire, are industriously adding fuel to the flames." He railed against the dissolution of the Union. "Will it remedy a single evil? Will it not aggravate those now complained of, and to their number add thousands, which, in the Union, can never exist?"*}

We complain of the personal liberty laws. Will our withdrawals from the Union repeal them? Will it not add to their number others more injurious and offensive?

We complain that our slaves escape to the free States, and that the laws of Congress intended for their recapture are not faithfully executed. Will a dissolution of the Union restrain them from escaping? Will the *abrogation* of the laws—consequent upon disunion—intended to return them to us, cause these laws to be *faithfully enforced*?

We complain that our slaves escape *through* the free States to Canada, whence we have no hope of getting them back. Will our condition be improved when the free States shall, by our act, be converted into another Canada, differing only from the other, in that it will be immediately upon our borders, and to reach it the slave will have no need of the underground railway?

We complain that we have not the right of transit through, and temporarily residence in, the free States with our slaves. One northern State now gives to us these rights. Others, we have to hope, may follow her example. One thing is manifest, we are not more likely to get them out of, than in, the Union, as it is a privilege granted us by no foreign State.

We complain that the soil of one of our States has been invaded by armed men, whose fiendish purpose was to incite insurrection among our slaves. When Virginia shall constitute a portion of a southern confederacy, will the danger of a repetition of this mad and most wicked undertaking be lessened? By whom were John Brown and his fellow-conspirators captured and placed in the hands of the law, that they might expiate upon the gallows the guilt of their most unnatural crimes? By the forces of the Federal Government. Will these forces prove more efficacious for our protection when we shall have renounced all allegiance to the Government and forfeited all claim to its interposition? Shall the hordes of northern fanatics, whose impudent interference with what does not in the least concern them, we so justly complain of, and from whom is our only danger of invasion to be apprehended, shall they be restrained by the strong arm of the States united, or shall they be let loose upon us, as were the Goths and Vandals upon southern Europe?

{*The* Congressional Globe *here inserted the following: "The adoption of the following resolution is recommended by the committee of thirty-three: Resolved, That each State be also respectfully requested to enact such laws as will prevent and punish any attempt whatever in such State to recognize or set on foot the lawless invasion of any other State or Territory."*}

We complain that northern Governors refuse to promptly deliver up, as they should, fugitives from justice—persons who have stolen our slaves, for example. When the North shall become to us a foreign nation, we will not have, in such a case, under any extradition treaty we will be able to make, even a pretext to demand such fugitive. We have reference made in the papers of this morning to a case now pending in Canada, where a fugitive slave, who slew a man in Missouri who was attempting to capture him, has been demanded. And although the authorities of Canada were disposed to surrender the murderer, so fanatical are the English people in their hatred to slavery, a writ of *habeas corpus* has been issued by the British courts to remove him to England, in order that he may be discharged.

We complain that equal and exact justice is not done us in the

Territories; at least, that there is a powerful party in the North that have declared their intention to prevent us carrying our slaves there.

The adjudication of the Supreme Court in the Dred Scott case, has put it out of the power of that party to do this, if they would. But if such a power existed and was exercised, I submit to gentlemen from the South if a remedy for this flagrant injustice to us is to be found in the absolute surrender of the Territories, for every purpose, to the North? Would this repair the wrong, or heal our wounded honor?

A leading journalist of Virginia, in an elaborate article—marked and sent to my address—urging the immediate secession of his State, because, as he says, "the North has deliberately, unjustly, and tyrannically driven us from the Territories," concludes one of his paragraphs with this heroic announcement: "We go forth with only the soil beneath our feet for our inheritance, asking but to be let alone by those who have proved themselves our enemies, and determined to fight if we are not let alone."

Is this the spirit of "the Old Dominion?" Certainly it is not. It is not the spirit of the men whom I represent. They are not prepared to retreat and surrender to the North our vast public domain, purchased with their blood and treasure. I do not comprehend, sir, that character of chivalry which, in one breath, recommends the breaking up of the Government, because of an *apprehended* denial to the people of the South of the right to carry slaves to the Territories; and in the next, announces its readiness to timidly abandon every character of right in and to such Territories, because, as the writer just referred to says, "the North have decided against slavery at the ballot-box."

If our connection with the Government is broken, Tennesseans will feel that they have brought humiliation and not honor upon themselves, if their interests in the Territories are thus to be surrendered to the North.

But, does any advocate of secession say we will have a part of the Territories, if need be, by force? What becomes, in that event, of the feast to which you invite my people, of a "peaceable secession?"

The truth is—and I want my people to know it—the purpose of the leaders of secession, who would seem to imagine that they had exclusive custody of southern rights and southern honor, is to *shamefully surrender all the Territories to the North*. There is neither honor or profit in such a course. As the Representative of a people who have made as great sacrifices and shed as much blood in the acquirement of these Territories as any in the Union, I *protest against it.*

{*Representative Hatton then objected to secessionist's claims that new slave territory will be acquired in Mexico and South America, although how that will be accomplished, "has not been explained."*}

Appeals are addressed to us in soft and winning phrase about "our sister States of the South." Eulogies are pronounced upon the "glorious little South Carolina;" and we are asked if we can hesitate to follow "her noble example."

Mr. Speaker, I have nothing unkind to say of South Carolina. No one of her sons is here to speak for her, to-day. Within her borders under the lead of Marion and Sumter, my ancestry suffered and sacrificed much that she might be free.[80] Her soil was wet with their blood, and in it, to-day, repose the bones of those who fell in her service. Her commercial metropolis was the birth place and early home of my father. Let no hostility to her people be attributed to me. Though she has acted most precipitously, wronged the Government, and injured my people, still my wish is, whether united or not with Tennessee, that "length of days may be in her right hand, and in her left riches and honor; may her ways be ways of pleasantness, and all her paths be peace."[81]

But whatever may be my feelings personally to her people, I owe it to the generous men who sent me here, to warn them against the folly of being controlled by her mad counsels, or in the least influenced by her example of weakness and wickedness. She advises rebellion against the best Government on earth; I say rebellion, for that is the true and manly word.

The doctrine of peaceable secession I utterly repudiate. As a remedy, under the Constitution, I believe it to be wholly without warrant. We have, however, reserved to us the great inherent right, that overrides all constitutions, of revolution. When it is no longer tolerable for Tennesseans to remain in the Union, I trust they will boldly proclaim themselves in rebellion, and meet its responsibilities like men. The right and the duty of rebellion usually go together. Government is instituted for the benefit of the governed. When so perverted that the aggregate good is more than overbalanced by the injuries it inflicts, it is the right, and, generally, *then* it becomes the *duty*, of the people to throw off such Government. This is, however, a question which it is unprofitable to discuss. Whether the withdrawal of a State is called secession or revolution, is now unimportant. The practical question is, "what profit" shall we have in doing what South Carolina advises?

Let us hear one of her own citizens upon the subject of secession: "It is no redress for the past, it is no security for the future. It is only a magnificent sacrifice of the present, without in anywise gaining in the future. Such is the intensity of my conviction on the subject, that if secession should take place—and of which I have no idea, for I cannot believe in such STUPENDOUS MADNESS—*I shall consider the institution of slavery as doomed*, and that the great God, in our blindness, has made us the instrument of its destruction."

This is the language of Mr. BOYCE,[82] late a Representative upon this floor from South Carolina, in an address, but a few years since, to the people of his State who were then threatening secession.

He thought it "stupendous madness"—"only a magnificent sacrifice of the present, without in any wise gaining in the future." If it took place, he said, he would "consider the institution of slavery doomed, and that the great God in their blindness had made them the instruments of its destruction."

The idea of making a nation out of South Carolina seemed to strike him as absurd. In the same address, he said:

> South Carolina cannot become a nation. God makes nations—not man. You cannot extemporize a nation out of South Carolina. It is simply impossible; we have not the resources. We could exist by tolerance; and what that tolerance would be, when we consider the present hostile spirit of the age to the institution of slavery, all may

readily imagine. I trust we may never have to look upon the painful and humiliating spectacle. From the weakness of our national Government a feeling of insecurity would arise, and capital would take the alarm and leave us. But it may be said, "Let capital go!" To this I reply, that capital is the life blood of a modern community; and in losing it, you lose the vitality of the State.

He could see no profit in secession—nothing but ruin.

The leaders in this movement in the cotton States, and others who are aspiring to position with them, tell us that they "loved the Union as our fathers made it." What is it now? Just what our fathers made it. If not, in what has it been changed? We have the same Constitution. There is not a law—not one—upon our Federal statute-book of which we complain. The adjudications of the Supreme Court, upon all questions affecting southern institutions, are precisely as we would have them. The statesmen of the South have dictated the entire policy of the Federal Government upon slavery since the formation of the Constitution. If there is an exception to this rule, I would ask to be informed of it. *There is none, sir.* What then becomes of this twaddle of gentlemen about their love of "the Union as it came from our fathers?"

As I have said before, there are serious grounds of complaint on our part against the North. *No one of them*, however, has its origins in the Constitution, in the Union, or in any law enacted by Congress. Most of them, all that are serious, may be remedied in the Union. All of them more effectually in it than out of it.

But as a reason for our hurrying out of this Union, we are told by the leaders in South Carolina and other cotton States that we are "oppressed, and have been for years;" that "the yoke of bondage must be thrown off;" "that we must be free." We, of the border States, have not been aware of our sad condition. Men of all parties, in Tennessee, at least, have innocently been of the opinion that they were "free." Until this storm of disunion broke over their heads, they were certainly happy and prosperous; as contented with their Government as any people on earth. But, it seems our contentment was the result of our ignorance and stupidity.

{Representative Hatton here continued to protest the action of South Carolina and plea for logic among his southern peers. "The remedies proposed are worse than the evils complained of," he lectured. Tennessee would not be bullied into secession. He reminded the House that abolitionists William Lloyd Garrison and Wendell Phillips saw disunion as a clear path to the end of slavery.}

But my time is nearly exhausted. I have spoken freely, candidly—I will not say boldly—my honest convictions. It has been my purpose, if possible, to throw into this great argument some word or thought—in the same spirit in which the widow cast her single mite into the treasury—that perchance might result in good to my country.

Convinced that anything like a reconstruction of the Government, if the further progress of dissolution is not checked, is impossible, my object has been to implore Representatives from all sections on this floor to moderation and liberality, forbearance and justice.

To my ardent and excited friends of the South let me say, in conclusion, as the liberties and free institutions which we have so highly prized, were acquired by one Revolution, they may be lost by another.

To the men of the North let me say, if you intend conciliation and compromise with your brethren of the South, leave no room to reproach yourselves for hesitation or reluctance. If the Government is to be subverted, see to it that its destruction is not attributable to your unreasonable and criminal obstinacy.

To members of all parties and from all sections, in this House, let me say: shall we not, in this hour of our country's peril, lift ourselves high above that narrow view, bounded by the contracted horizon of self, of party, or of section, and thereby preserve to mankind the only example of well-regulated liberty in the world? Or shall we—indifferent to all the memories of the past; heedless to the claims of humanity; wrapped in a stolid selfishness, see the glory of our fathers sink into their childrens' shame? I beseech you, brethren, to consider well the momentous issues before us; act upon them justly, firmly, as becometh men, to whose keeping have been intrusted the highest privileges ever given to man, and who are responsible to posterity and to God for their transmission, unimpaired to those who are to come after us.

When before Milan, Napoleon I, in addressing his army, drawn up around him, told them that when they returned to their homes in France, their countrymen, pointing to them, would say: "He belonged to the army in Italy."

Mr. Speaker, if, on account of our wicked perverseness and want of patriotism, our country is not saved, and revolution and civil war ensue; when the youth of the country shall have been cut down like grass, our cities and villages burned, and our fields laid waste; when our ears shall be greeted by the weeping of widows and wailing of their children, with merited scorn and maledictions, we will be pointed at by our fellow-citizens, who will say, as in shame we avert our faces, "He was a member of the Thirty-Sixth Congress!"

Source: *Congressional Globe*, 36th Cong., 2nd Sess., Appendix, 170–74.

REESE BOWEN BRABSON,
3RD DISTRICT
EAST TENNESSEE (OPPOSITIONIST)
March 4, 1861

Born at Brabson's Ferry in Knox County, Reese B. Brabson (1817–1863), graduated from Maryville College in 1840, was admitted to the bar in 1848, and began his law practice in Chattanooga. He served in the state house of representatives (1851–1852) and then as an Opposition Party member in the Thirty-Sixth Congress. He declined to run for reelection, returned to Chattanooga, and resumed his profession in the law.

Like Representative Hatton, Brabson was a Unionist who thought secession folly—"rash, ill-advised, and precipitate." He, too, enumerated the South's complaints against the North and found that breaking up the Union would not solve any of them. Not only did Brabson believe that secession was not "a remedy for any of the evils of which the South complains," he did not find any constitutional basis for the doctrine itself. Speaking in the early morning of March 4, only hours before Lincoln was to be inaugurated, Brabson reminded his colleagues that if the South had not left the Union and removed their representatives and senators from the Congress, Democrats would control executive appointments and congressional appropriations. Lincoln would have no "power to make war," and would have "but little influence in forming and controlling public opinion."

On the report from the committee of thirty-three on the disturbed condition of the country.

Mr. BRABSON said:

Mr. SPEAKER: When I took my seat as a member of the Thirty-Sixth Congress, I determined not to occupy the attention of the House with any remarks of a general character, believing I could in a quiet way better serve my constituents and my country. But the extraordinary and unhappy state of things which surround us makes it imperative on me to give utterances to the sentiments which I entertain. I am fully aware of the dangers which lie in the path I must tread; but I would be unworthy the confidence of the intelligent and gallant people whom I represent, were I to shrink from the discharge of my duty.

The question is not who shall direct the machinery of this Government, but whether we shall have a Government of the United States at all? Startling events occur with such rapidity that the stoutest hearts tremble at what they foresee. The greatest Government on earth, commanding the respect and admiration of the world, is to be hurled to the dust unless the currents of events is changed, and changed quickly. No one can look upon these vacant seats, occupied at the commencement of this session by intelligent and able Representatives from seven States, without feelings of sadness and sorrow. And it is to be deeply regretted that, while every honorable effort is being made to stay the tide of ruin that is sweeping over our country by the conservative men of the nation, we hear it said by gentlemen from both sections, that nothing can be done to avert impending ruin; that the alienation of feeling between the North and South, the bitterness of party strife, the fierce conflict of sectional passions, destroy all hope of an adjustment. But, sir, I acknowledge no difficulty which may not be settled, no dangers which may not be averted by wisdom, prudence, and patriotism; and whether the members of this House are imbued sufficiently with these virtues to meet the issues as become the Representatives of thirty-one million freemen, I have every confidence that the American people can and will meet the emergency successfully.

It is not to be denied that passion, prejudice, and bitter party feelings, have had too much to do in bringing about our present difficulties; and the sooner we divest ourselves of those unpatriotic and unstatesmanlike feelings, the sooner all our difficulties will be settled, and our country move on the march of greatness and prosperity to that destiny which awaits us, if we remain a united people. Born to an inheritance such as was never vouchsafed to man before, we certainly should not trifle with it, and hastily and passionately destroy it, but realizing the most solemn responsibility which can rest upon men, put forth every energy of our nature to protect and preserve that inheritance, and transmit it, unimpaired, to posterity. Should we fail so to do, posterity will not hold us guiltless. Amid the storm of revolution which is sweeping over our country, it would be criminal in me to add to its fury by indulging in crimination and recrimination.

Could we but calmly and dispassionately inquire into and ascertain the causes of all our troubles, we would be the better able to apply the remedy. What is the ground of complaint, and what is the remedy? Whatever ground of complaint there may be in relation to the execution of the laws by the present Administration, I do not suppose there can be any just cause of complaint against the laws of the United States upon the subject of slavery. Congress has passed no law, since the decision of the Supreme Court in the Dred Scott case, upon the subject of slavery. If Congress has passed no law affecting the rights of slavery; if the Supreme Court of the United States, by its decisions, guards and protects the South, where is the evil which has produced so much mischief? It is not in the Government of the

United States, but its existence is found in the moral and religious training of the northern mind, which manifests itself in the election of a sectional President and Vice President of the United States, by a sectional organization, and upon a sectional principle.

The passage of personal liberty bills, the raid into Virginia, the utterance of wicked and fanatical sentiments calculated to stir up insurrection in the South, all have their foundation in hostility to the institution of slavery. These things, in my opinion, furnish just cause of complaint against the northern States and northern people; and, in my judgment, the South can never submit with honor to the enforcement of those principles by congressional legislation. We can never submit to any inequality in the Territories, which are common property, but will demand our rights to enter them, as long as they remain Territories, with our property recognized as such by the laws of the State from which we remove. Is there anything unreasonable in the proposition that the people of Tennessee may go to the Territories of the United States with their property and reside there? By what authority shall Congress say that Territories shall be appropriated to the use and benefit of the people of a particular section because they do not own a particular species of property? If this is to be the policy of the incoming Administration, I say to you frankly, we can never live in peace. It is true, Congress has passed no law applying such principles to the Territories, since the decision of the Supreme Court to which I have referred; and, in my opinion, the rights of the South are protected against such legislation by the Dred Scott decision. But in the face of that decision, the Republicans claim that Congress has the power, and should exercise it when necessary, to exclude slavery and, consequently, slaveholders, from the Territories.

The fact that a large party asserts that the Constitution gives to the majority in Congress the power to exclude the minority from the common Territories because that minority own slaves, is of itself sufficient to excite the people of the South, and does give them just cause of complaint. The election of a sectional President, upon a sectional platform, and by a purely sectional vote; the raid of John Brown; the personal liberty bills; the preventing the execution of the fugitive slave law by mobs; the flooding the country with incendiary pamphlets, are the principal grounds of complaint, and all tend to chafe and fret and interfere with the southern people and their rights, and have proved fatal to the peace and good order of society; and, if persisted in, will prove destructive to the Government itself, and the best interest of the American people. It would be an act degrading to me, and for which I would receive the just indignation of an insulted and injured constituency, were I to return to my home in Tennessee, and say to the gallant men of Monterey, Vera Cruz, Cerro Gordo, Chapultepec, Churubusco, and the City of Mexico, and the children of the brave men who fell on those bloody fields, that I had consented to deprive them of the right to enter and reside within the Territories won by their valor; when the fact is, I have no doubt, I represent upon this floor more widows and orphans—made widows and orphans by the Mexican war—than some of the northern States had soldiers in that war. But, Mr. Speaker, is the remedy for all the evils which now afflict our country secession? I think not. I do not believe secession a remedy for any of the evils of which the South complains; nor do I believe the doctrine finds any sanction in the Constitution.

Upon a mere question of policy, I have never been able to see how we could secure our constitutional rights in the Territories by destroy-ing the Constitution, and by our own act abandoning the Territories; how can we better secure the return of the fugitive slave labor, by abandoning the fugitive slave law, and all our rights under it; how can we be more secure from the wicked and fanatical sentiments of north-ern fanatics, by removing every constitutional and legal restraint from those who give utterance to such sentiments, is past my comprehension. I adopt the sentiments of the hero of the Hermitage, whose bones lie moldering beneath the sod of Tennessee, when he says: "It is the right of mankind generally to secure, by all means in their power, the blessings of liberty and happiness; but when, for those purposes, any body of men have voluntarily associated themselves under a particular form of government, no portion of them can dissolve the association without acknowledging the correlative right in the remainder, to decide whether that dissolution can be permitted consistently with their rights and the general welfare."[83]

Mr. Speaker, there can be no permanent security in any new Government founded upon the principle that any one of the States may, at will, break up and destroy the Government. Is there not evidence of South Carolina's disposition to secede from the new confederacy? Hon. J. W. Spratt,[84] of South Carolina, has already sounded the alarm, and heralds a new crusade for the emancipation of the South. If the constitutional provision of the new Government prohibiting the foreign slave trade should become permanent, Mr. Spratt says: "Our whole movement is defeated. It will abolitionize the border States. It will brand our institutions. Slavery cannot share a Government with Democracy; it cannot bear a brand upon it; thence another revolution. It may be painful, but we must make it. The constitution cannot be changed without it. It is doubtful if another movement will be so peaceful; but no matter."

Mr. Spratt is not the only one in South Carolina who is now agitating the question of seceding from the southern confederacy, unless the African slave trade is constitutionally recognized. How long will the southern confederacy last, organized upon such principles? When a people are oppressed by their Government, they have the undoubted right of revolution to free themselves from that oppression; but no people, for slight causes, will resort to that remedy. Will the people consent to trust their lives, their fortunes, their peace and security, in a Government recognizing the principle that any one member, when affronted, may destroy the Government? I think not.

But, sir, I will not discuss the right of secession. Seven States have already dissolved their connection with the United States Government, and others may soon follow. They have not only dissolved their connections with this Government, but have ordained and established a separate and independent provisional government, elected a president and vice president, and have appointed officers to the various offices in their new government. They have armed, and are arming, their citizen soldiers. They have taken possession of the forts, arsenals, and dock-yards, within their respective limits; and Louisiana has taken possession of the mint at New Orleans. The secession of the seven States is regarded by the people of the border States as rash, ill-advised, and precipitate; and we have a right to complain of their action.

The seven grain-growing and tobacco States are more interested in the permanent settlement of the slavery question than their sister States further south, because they are more exposed to the depredations of northern fanatics; yet, they have not been consulted by the seceding States, but left to defend themselves as best they can. We have the more right to complain, because they have left us here in the minority, when the opposition to Mr. Lincoln's policy was in the majority, and when, in the next Congress, the majority against the Republicans would be, I believe, twenty or twenty-one, if the southern States were all represented here. It would have been impossible for the incoming Administration, for the next two years, to ingraft upon the legislation of the country the policy of the Republican party. The President could not make an appointment of any importance without the consent of his opponents in the Senate of the United States. The majority in the Senate, if all the southern States were represented in that body, could, in effect, select the President's Cabinet. The President can pass no law, cannot draw a dollar from the Treasury, without an appropriation from Congress. He has no power to make war; and, if we are to judge the future by the past, he can have but little influence in forming and controlling public opinion.

With both branches of Congress opposed to the incoming Administration, the principles of whose party were voted down by a popular majority of over one million votes, the decision of the Supreme Court maintaining the rights of the South in the Territories; with all these facts before us, we are asked to say, that the seceding States have acted with prudence, wisdom, and a due regard for the rights and interests of the border States. They have not only abandoned the border States, but have incorporated into the constitution of their new government a provision, giving the congress of the "confederated States of North America" the power to carry out the recommendation of Governor Gist, of South Carolina, and the Governor of Mississippi,[85] to prohibit the citizens of all the States not joining the confederacy from taking slaves into the seceding States, unless the citizens accompany them with the intention of permanently residing there.

I have said that the border States were more interested in the final and permanent settlement of the question of slavery than the cotton States, and I have sometimes thought there were other causes than the question of slavery for the precipitate action of the seceding States, which especially operated on South Carolina to induce her to take the initiative in the movement. She could not have been very much concerned about the safety of her slaves, guarded as she is by North Carolina, Virginia, Tennessee, and Kentucky; and I take it for granted, those gallant States are as sensitively alive to their honor, and quite as capable of taking care of it, as any State in the Union. South Carolina desired a separation from the United States Government upon a question of very grave importance to her, as always insisted upon by her statesmen. Her public men have uniformly insisted that the revenue policy of the United States Government was unjust and oppressive; and to get clear of that principle, I am inclined to think, she embraced the occasion of the election of a sectional President and Vice President to dissolve her connection with the Government of the United States.[86] I am supported in these positions by the line of argument pursued by one of the leading secession journals of South Carolina, upon the action of the southern congress at Montgomery, Alabama, in adopting, as that paper says, the tariff of 1857. The Charleston Mercury says:

> We regret that any provisional government was formed at all, and in one or two important particulars confess to disappointment and surprise at the government and laws enacted. It seems that the United States protective tariff of 1857 has been adopted, and that a positive condemnation of the institution of slavery, through the slave trade, has been inserted into the constitution itself. Neither of these did we expect. We did not suppose that any southern government, whether for a month or a year, would sanction the policy of protective tariffs. The tariff of 1857 is odious and oppressive in its discriminations. It was made to favor northern enterprise at the expense of the people of the South—a huge free list for

them—the burden of taxation for us to bear, and we maintain is adverse to revenue, unjust in principle, and oppressive in practice. Whether this is brought about by a partial remission of duties, or a partial imposition, it is still the same in effect. We enter our protest against the scheme and policy, both as regards ourselves, and in the results, so far as foreign nations are concerned, and their friendship, at this time, is valuable to us. In each respect free trade is the true policy of the confederate States.

We deem it also unfortunate and *mal apropos* that the stigma of illegitimacy and illegality should be placed upon the institution of slavery by a fundamental law against the slave trade. In our opinion, it is a matter of policy, and not of principle, to be decided now and hereafter, from sound views of the necessity and safety of our people. We think it is a proper subject of legislation. * * * *

Every principle of right government and every dictate of policy seem to be against the Mississippi scheme. But there is a graver matter than its absurdity behind this scheme. It is nothing else than *the policy of reconstructing the Union*. Take the Constitution of the United States as it is, with all its constructive powers, and get the frontier States in the confederacy with us, will the Constitution ever be altered! Will we ever be freed from the same troubles and dangers we have been contending against for the last thirty years? Maryland, Kentucky, and Missouri have been protective tariff States, and all of them in favor of internal improvements. Suppose the Constitution of the United States is taken as it is, with its consolidation constructions, to obtain their union with us: will they consent to have it altered so as to prevent constructive abuses? And, if not altered, will we not have the same battle to fight over again with them, after a few years, which we have been compelled to fight with the northern States? We will only have changed masters. But will a southern confederacy exist at all with such a policy? Will not all the northern States come again into the Union with us? Why should they not? They are satisfied with the Constitution of the United States as it is, open to their interpretation. It establishes a capital despotism under their power. Of course they will seek to reconstruct the Union. And will it not be done? Yes, certainly, under this scheme. After all, we will have run round a circle and end where we started. The Union will be restored, with a few guarantees about negroes, such as the frontier States want, but which are of no consequence to the cotton States; and we will again enter upon the broad road of consolidation and ruin.

The majorities in Congress against the Republicans would have been abundantly able to protect the rights of the South upon the slavery question; but many southern men would support a revenue tariff, giving individual protection to home industry, which the Mercury regards as unjust in principle and oppressive in practice. The editor of that paper thinks the policy of the "confederate States of North America" will lead to a restoration of the Union, "with a few guarantees about negroes, such as the frontier States want, but which are of no consequence to the cotton States." This leading and influential secession journal sustains me in the position that the border States are more interested in quieting the agitation of the slavery question than the cotton States. Maryland, Virginia, Kentucky, and Missouri, have over fifteen hundred miles of border on the free States, and must be the first to be interfered with by the northern fanatics; and yet they stand here to defend their constitutional rights in the Union, demanding firmly, though respectfully, such constitutional guarantees as will place beyond the reach of politicians the question of slavery, and forever silence the agitation of a subject which ought never to have been brought into the political arena. With all the interest these States have in slavery, they are still here; and I would suffer martyrdom before I would forsake them in this their hour of trial and difficulty.

I mention these things because I believe, if the cotton States had remained in the Union instead of seceding, and the South had unitedly made known her grievances, and demanded in a firm and manly tone a settlement of all the difficulties between the North and South, upon a basis alike honorable to both sections, we might have been saved the perils of revolution.

Additional constitutional guarantees become the more necessary for the border States, since they have been thrown into the minority by the rash action of the cotton States.

The position of the middle and border States is painful and embarrassing; but, sir, shall we despair of the Republic? Is there no hope for the Constitution and for constitutional liberty? A Government like ours, under the protection of which the country has grown great and prosperous, should not be abandoned to sectionalism without a struggle. From three million we have increased to thirty-one million people, under the Constitution and Union; from thirteen to thirty-four States. We occupy a front rank among the nations of the earth. The white-winged sails of our commerce cover every sea; the stars and stripes, the flag of the Union, is wafted by every breeze, into every port under the sun, and where ever unfurled is honored and respected. The American citizen, however humble, knows, whether at home or abroad, on the land or on the seas, the strong arm of his Government is over him to guard and protect. He feels that he is an American citizen.

For such a Government as this will not gentlemen forget their party feuds and rise superior to their miserable party platforms, remembering that, while they have a party to serve, they have a country to save? Of what use will your miserable platforms be when civil war with all its horrors, has swept over the land, not only, in its maddening course, overturning the Government of our fathers, but blotting out forever the last hope of liberty throughout the world?

I have been astonished, the present session of Congress, to see the apparent indifference manifested by the Republican members of this House. State after State has gone out, and others preparing to go. Whether rightfully or wrongfully, they have gone. Business of every kind is prostrated; commerce paralyzed; the whole country upon the verge of bankruptcy; and the Government of the United States forced to ask the indorsement of her bonds by the States, that they may find a purchaser in the market at a heavy discount. And yet, gentlemen affect to believe that all this is merely an "artificial" matter, of momentary importance, that will soon pass away. The vote of Virginia, which was the first to stay the tide of secession; the overwhelming and crushing defeat of the precipitators in Tennessee, and then in Missouri, are seized upon by some men in the North, and urged as evidence of a determination on the part of those States to consent to the doctrines and principles of the Republican party.[87] I beg all such to undeceive themselves. I have no right to speak for the proud old State of Virginia, the memory of whose mighty dead has been vindicated by her noble sons, who have put the seal of their condemnation upon sectionalism north and south; but for Tennessee I may venture to say that no such interpretation can be given to her vote on the 9th of February. She has rights under the Constitution, and in the Union, which no true son of hers will ever basely surrender at the bidding of any power on earth. By her vote, Tennessee appeals to the conservative element of the whole country, to come to the rescue of the Constitution and Union; not with fire and sword, not with the swift-winged messengers of death, but with the principles of concession and compromise, which should characterize the action of a great and free people. Shall that appeal be in vain to both sectional parties? Do gentlemen prefer peace to war? Do they prefer a united to a divided people? Do they prefer union to disunion?

I am satisfied there are men, north and south, who have long labored for the destruction of this, the best Government on earth; and unless the people, by whom and for whom the Government was made, interpose, I fear these agitators will accomplish their long-cherished and wicked designs. The people are deeply interested in the settlement of the vexed question of slavery, the agitation of which more seriously affects them than the men who occupy high places in the Government. If war result from the action of the politicians, the brave and hardy sons of toil are the ones to meet the issue then. If any foreign Government had insulted the flag, the question would be quite a different one; but to place one section of a great country like ours in hostile array against the other, for causes such as now distract our people, and thus by war destroy the people of both sections, is too monstrous to contemplate. Governments should have no other object than to guard, protect, and advance the interests and happiness of the governed; and those who have sought and obtained the confidence of the people should remember that—

> Princes and lords may flourish or may fade;
> A breath can make them, as a breath has made;
> But a brave populace, their country's pride,
> When once destroyed, can never be supplied.[88]

I appeal to the Representatives of the people upon this floor to avert the impending storm.

I ask you, in the name of a common country, of humanity, and of liberty itself, to settle the difficulties. Shall we, when we leave this noble edifice, these gorgeous marble Halls, look for the last time upon the proud flag of the Union, waving from the dome of this Capitol? Shall column after column of this noblest and best Government ever devised by man crumble and fall, because the representatives of the people prefer some miserable dogma to the Constitution of our fathers, and the best interests of thirty-one million freemen? Forbid it, my countrymen; forbid it, Heaven! If it were possible for the spirits of the departed good and great to revisit this earth and participate in the affairs of man, I would implore them to bend the bolted heavens and come down, and shed the light of other days around us. Shall we have no settlement, no compromise? Shall the dark and lowering clouds of revolution continue to sweep over our once happy land? Will this House adjourn, refusing to do anything? We have already the action of some of the States, moving in the right direction, in the repeal and modification of their personal liberty bills; and over one million petitioners have implored us to adjust and settle the difficulties. Will you do it?

If the wild passions of party have so blinded Representatives, north and south, as to induce them to refuse concession, compromise, and settlement, I, for one, will appeal from your partisan and prejudiced decision to the people of the United States, feeling unwilling that this Government, which cost the toil and suffering of seven years, shall be destroyed by the politicians and demagogues who infest this Capitol. I am satisfied that appeal will not be in vain. The recollections of the past, the anticipation of the future, the certainty that we cannot better our condition by destroying the Government, will all urge the great American people to the rescue of their imperiled Constitution and Union, and drive from power and place those whose devotion to party and party dogmas is superior to their devotion to their country.

But, sir, I am told I am a submissionist. I am always ready to submit to the Constitution of my country and the laws passed in conformity to it. But, sir, I am unwilling to run away from this Capitol, and yield everything, Constitution, Union, fame, glory, and property, at the bidding of any party, however powerful that party may be. I should feel unworthy the confidence of a gallant people were I to surrender all their rights at discretion. This, to my mind, is the worst form of submission. But, sir, if we are to be driven to the necessity of taking the sword for the purpose of maintaining our constitutional rights, my advice will be, to draw that sword in the Union; for I would feel more like a soldier marching in defense of my constitutional rights under the stars and stripes, than under any other flag.

Source: *Congressional Globe*, 36th Cong., 2nd Sess., Appendix, 293–95.

CHAPTER FIVE

Proposed Constitutional Amendments

December 1860–January 1861

Of the sixty-eight compromise resolutions cast in the form of constitutional amendments proposed over Secession Winter, Tennesseans suggested nine, second only to Virginia which produced sixteen. Tennessee's elected officials, like those from other states, were concerned with protecting slavery in the United States Constitution. Of the fifty-nine articles (or subparts) contained in the nine amendments, only seven did not deal with the peculiar institution. The primary goal of these amendments was to protect slavery in the territories, the District of Columbia, federal installations in slave states, and the transit of slaves into and through free states and territories. Eight proposed strengthening the 1850 Fugitive Slave Act, five prohibited Congress from interfering with slavery in the states, and four recommended the nationalization of slavery. None advocated prohibiting protective tariffs. Collectively they illustrate the issues that were most near and dear to Tennesseans during the secession crisis.

Representative Thomas Amos Rogers Nelson (Oppositionist) US House of Representatives

December 12, 1860

JOINT RESOLUTION to amend the Constitution of the United States.

Be it resolved by the Senate and the House of Representatives of the United States of America in Congress assembled, two-thirds of both houses concurring, That the following articles be proposed to the legislatures of the several States as amendments to the Constitution of the United States; all or any of which articles, when ratified by three-fourths of said legislatures, shall be valid to all intents and purposes as part of the said Constitution, viz:

ARTICLE XIII. In all that territory ceded by France to the United States, under the name of Louisiana, and in all the territory ceded by Mexico to the United States, which lies north of thirty-six degrees and thirty minutes north latitude, which is not included within the limits of any State, slavery and involuntary servitude, otherwise than in the punishment of crimes, whereof the parties shall have been duly convicted, shall be, and is hereby, forever prohibited.

In all territories, or parts of territories, south of said line of thirty-six degrees and thirty minutes, slavery may exist, and shall be protected by such rules and regulations as Congress may prescribe. When such Territories form constitutions with a view to their admission into the Union as States, or when new States may be formed, as now provided for, out of any State or States, any part of which is situate south of a line thirty-six degrees and thirty minutes of north latitude, extending from the Atlantic to the Pacific ocean, such Territory or new State, applying for admission into the Union, may continue or abolish slavery, and shall be admitted on the same footing as other States.

No law shall be passed by Congress interfering with or prohibiting the slave trade in the slaveholding States, or in the Territories, or new States, now existing, or which may be created south of said line.

Congress shall not abolish slavery in the District of Columbia.

The importation of persons from Africa, or any foreign State or country, to be held as slaves or in involuntary servitude, shall not be allowed.

ARTICLE XIV. Congress shall provide by law for the arrest of fugitive slaves and servants escaping from one State or Territory into another, and for their return to their owners or masters.

If such fugitives cannot be arrested, Congress may enact laws providing for indemnity from the persons, counties, or towns, by whom or in which the escape may have been aided.

All laws or customs interfering with these provisions shall be null and void.

Congress may enact such statutes as may be deemed proper to enforce these amendments.

ARTICLE XV. The electors shall meet in their respective States and vote by ballot for President and Vice-President; one of whom shall be an inhabitant north of said line of thirty-six degrees and thirty minutes of north latitude, extending from the Atlantic to the Pacific ocean; the other, an inhabitant south of said line; and both of whom shall not be inhabitants of the same State.

Source: 36th Cong., 2nd Sess., House of Representatives Report No. 31 (Journal of the Committee of Thirty-Three), 3–4.

SENATOR ANDREW JOHNSON
(DEMOCRAT)
US SENATE
December 13, 1860

Mr. JOHNSON, of Tennessee. I introduce the following resolution, with a view of referring it at the proper time:

Resolved, That the select committee of thirteen be instructed to inquire into the expediency of establishing, by constitutional provision: 1. A line running through the territory of the United States, not in-cluded within the States, making an equitable and just division of said territory, south of which line slavery shall be recognized and protected as property, by ample and full constitutional guarantees, and north of which line it shall be prohibited. 2. The repeal of all acts of Congress in regard to the restoration of fugitives from labor, and an explicit declaration in the Constitution, that it is the duty of each State for itself to return fugitive slaves when demanded by the proper authority, or pay double their cash value out of the treasury of the State. 3. An amendment of the Constitution, declaring that slavery shall exist in navy-yards, arsenals, &c., or not, as it may be admitted or prohibited by the States in which such navy-yards, arsenals, &c., may be situated. 4. Congress shall never interfere with slavery in the District of Columbia, so long as it shall exist in the State of Maryland, nor even then, without the consent of the inhabitants and compensation to the owners. 5. Congress shall not touch the representation of three fifths of the slaves, nor the inter-State trade, coastwise or inland. 6. These provisions to be unamendable, like that which relates to the equality of the States in the Senate.

Source: *Congressional Globe*, 36th Cong., 2nd Sess., 83.

REPRESENTATIVE THOMAS AMOS ROGERS NELSON (OPPOSITIONIST) US HOUSE OF REPRESENTATIVES
December 27, 1860

Mr. Nelson withdrew his joint resolution to amend the Constitution of the United States, and in place thereof submitted the following, which he stated was identically the same as that submitted by Mr. Crittenden to the special committee of the Senate.

JOINT RESOLUTION proposing certain amendments to the Constitution of the United States.

Whereas serious and alarming dissensions have arisen between the northern and southern States, concerning the rights and security of the rights of the slaveholding States, and especially their rights in the common territory of the United States; and whereas it is eminently desirable and proper that those dissensions which now threaten the very existence of this Union, should be permanently quieted and settled by constitutional provisions which shall do equal justice to all sections, and thereby restore to the people that peace and good will which ought to prevail between all the citizens of the United States: Therefore—

Resolved by the Senate and House of Representatives of the United

States of America in Congress assembled, two thirds of both Houses concurring, That the following articles be, and are hereby, proposed and submitted as amendments to the Constitution of the United States, which shall be valid to all intents and purposes as part of said Constitution when ratified by conventions of three-fourths of the several States:

ARTICLE 1. In all the territory of the United States now held or hereafter acquired, situate north of latitude thirty-six degrees and thirty minutes, slavery or involuntary servitude, except as a punishment for crime, is prohibited while such territory shall remain under territorial government. In all the territory south of said line of latitude slavery of the African race is hereby recognized as existing, and shall not be interfered with by Congress, but shall be protected as property by all the departments of the territorial government during its continuance; and when any territory, north or south of said line, within such boundaries as Congress may prescribe, shall contain the population requisite for a member of Congress, according to the then Federal ratio of representation of the people of the United States, it shall, if its form of government be republican, be admitted into the Union, on an equal footing with the original States, with or without slavery, as the constitution of such new State may provide.

ARTICLE 2. Congress shall have no power to abolish slavery in places under its exclusive jurisdiction, and situate within the limits of States that permit the holding of slaves.

ARTICLE 3. Congress shall have no power to abolish slavery within the District of Columbia so long as it exists in the adjoining States of Virginia and Maryland, or either, nor without the consent of the inhabitants, nor without just compensation first made to such owners of slaves as do not consent to such abolishment. Nor shall Congress at any time prohibit officers of the federal government or members of Congress, whose duties require them to be in said District, from bringing with them their slaves, and holding them as such during the time their duties may require them to remain there, and afterwards taking them from the District.

ARTICLE 4. Congress shall have no power to prohibit or hinder the transportation of slaves from one State to another, or to a Territory in which slaves are by law permitted to be held, whether that transportation be by land, navigable river, or by the sea.

ARTICLE 5. That in addition to the provisions of the third paragraph of the second section of the fourth article of the Constitution of the United States, Congress shall have power to provide by law, and it shall be its duty so to provide, that the United States shall pay to the owner who shall apply for it, the full value of his fugitive slave, in all cases, when the marshal, or other officer, whose duty it was to arrest said fugitive, was prevented from so doing by violence or intimidation, or when, after arrest, said fugitive was rescued by force, and the owner thereby prevented and obstructed in the pursuit of his remedy for the recovery of his fugitive slave, under the said clause of the Constitution and the laws made in pursuance thereof. And in all such cases, when the United States shall pay for such fugitive, they shall have the right, in their own name, to sue the county in which said violence, intimidation, or rescue was committed, and to recover from it, with interest and damages, the amount paid by them for said fugitive slave. And the said county, after it has paid said amount to the United States, may, for its indemnity, sue and recover from the wrong-doers, or rescuers, by whom the owner was prevented from the recovery of his fugitive slave, in like manner as the owner himself might have sued and recovered.

ARTICLE 6. No future amendment of the Constitution shall affect the five preceding articles, nor the third paragraph of the second section of the first article of the Constitution, nor the third paragraph of the second section of the fourth article of said Constitution; and no amendment shall be made to the Constitution which shall authorize or give to Congress any power to abolish or interfere with slavery in any of the States by whose laws it is or may be allowed or permitted.

And whereas, also, besides those causes of dissension embraced in the foregoing amendments proposed to the Constitution of the United States, there are others which come within the jurisdiction of Congress, and may be remedied by its legislative power; and whereas it is the desire of Congress, as far as its power will extend, to remove all just cause for the popular discontent and agitation which now disturb the peace of the country and threaten the stability of its institutions: Therefore—

1. *Resolved by the Senate and House of Representatives of the United States of America in Congress assembled,* That the laws now in force for the recovery of fugitive slaves are in strict pursuance of the plain and mandatory provisions of the Constitution, and have been sanctioned as valid and constitutional by the judgment of the Supreme Court of the United States; that the slaveholding States are entitled to the faithful observance and execution of those laws, and that they ought not to be repealed or so modified or changed as to impair their efficiency; and that laws ought to be made for the punishment of those who attempt by rescue of the slave or other illegal means, to hinder or defeat the due execution of said laws.

2. That all State laws which conflict with the fugitive slave acts, or any other constitutional acts of Congress, or which in their operation impede, hinder, or delay the free course and due execution of any of said acts, are null and void by the plain provisions of the Constitution of the United States. Yet those State laws, void as they are, have given color to practices and led to consequences which have obstructed the due administration and execution of acts of Congress, and especially the acts for the delivery of fugitive slaves, and have thereby contributed much to the discord and commotion now prevailing. Congress, therefore, in the present perilous juncture, does not deem it improper, respectfully and earnestly, to recommend the repeal of those laws to the several States which have enacted them, or such legislative corrections or explanations of them as may prevent their being used or perverted to such mischievous purposes.

3. That the act of the eighteenth of September, eighteen hundred and fifty, commonly called the fugitive slave law, ought to be so amended as to make the fee of the commissioner, mentioned in the eighth section of the act, equal in amount in the cases decided by him, whether his decision be in favor of or against the claimant. And to avoid misconstruction, the last clause of the fifth section of said act, which authorizes the person holding a warrant for the arrest or

detention of a fugitive slave to summon to his aid the *posse comitatus*, and which declares it to be the duty of all good citizens to assist him in its execution, ought to be so amended as to expressly limit the authority and duty to cases in which there shall be resistance or danger of resistance or rescue.

4. That the laws for the suppression of the African slave trade, and especially those prohibiting the importation of slaves in the United States, ought to be made effectual, and ought to be thoroughly executed, and all further enactments to those ends ought to be properly made.

{*The four attached resolutions were a part of Crittenden's submission to the Senate on December 18, but were not a part of his proposal to the Special Committee of Thirteen on December 22. On January 3, 1861, Crittenden added two additional articles both borrowed from an amendment proposed by Senator Stephen A. Douglas. The additions read: "The elective franchise and the right to hold office, whether federal, State, territorial, or municipal, shall not be exercised by persons who are, in whole or in part, of the African race" and "The United States shall have the power to acquire, from time to time, districts of country in Africa and South America, for the colonization, at the expense of the Federal Treasury, of such free negroes and mulattoes as the several States may wish to have removed from their limits, and from the District of Columbia, and such other places as may be under the jurisdiction of Congress."*}

Source: 36th Cong., 2nd Sess., House of Representatives Report No. 31 (Journal of the Committee of Thirty-Three), 16–19.

Representative Emerson Etheridge
(Oppositionist)
US House of Representatives
January 7, 1861

The Clerk read Mr. ETHERIDGE's resolution, as follows:
A joint resolution providing for amendments to the Constitution of the United States

Be it resolved by the Senate and House of Representatives of the United States of America in Congress assembled, That the following amendments to the Constitution of the United States be proposed to the several States for their adoption or ratification:

ARTICLE 1. Congress shall have no power to interfere with slavery in any of the States of the Union.

ART. 2. Congress shall have no power to interfere with or abolish slavery in any of the navy-yards, dock-yards, arsenals, forts, or other places ceded to the United States, within the limits of any States where slavery exists.

ART. 3. Congress shall have no power to interfere with or abolish slavery in the District of Columbia, without the consent of the States of Maryland and Virginia; nor without the consent of the inhabitants of said District; nor without making just compensation to the owners.

ART. 4. Congress shall have no power to prohibit the removal or transportation of slaves from one slave State to another slave State.

ART. 5. The migration or importation of persons held to service or labor for life, or a term of years, into any of the States, or the Territories belonging to the United States, is perpetually prohibited; and Congress shall pass all laws necessary to make said prohibition effective.

ART. 6. In all that part of the territory of the United States, not included within the limits of any State, which lies north of the parallel of 36°30' of north latitude, slavery, or involuntary servitude, except for crime, whereof the party shall have been duly convicted, shall be prohibited; and in all that territory of the United States, not included within the limits of any State, which lies south of said parallel of 36°30' of north latitude, neither Congress nor any Territorial Legislature shall have power to pass any law abolishing, prohibiting, or in any manner interfering with the right to hold slaves; and wherever, in any portion of the territory owned by the United States north or south of the said parallel of 36°30', there shall be, within an area of not less than sixty thousand square miles, a population equal to the ratio of representation for a member of Congress, the same shall be admitted by Congress into the Union as a State, upon the same footing with the original States in all respects whatever, with or without slavery, as its constitution may determine.

ART. 7. No territory beyond the present limits of the United States and the Territories thereof shall be hereafter acquired by, or annexed to, the United States, unless the same be done by a concurrent vote of two thirds of both Houses of Congress, or, if the same be acquired by treaty, by a vote of two thirds of the Senate.

ART. 8. Article four and section two of the Constitution of the United States shall be so amended as to read as follows: A person charged in any State with treason, felony, or other crime, (*against the laws of said State,*) who shall flee from justice and be found in another State, shall, on demand of the executive authority of the State from which he fled, be delivered up, to be removed to the State having jurisdiction of the crime.

Source: *Congressional Globe*, 36th Cong., 2nd Sess., 279.

State Representative George R. Gantt (Democrat) Tennessee General Assembly
January 11, 1861

Representative George R. Gantt (1824–1897) represented Maury County as a Democrat. He was born in Maury County, studied law in Columbia, and began his law practice there. During

the war he served as a lieutenant colonel in the 9th Battalion,
Tennessee Cavalry (Confederate).

Mr. Gantt offered House Resolution No. 21, as follows:

The success of the Black Republican party, and the secession of the Cotton States may be treated as accomplished facts. These events press upon Tennessee questions of the gravest and highest moment. She cannot waive them—her safety and her honor demand that she must meet them.

She is vitally interested in slavery as a political institution, and in slaves as property. Her slaves are entitled to the status of all other property, both under the Federal Constitution and the local law; but whilst every other species of property is permitted to spread freely throughout the States and Territories, at the will of the owner, this alone is marked out for destruction, by the sentiment which called the Black Republican party into being. The basis of its organization is hatred to slavery; and so exclusively is the case, that if the sentiment of hate were withdrawn it would perish in an hour. It denies that the Constitution recognizes and protects slaves as property; it holds that it has the power to exclude slave property from the common Territories, in the face of an express decision of the Supreme Court of the United States; its avowed policy is that slavery is a wrong and to be dealt with as such—a sin for which not only the slave-holding States are responsible, but which rests also upon the non-slaveholding States; that it is to be confined in perpetual siege in the States where it now exists, and placed in a course of ultimate extinction. Its President elect champions the sentiment that it is and must continue to be the subject of a perpetual struggle, until it prevais {*sic*} everywhere, or is abolished everywhere in the broad borders of the Republic.

This sentiment has taken possession of all the State governments in the North; and, finally, in the recent Presidential election, by a purely sectional vote, has elected its candidate to the office of President. On the fourth of March next, it will be duly installed into all the chief seats of power in the Federal Union. The purse, the sword, the army, the navy, then pass into its hands. It cannot be doubted for a moment that this power will be used to the prejudice of slave property, which will then be exposed to its attacks. As property, it will not receive the fostering care of the General Government, but it will be outlawed—treated as a sin—dealt with as a wrong.

Already in a minority on this question, the secession of the Cotton States leaves us in a hopeless minority. It takes not the prescience of prophecy to foretell, that in a few years, under these circumstances if we tamely submit to the domination of this anti-slavery spirit, that in all the boundaries of Tennessee, "the sun will not rise upon a slave, or set upon a master." Our slave property is interwoven with the whole frame work of our society, and identified with all our industrial pursuits; its destruction involves degradation and ruin. It is vain to think of protecting it under the present forms of the Constitution. Tennessee has loved the Federal Union, and loudly cherished the hope that it was destined to be perpetual; and now, surrounded by the great and impressive facts of the hour, she feels it her solemn duty to make a last effort for the reconstruction of that Union, and the protection of her honor and property therein; failing in this, she will be driven to resume her delegated powers, and unite her destiny with her sister Slave States in a Southern Union.

Tennessee desires the co-operation of her sister Slave States in the effort she proposes to make, and earnestly invites them to join her in the same. Therefore,

Be it resolved by the General Assembly of Tennessee:

1. That the Governor appoint a commission of not less than ten of our ablest and wisest citizens, to meet in convention a similar commission on behalf of the other Slave States, in the city of Louisville, Kentucky, between the 20th and 25th of January, 1861.

2. That said Convention adopt a basis of settlement, upon which, if possible, the Union may be reconstructed, and by which the rights of property and honor of the slave States may be rendered secure from injury or attack.

3. That the delegates composing said Convention, repair with the ultimatum adopted by them, to the city of Washington, and lay the same before the Congress of the United States, and urge that body to submit it, in the form of an amendment or amendments to the Federal Constitution, on or before the 20th day of February, 1861.

4. That while Tennessee will abide by the ultimatum agreed upon by the Convention, she deems it proper to express her own view of what it should embrace, and which is as follows:

1. A declaratory amendment to the Federal Constitution, to the effect that, under it, African slavery, as it exists in the slave States, is property, and entitled by it, as well as the local law to the status, of every other species of property.

2. An amendment which will compel the States to surrender on demand, slaves escaped from their owners, or on refusal, to pay double their value, by suit in the Federal Court, at the instance of the owner.

3. An amendment whereby this property shall be rendered secure in transit through the non-slaveholding States, and whilst in such States temporarily sojourning with the owner.

4. An amendment running a line on the northern borders of the slave States, until it touches our territories, and then west, on the parallel of thirty-six degrees and thirty minutes, until it touches the boundary of the State of California, and then with her boundary to the Pacific Ocean; and declaring that in all the States and Territories south of said line, slavery shall exist, and in all north of it shall be forever prohibited.

5. *Resolved*, That the Governor of Tennessee appoint a Commissioner upon the impending crisis to each of the slaveholding States whose Legislatures are now in session, or may be in session before the adjournment of this General Assembly.

6. *Resolved*, That copies of these resolutions be transmitted to the Governors of the several slave States by the Governor of Tennessee.

Which resolutions lie over under the rule.

Source: *House Journal of the Extra Session of the Thirty-Third General Assembly of the State of Tennessee, which Convened at Nashville, on the First Monday in January, A.D. 1861* (Nashville: J. O. Griffith and Company, Public Printers, 1861), 43–45.

JOINT SELECT COMMITTEE ON FEDERAL RELATIONS
TENNESSEE GENERAL ASSEMBLY
January 14, 1861

Mr. Barksdale[1] from the Joint Select Committee on Federal Relations, reported that they had had under consideration House Resolutions, Nos. 24 and 25; and also Senate Resolution, No. 5, and recommend resolutions in lieu, which are herewith submitted.

BARKSDALE, *Chairman.*

Which resolutions in lieu, are as follows:

{*Chairman Barksdale introduced the committee's resolutions with the same preamble used by George R. Gantt in his House Resolution No. 21 three days earlier.*}

Therefore be it resolved by the General Assembly of Tennessee,
That a Convention of all the slave-holding States shall assemble as early as practicable, to define and adopt a basis upon which, if possible, the Union may be reconstructed, and that in the opinion of the General Assembly of the State of Tennessee, said basis of adjustment should embrace the following propositions, as amendments to the Federal Constitution, to-wit:

1. A declaratory amendment to the Federal Constitution, to the effect that, under it African slavery as it exists in the slave States, is property, and entitled by it, as well as the local law to the States of every other species of property.

2. In all the territory of the United States now held, or hereafter acquired, situated north of latitude thirty-six degrees and thirty minutes, slavery or involuntary servitude, except as a punishment for

crime, is prohibited, while such territory shall remain under territorial government. In all the territory south of said line of latitude, slavery of the African race is hereby recognized as existing, and shall not be interfered with by Congress, nor by the territorial Legislature; but shall be protected as property by all the departments of the government during its continuance; and when any territory, north or south of said line, within such boundaries as Congress may prescribe, shall contain the population requisite for a member of Congress, according to the then federal ratio of representation of the people of the United States, it shall, if its form of government be republican, be admitted into the Union on an equal footing with the original States, with or without slavery, as the Constitution of such new State may provide.

3. Congress shall have {no} power to abolish slavery in places under its exclusive jurisdiction, and situate within the limits of States that permit the holding of slaves.

4. Congress shall have no power to abolish slavery within the District of Columbia, so long as it exists in the adjoining States of Virginia and Maryland, or either, nor without the consent of the inhabitants, nor without just compensation made to such owners of slaves as do not consent to such abolishment. Nor shall Congress at any time prohibit officers of the Federal Government or members of Congress, whose duties require them to be in said District, from bringing with them, their slaves, and holding them as such, during the time their duties may require them to remain there, and afterwards taking them from the District.

5. Congress shall have no power to prohibit or hinder the transportation of slaves from one State to another, or to a territory in which slaves are by law permitted to be held, whether that transportation be by land, navigable rivers, or by the sea.

6. That, in addition to the provisions of the third paragraph of the second section of the fourth article of the Constitution of the United States, Congress shall have power to provide by law, and it shall be its duty to so provide, that the United States shall pay to the owner who shall apply for it, the full value of his fugitive slave, in all cases, when the marshal or other officer, whose duty it was to arrest said fugitive,

was prevented from so doing by violence or intimidation, or when, after arrest, said fugitive was rescued by force, and the owner thereby prevented and obstructed in the pursuit of his remedy for the recovery of his fugitive slave, under the said clause of the Constitution and the laws made in pursuance thereof. And in all such cases when the United States shall pay for such fugitive, they shall have the right, in their own name, to sue the county in which said violence, intimidation, or rescue was committed, and to recover from it, with interest and damages, the amount paid by them for said fugitive slave. And the said county, after it has paid said amount to the United States, may, for its indemnity, sue and recover from the wrong-doers, or rescuers, by whom the owner was prevented from the recovery of his fugitive slave, in like manner as the owner himself might have sued and recovered.

7. No future amendment of the Constitution shall affect the five preceding articles, nor the third paragraph of the second section of the first article of the Constitution, nor the third paragraph of the second section of the fourth article of said Constitution, and no amendment shall be made to the Constitution which will authorize or give to Congress any power to abolish or interfere with slavery in any of the States by whose laws it is or may be allowed or permitted.

8. An amendment whereby this property shall be rendered secure in transit through the non slaveholding States, and whilst in such States temporarily sojourning with the owner.

9. For amendment to the effect, that all fugitives are to be deemed those offending the laws within the jurisdiction of the State, and who escape therefrom to other States, and that it is the duty of each State to suppress armed invasion of another State.

Source: *House Journal of the Extra Session of the Thirty-Third General Assembly of the State of Tennessee, Which Convened at Nashville, on the First Monday in January, A. D. 1861* (Nashville: J. O. Griffith and Company, Public Printers, 1861), 63–66.

TENNESSEE GENERAL ASSEMBLY
January 22, 1861

Resolutions proposing amendments to the Constitution of the United States.

Resolved by the General Assembly of the State of Tennessee, That a Convention of delegates from all the slaveholding States should assemble at Nashville, Tennessee, or such other place as a majority of the States co-operating may designate, on the fourth day of February, 1861, to digest and define a basis upon which, if possible, the Federal Union and the Constitutional rights of the slave States may be perpetuated and preserved.

Resolved, That the General Assembly of the State of Tennessee appoint a number of delegates to said Convention, of our ablest and wisest men, equal to our whole delegation in Congress; and that the Governor of Tennessee immediately furnish copies of these resolutions to the Governors of the slaveholding States, and urge the participation of such States in said Convention.

Resolved, That in the opinion of this General Assembly, such plan of adjustment should embrace the following propositions as amendments to the Constitution of the United States.

1. A declaratory amendment that African slaves as held under the institutions of the slaveholding States, shall be recognized as property, and entitled to the *status* of other property, in the States where slavery exists, in all places within the exclusive jurisdiction of Congress in the slave States, in all the Territories south of 36 deg. 30 min., in the District of Columbia, in transit and whilst temporarily sojourning with the owner in the non-slaveholding States, and Territories north of 36 deg. 30 min., and when fugitives from the owner, in the several places above named, as well as in all places in the exclusive jurisdiction of Congress in the non-slaveholding States.

2. That all the territory now owned, or which may be hereafter acquired by the United States south of the parallel of 36 deg. 30 min., African slavery shall be recognized as existing, and be protected by

all the departments of the Federal and Territorial Governments; and in all north of that line, now owned or to be acquired, it shall not be recognized as existing; and whenever States formed out of any of said territory south of said line, having a population equal to that of a Congressional District, shall apply for admission into the Union, the same shall be admitted as slave States; whilst States north of the line, formed out of said territory, and having a population equal to a Congressional District, shall be admitted without slavery; but the States formed out of said territory north and south, having been admitted as members of the Union, shall have all the powers over the institution of slavery possessed by the other States of the Union.

3. Congress shall have no power to abolish slavery in places under its exclusive jurisdiction, and situate within the limits of States that permit the holding of slaves.

4. Congress shall have no power to abolish slavery within the District of Columbia, as long as it exists in the adjoining States of Virginia and Maryland, or either, nor without the consent of the inhabitants, nor without just compensation made to such owners of slaves as do not consent to such abolishment. Nor shall Congress at any time prohibit the officers of the Federal Government, or members of Congress, whose duties require them to be in said District, from bringing with them their slaves, and holding them as such during the time their duties may require them to remain there, and afterwards taking them from the District.

5. Congress shall have no power to prohibit or hinder the transportation of slaves from one State to another, or the territory in which slaves are permitted by law to be held, whether that transportation be by land, navigable rivers, or by sea.

6. In addition to the Fugitive Slave clause, provide, that when a slave has been demanded of the Executive authority of the State to which he has fled, if he is not delivered, and the owner permitted to carry him out of the State in peace, the State so failing to deliver shall pay to the owner the value of such slave, and such damages as he may have sustained in attempting to reclaim his slave, and secure his

right of action in the Supreme Court of the United States, with execution against the property of such State and of the individuals thereof.

7. No future amendment of the Constitution shall affect the six preceding articles, nor the third paragraph of the second section of the first article of the Constitution, nor the third paragraph of the second section of the fourth article of said Constitution; and no amendment shall be made to the Constitution which will authorize or give to Congress any power to abolish or interfere with slavery in any of the States by whose laws it is, or may be, allowed or permitted.

8. That slave property shall be rendered secure in transit through, or whilst temporarily sojourning in non-slaveholding States or Territories, or in the District of Columbia.

9. An amendment to the effect that all fugitives are to be deemed those offending the laws within the jurisdiction of the State, and who escape therefrom to other States; and that it is the duty of each State to suppress armed invasions of another State.

Resolved, That said Convention of the slaveholding States having agreed upon a basis of adjustment satisfactory to themselves, should, in the opinion of this General Assembly, refer it to a Convention of all the States, slaveholding and non-slaveholding, in the manner following:

It should invite all States friendly to such plan of adjustment, to elect delegates in such manner to reflect the popular will, to assemble in a Constitutional Convention of all the States, North and South, to be held at Richmond, Virginia, on the——day of February, 1861, to revise and perfect such plan of adjustment, for its reference for final ratification and adoption by a Convention of the States respectively.

Resolved, That should a plan of adjustment satisfactory to the South not be acceded to by a requisite number of States to perfect amendments to the Constitution of the United States, it is the opinion of this General Assembly that the slaveholding States should adopt for themselves the Constitution of the United States, with such amendments as may be satisfactory to the slaveholding States, and that they should invite into the Union with them all the States in the North which are willing to abide such amended Constitution and frame of government, severing at once all connections with States refusing such reasonable guarantees to our future safety; such renewed conditions of Federal Union being first submitted for ratification to Conventions of all the States respectively.

Resolved, That the Governor of the State of Tennessee furnish copies of these resolutions immediately to the Governors of the non-slaveholding States.

W. C. WHITTHORNE,[2]
Speaker of the House of Representatives.
TAZ. W. NEWMAN,[3]
Speaker of the Senate.

Passed January 22, 1861.

Source: *Public Acts of the State of Tennessee, Passed at the Extra Session of the Thirty-Third General Assembly, for the Year 1861* (Nashville: E. G. Eastman & Co., Public Printers, Union and American Office, 1861), 49–52.

Also see Lucius E. Chittenden, ed., *A Report of the Debates and Proceedings in the Secret Sessions of the Conference Convention, for Proposing Amendments to the Constitution of the United States, Held at Washington, D.C., in February, A.D. 1861* (New York: D. Appleton & Company, 1864), 454–55. Resolutions were read to the US House of Representatives on January 28, 1861; *Congressional Globe,* 36th Cong., 2nd Sess., 599; House Misc. Doc. No. 27.

STATE SENATOR JOHN WATKINS RICHARDSON
(OPPOSITIONIST)
TENNESSEE GENERAL ASSEMBLY
January 22, 1861

Dr. John W. Richardson (1809–1872) was born in Virginia and brought to Rutherford County when six years old. A graduate of Transylvania University in Lexington, Kentucky, Richardson practiced medicine in Murfreesboro from 1830 until his death.

He published numerous tracts on medical, political, and reli-
gious subjects, and served as president of the state medical society
on several occasions. In 1861, he represented Rutherford and
Williamson Counties as a member of the Opposition Party.

Mr. Richardson offered the following in lieu of the terms of adjustment as proposed in the third resolution:

Article 1. In all the territory of the United States now held, or hereafter acquired, situated North of latitude thirty-six degrees and thirty minutes, slavery or involuntary servitude, except as a punishment for crime, is prohibited, while such territory shall remain under territorial government. In all the territory South of said line of latitude slavery of the African race is hereby recognized as existing, and shall not be interfered with by Congress; but shall be protected as property by all the departments of the territorial government during its continuance; and when any territory, North or South of said line, within such boundaries as Congress may prescribe, shall contain the population requisite for a member of Congress, according to the then Federal ratio of representation of the people of the United States, it shall, if its form of government be republican, be admitted into the Union on an equal footing with the original States, with or without slavery, as the Constitution of such new State may provide.

Art. 2. Congress shall have no power to abolish slavery in places under its exclusive jurisdiction, and situate within the limits of States that permit the holding of slaves.

Art. 3. Congress shall have no power to abolish slavery within the District of Columbia, so long as it exists in the adjoining States of Virginia and Maryland, or either, nor without the consent of the inhabitants, nor without just compensation first made to such owners of slaves as do not consent to such abolishment. Nor shall Congress at any time prohibit officers of the Federal Government or members of Congress, whose duties require them to be in said District, from bringing with them their slaves, and holding them as such, during the time their duties may require them to remain there, and afterwards taking them from the District.

Art. 4. Congress shall have no power to prohibit or hinder the transportation of slaves from one State to another, or to a territory in which slaves are by law permitted to be held, whether that transportation be by land, navigable rivers, or by the sea.

Art. 5. That in addition to the provisions of the third paragraph of the second section of the fourth article of the Constitution of the United States, Congress shall have power to provide by law, and it shall be its duty to so provide, that the United States shall pay to the owner who shall apply for it the full value of his fugitive slave, in all cases, when the marshal or other officer, whose duty it was to arrest said fugitive, was prevented from so doing by violence or intimidation, or when, after arrest, said fugitive was rescued by force, and the owner thereby prevented and obstructed in the pursuit of his remedy for the recovery of his fugitive slave, under the said clause of the Constitution and the laws made in pursuance thereof. And in all such cases, when the United States shall pay for such fugitives, they shall have the right, in their own name, to sue the county in which said violence, intimidation or rescue was committed, and to recover from it, with interest and damages, the amount paid by them for said fugitive slave. And the said county, after it has paid said amount to the United States, may, for its indemnity, sue and recover from the wrong-doers, or rescuers, by whom the owner was prevented from the recovery of his fugitive slave, in like manner as the owner himself might have sued and recovered.

Art. 6. No future amendment of the Constitution shall affect the five preceding articles, nor the third paragraph of the second section of the first article of the Constitution, nor the third paragraph of the second section of the fourth article of said Constitution, and no amendment shall be made to the Constitution which shall authorize or give to Congress any power to abolish or interfere with slavery in any of the States by whose laws it is or may be allowed or permitted.

{Richardson's amendment is identical to Crittenden's of December 18th, excluding the attached four resolutions. (See Thomas A. R. Nelson's amendment of December 27.) The Tennessee Senate declined Senator Richardson's substitute proposal by a vote of 16–8.}

Source: *Senate Journal of the Extra Session of the Thirty-Third General Assembly of the State of Tennessee, Which Convened at Nashville, on the First Monday in January, A. D. 1861* (Nashville: J. O. Griffith and Company, Public Printers, 1861), 77–79.

CHAPTER SIX

SEPARATION

April, May, June 1861

The sixty days from April 15 to June 18 were fateful for the state of Tennessee. President Abraham Lincoln issued a call for troops two days after the surrender of Fort Sumter to "suppress" the southern rebellion and to "cause the laws to be duly executed." He emphasized that his main purpose was to retake federal property, and that "the utmost care will be observed, consistently with the objects aforesaid, to avoid any devastation, any destruction of, or interference with, property, or any disturbance of peaceful citizens in any part of the country."

Governor Harris rejected the president's request, and, in his opening address to a second special session of the general assembly on April 25, argued that Tennessee should instead declare its independence from the United States. Without suggesting there was a constitutional right of secession, Harris reasoned that "all admit the moral right asserted by our fathers, of each and every people to resist wrong, and to maintain their liberties by whatever means may be necessary." While never mentioning the attack on the federal fort in Charleston Harbor, the governor invoked a "long train of abuses" by "the anti-republican spirit" in the North and the "encroachment of Abolition power." The crisis had been brought on, he declared, by the "unprovoked and tyrannical usurpation" of the southern people.

On May 6, the legislature responded by calling a referendum for June 8 of the state's voters on two issues: a declaration of independence and the adoption of the Provisional Constitution of the Confederate States of America. The next day, Governor Harris, not waiting for the results of the June election, appointed three commissioners to meet with Henry W. Hilliard, a commissioner representing President Jefferson Davis, to negotiate

a military league with the authorities of the Confederate States.
Assuming that Tennessee would join the Confederacy, the
"Convention Between the State of Tennessee and the Confederate
States of America" bound the state to the Confederate govern-
ment and placed its military operations under the "control and
direction" of President Davis. Having obligated the state to an
alliance with the southern Confederacy, the legislature prepared
an open letter to the male voters of the state justifying the separa-
tion of Tennessee from the United States. The message, published
on May 9, set out to sway public opinion in favor of secession
well in advance of the June 8 referendum. Governor Harris's
June 18 address to the general assembly, following the assent of
the voters to secede ten days earlier, and issued during the East
Tennessee Convention at Greeneville, was congratulatory in
tone and recommended to the legislature several items that would
complete the state's separation from the United States.

PRESIDENT ABRAHAM LINCOLN'S PROCLAMATION CALLING MILITIA AND CONVENING CONGRESS
April 15, 1861

By the President of the United States
A Proclamation.

Whereas the laws of the United States have been for some time
past, and now are opposed, and the execution thereof obstructed, in
the States of South Carolina, Georgia, Alabama, Florida, Mississippi,
Louisiana and Texas, by combinations too powerful to be suppressed
by the ordinary course of judicial proceedings, or by the powers vested
in the Marshals by law,

Now therefore, I, Abraham Lincoln, President of the United
States, in virtue of the power in me vested by the Constitution, and
the laws, have thought fit to call forth, and hereby do call forth, the

militia of the several States of the Union, to the aggregate number of seventy-five thousand, in order to suppress said combinations, and to cause the laws to be duly executed. The details, for this object, will be immediately communicated to the State authorities through the War Department.

I appeal to all loyal citizens to favor, facilitate and aid this effort to maintain the honor, the integrity, and the existence of our National Union, and the perpetuity of popular government; and to redress wrongs already long enough endured.

I deem it proper to say that the first service assigned to the forces hereby called forth will probably be to re-possess the forts, places, and property which have been seized from the Union; and in every event, the utmost care will be observed, consistently with the objects aforesaid, to avoid any devastation, any destruction of, or interference with, property, or any disturbance of peaceful citizens in any part of the country.

And I hereby command the persons composing the combinations aforesaid to disperse, and retire peaceably to their respective abodes within twenty days from this date.

Deeming that the present condition of public affairs presents an extraordinary occasion, I do hereby, in virtue of the power in me vested in the Constitution, convene both Houses of Congress. Senators and Representatives are therefore summoned to assemble at their respective chambers, at 12 o'clock, noon, on Thursday, the fourth day of July, next, then and there to consider and determine such measures, as, in their wisdom, the public safety, and interest may seem to demand.

In Witness Whereof I have hereunto set my hand, and caused the Seal of the United States to be affixed.

Done at the city of Washington this fifteenth day of April in the year of our Lord, One thousand, Eight hundred and Sixty-one, and of the Independence of the United States the Eighty-fifth.

ABRAHAM LINCOLN

By the President

WILLIAM H. SEWARD, Secretary of State.

Source: Roy P. Basler, ed., *The Collected Works of Abraham Lincoln*, vol. IV (New Brunswick: Rutgers University Press, 1953), 331–32.

GOVERNOR HARRIS'S
LEGISLATIVE MESSAGE
April 25, 1861

Gentlemen of the Senate and House of Representatives:

The President of the United States—elected according to the forms of the Constitution, but upon principles openly hostile to its provisions—having wantonly inaugurated an internecine war between the people of the slave and non-slave holding States, I have convened you again at the seat of Government, for the purpose of enabling you to take such action as will most likely contribute to the defence of our rights, the preservation of our liberties, the sovereignty of the State, and the safety of our people; all of which are now in imminent peril by the usurpations of the authorities at Washington, and the unscrupulous fanaticism which runs riot throughout the Northern States.

The war thus inaugurated is likely to assume an importance nearly, if not equal, to the struggle of our revolutionary fathers, in their patriotic efforts to resist the usurpations and throw off the tyrannical yoke of the English Government; a war the duration of which and the good or evil that must result from it, depends entirely, in my judgment, upon the readiness with which the citizens of the South harmonize as one people, and the alacrity with which they respond to the demands of patriotism.

I do not think it necessary to recapitulate, at this late hour, the long train of abuses to which the people of Tennessee, and our sister States of the South have been subjected by the anti-republican spirit that has for many years been manifesting itself in that section, and which has at last declared itself our open and avowed enemy. In the message which I addressed to you at your called session in January last,[1] these things were somewhat elaborately referred to, as constituting, in my judgment, the amplest reason for considering ourselves in imminent danger, and as requiring such action on the part of the Legislature as would place the State in an attitude for defence, whenever the momentous crisis should be forced upon us; and, also, as presenting to the North the strongest argument for peace, and if possible, securing a reconstruction of the Union, thus already dissolved by the most authoritative, formal, and matured action of a portion of the slaveholding States. Minor differences upon abstract questions—the ardent devotion of our people to the preservation of the Union, originating with their great loyalty to the Government—and a more hopeful view of the subject than I had been able to take, coupled with the supposed peaceful intentions of the authorities at Washington, have resulted in leaving the State poorly prepared for the sad realities which are now upon us.

But unfortunate as this may be, I am nevertheless encouraged with the belief that we are at last, practically, a united people. Whatever differences may have heretofore existed amongst us, growing out of party divisions, as to the right of Secession as a Constitutional remedy against Federal usurpation, all admit the moral right asserted by our fathers, of each and every people to resist wrong, and to maintain their liberties by whatever means may be necessary; "that Governments derive their just powers from the consent of the governed, and that whenever any form of government becomes destructive of the ends for which it was created, it is the right of the people to alter and abolish it, and to institute a new government, laying its foundations on such principles, and organizing its powers in such form as shall to them seem most likely to effect their safety and happiness."[2] Standing by this common sentiment, with the bloody and tyrannical policy of the Presidential usurper fully before us; in the face of his hordes of armed soldiery, marching to the work of Southern subjugation; the people of the proud Commonwealth of Tennessee—true to their honor, true to the great principles of free institutions, true to the lessons of their fathers, and true to their brethren of the South, the subjects of a common oppression—have united, almost with one voice, in declaring their fixed resolve to resist the tyrant; and in pledging their lives, their fortunes, and their sacred honor to the maintenance of their rights, and the rights of their sister States of the South.

It cannot be overlooked that, in assuming an attitude of this character—forced upon us by the remarkable exigency of the times—we are, in effect, dissolving our connection with the Federal Union. As established by our fathers, that Union no longer exists. However much we may have cherished it heretofore, no intelligent and candid man can deny that it has ceased to be a blessing, and has become a curse; that it is no longer a high and sacred means of protection, but an engine of oppression; that it has ceased to be a bond of brotherhood, and has become a hateful connection between communities at war. It would be idle, therefore, to speak of ourselves any longer as members of the Federal Union; and while it is believed by many, whose opinions are entitled to the highest respect, that, by reason of the subversion of the Constitution by the authorities in power, inaugurating a revolution between the States thereof, each and every individual is already released from his former obligations to that government, yet, as best comporting with the dignity of the subject, and also from a due regard to those who may hold a different opinion—and farther still, that all the world may be advised of our action—I respectfully suggest that our connection with the Federal Union be formally annulled in such manner as shall involve the highest exercise of sovereign authority by the people of the State, and best secure that harmony, so much to be desired, in times like the present, upon questions even of mere detail. Until this is done many conscientious citizens may feel embarrassed in their action from their supposed relation to the General Government. In emergencies like the present, while it is our duty to act with due deliberation and prudence, unbiased as far as possible by excitement or prejudice, it is nevertheless of the highest importance that we should act with promptitude and decision.

Whatever the grounds of hope may have been supposed to exist heretofore for an adjustment of the difficulties between the two sections of the Federal Union; however anxious we may have been to continue members of the same common family with the people of the North, such hope and expectation no longer exist in the mind of any rational man, who desires to maintain the honor and equality of the State, and the inviolability of her peculiar institutions.

The present administration, elected upon avowed purposes of hostility to the South—purposes which all knew then as well as now, could not be carried into effect, without an internecine war and a dissolution of the Union—has exerted every energy, resorted to every strategy, and disregarded every constitutional barrier, in order to hasten the accomplishment of the unholy mission for which the people of the Northern section had elevated it to power. They have lost no time—they have neither hesitated or faltered. The low duplicity in which their Administration was inaugurated—trusting, while conceding nothing, to lull the South into a fatal security, furnishing ground for divisions in the border slave States, while constant though secret preparation for the work of subjugation was going on, is now exposed and leaves us no alternative but independence out of the Union, or subjugation in it. The dishonorable and treacherous practices which have so far characterized the authorities at Washington, admonish us, that in the impending struggle we are scarcely to expect the rules of honorable warfare. Having its origin in a disordered moral sentiment of the North—not finding the ordinary restraints of patriotism among their people—deriving its power from a usurpation and perversion of the functions of government—having no middle-ground short of positive subjugation of the South, or a defeat which exposes its disgrace to the civilized world—I fear the time has passed when peace can be hoped for by the mere moral force of a united South, without a trial of arms. Having succeeded in confusing and dividing the border slave States, they have had ample time for military preparations. The veil which concealed their recent movements has been thrown aside. The note of war has been sounded, and in the imperial proclamation, recently issued, the people of the Confederate States and all who sympathize with them are treated as rebels, and twenty days is allowed them to "disperse" and return to their allegiance to the authorities at Washington. Without waiting for the expiration of the twenty days, in addition to the regular army and naval forces, militia forces, a militia force of seventy-five thousand has been called into the field to execute this edict, by the power of arms. As if purposely intended to add additional insult to the people of Tennessee, I have been called upon, as their Governor, to furnish a portion of these troops. I have answered that demand as in my judgment became the honor of the State, and leave the people to pass upon my action.

The Federal Union of the States, thus practically dissolved, can never be restored; or if ever thus restored, it must, by the very act, cease to be a Union of free and independent States, such as our fathers established. It will become a consolidated, centralized Government, without liberty or equality, in which some will reign and others serve—the few tyrannize and the many suffer. It would be the greatest folly to hope for the reconstruction of a peaceful Union, upon terms of fraternity and equality, at the end of an internecine war. There can be no desirable Union without fraternity. And if we could not have that, before the unholy crusade which is now being waged against us, we cannot have it after they shall have wantonly imbrued their unholy hands in the innocent blood of our people, from no worthier motive than a desire to destroy our equality and subvert our liberties.

Therefore, I respectfully recommend the perfecting of an Ordinance by the General Assembly, formally declaring the independence of the State of Tennessee of the Federal Union, renouncing its authority, and re-assuming each and every function belonging to a separate sovereignty; and that said Ordinance, when it shall have been thus perfected by the Legislature, shall, at the earliest practicable time, be submitted to a vote of the people, to be by them adopted or rejected.

When the people of the State shall formally declare their connection with the remaining States of the Union dissolved, it will be a matter of the highest expediency,—I might almost say of unavoidable political necessity—that we shall at the same time, or as soon thereafter as may be, connect ourselves with those with whom a common interest, a common sympathy, and a common destiny identify us, for weal or for woe. That each of the Southern States, as they throw off their connection with the Federal Government, should take an independent position in the contest, without that concert of action which alone can be secured by political unity, is a proposition which surely no one will assent to, who anticipates the dangers of the hour and the necessity for perfect harmony in the work of our general defence.

Such a political Union with the people of the Confederate States is rendered essential, by the fact, that we have made no provision for arming, organizing, provisioning, and embodying our military forces, while the Government of the Confederate States, foreseeing this invasion, has had an eye to the necessities of the emergency, and stands prepared generously to lend us its assistance in this unprovoked and cruel struggle. If we accept that assistance, we should do it in a spirit of mutual trust and confidence, prepared to share its burdens equally, while we avail ourselves of its advantages. A Government thus perfectly organized can more thoroughly command the resources and aggregate the revenues of the country than isolated States, fighting without unity, and moving without a common and responsible head. These resources, being thus concentrated, because it is natural intuition to rally round such a Government, in such an emergency, for self-preservation and defence, can be disbursed with more efficiency, and with less cost to the people than when the revenues, necessary to support the war, are scattered by divided counsels and not controlled by a common bureau. The same may be said with regard to military operations. Unity of movement, to secure unity of purpose in attack or defence, is absolutely necessary to success. The people of the whole South, thus united by a firm political compact, moving under the direction of one Government, and animated by the sense of common perils and by a unanimous determination to maintain their rights, liberties, and institutions, are invincible, and must speedily conquer an honorable peace. The war must necessarily be protracted or brief in proportion to the union among themselves.

I, therefore, further recommend that you perfect an ordinance, with a view to our admission as a member of the Southern Confederacy, (which, it is evident, must soon embrace the entire slaveholding States of the South,) to be submitted in like manner, and at the same time, but separately, for adoption or rejection by the people; so that they may have the opportunity to approve the former and reject the latter, or adopt both, as in their wisdom may seem most consistent with the future welfare of the State. However fully satisfied the Executive and Legislature may be, as to the urgent necessity for the speedy adoption of both these propositions, it is our duty to furnish the amplest means for a fair and full expression of the popular will.

In the opening of a revolution, fraught with such consequences, and the close of which no one can foresee, it is a matter of the highest moment that we determine, as speedily as possible our future political relations, delaying only long enough to reach the will and voice of the people. Under existing circumstances, I can see no propriety for encumbering the people of the State with the election of delegates, to do that which it is in your power to enable them to do directly for themselves. The most direct as well as the highest act of sovereignty, according to our theory, is that by which the people vote, not merely for men, but for measures submitted for their approval or rejection. Since it is only the voice of the people that is to be heard, there is no reason why they may not as readily and effectively express themselves upon an ordinance framed and submitted to them by the Legislature, as if submitted to them by a Convention. The Southern States, all of whom are now engaged in resistance to the encroachment of Abolition power, will necessarily encounter embarrassments, arising from a want of unity of action, until such time as they shall all be united under a common Government.

The mode of action suggested, in addition to the advantage of its being the speediest of all others, will be attended with less expense to the State, which is of far greater importance now than at any former period of our history, owing to the general embarrassment of the people, which must continue at least during these troubles, and to the heavy appropriations that you will have necessarily to make to defray the expense of our defences.

If, however, it should be deemed advisable that a Convention, representing the sovereignty of the people, should be called by the General Assembly, in preference to submitting an ordinance of independence directly to them, though I deem the latter measure more expedient, under the circumstances, I am not prepared to say that harmony and unanimity will not thus be effected. The Senators and Representatives, coming as they do, directly from their constituents, are the best judges of this measure. It cannot be regarded other than a question of detail, inasmuch as a very large majority of the people regard themselves as being forever absolved from all obedience to a Government that has developed the coldest and most deliberate purpose to inaugurate a civil and sanguinary war among them.

I deem it proper to remark in this connection that the Constitution of the Confederate States, while it retains all that is valuable of the Constitution of the former United States, is an improvement in many essential points upon that instrument, as conceded by those even who are unfriendly to the mode and manner in which it originated.

The only additional matter to which I shall call your attention—and first in importance—is the necessity of such legislation as will put the State upon war footing immediately. I will not insult your intelligence or question your patriotism so far as to resort to argument to prove the necessity of this measure, but content myself by recommending the passage of a law regulating the raising and thorough organization of an efficient volunteer force for immediate service, in any emergency which may arise, and a thorough and perfect organization of the militia, so that in case of necessity the whole force of the State can be speedily brought into action.

In my message to your extra session in January last, I laid before you the report of the Keeper of Public Arms, showing the number, character, and condition of the arms of the State, to which I refer you for information on that subject. Since that report was made, I have ordered and received at the arsenal, fourteen hundred rifle muskets. If upon this subject further or more accurate information is desired, it shall be laid before you by the report of the proper officer.

It requires no argument from me to prove the absolute necessity of an immediate appropriation of a sum sufficient to thoroughly arm and equip such military force as the State may probably need in the prospective difficulties which lie before us. In addition to which, I respectfully recommend that you appropriate a sum sufficient to provision and maintain such force as is intended for the field, and an ample contingent military fund, to be subject to the order and disbursement of a Military Board, under such restrictions as you may see proper to impose.

The establishment of a Military Board, to consist of at least three persons, and invested with power to make all needful rules and regulations for organization and maintenance, I regard as indispensably necessary to a perfect military organization and equipment in the State, and the fact that the Legislature cannot foresee and provide for the various contingent expenses necessarily incidental to a state of war, justifies and makes necessary the contingent military fund referred to.

I trust gentlemen, that I have not so far mistaken your intelligence and patriotism, as to render necessary that I should invoke you in the name of all that is sacred and dear to us as a people—even the sanctity of our domestic firesides—to forget past differences, and whatever may tend in the least to distract your counsels in the present momentous crisis, in which we have been involved by the unprovoked and tyrannical usurpation of a people who, forgetting the lessons of their fathers, have overthrown the fairest government upon earth, in the mere wantonness of an unnatural sectional prejudice amounting to a sectional hate, and a disregard of those great principles of justice and equality upon which the Federal Union was based. I trust that to-day there are in Tennessee no Whigs, no Democrats; but that we are one people—all patriots, all brothers, recognizing a common interest and a common destiny; and that we will stand as one man in defence of our honor and of our rights. I pray you to cultivate a feeling of this kind, and to disseminate it amongst your constituents. It is only by such united and determined action, on the part of the people of the whole South, that we can hope to avoid the calamities of the bloodiest and most devastating civil war that has afflicted any nation in the history of the civilized world.

I trust that a few days will be amply sufficient to dispose of the business which I have laid before you. Your presence may soon be needed in the field, and if not, will be required at home for counsel among your constituents.

Trusting that an All Wise Providence may watch over your deliberations, and direct you in the adoption of such measures, as may most subserve the maintenance of the rights and liberties of the people, I submit the determination of these matters to your hands.

ISHAM G. HARRIS.

Source: *Senate Journal of the Second Extra Session of the Thirty-Third General Assembly of the State of Tennessee, Which Convened at Nashville on Thursday, the 25th Day of April, A. D. 1861* (Nashville: J. O. Griffith and Company, Public Printers, 1861), 5–13.

DECLARATION OF INDEPENDENCE AND ORDINANCE DISSOLVING THE FEDERAL RELATIONS BETWEEN THE STATE OF TENNESSEE AND THE UNITED STATES OF AMERICA
May 6–7, 1861

CHAPTER I.

AN ACT to submit to a vote of the people a Declaration of Independence, and for other purposes.

SECTION I. *Be it enacted by the General Assembly of the State of Tennessee,* That immediately after the passage of this act, the Governor of this State shall, by proclamation, direct the sheriffs of the several counties in this State to open and hold an election at the various voting precincts in their respective counties, on the 8th day of June, 1861; that said sheriffs, or in the absence of the sheriffs, the coroner of the county, shall immediately advertise the election contemplated by this act; that said sheriffs appoint a deputy to hold said election for each voting precinct, and that said deputy appoint three judges and two clerks for each precinct; and if no officer shall, from any cause, attend any voting precinct to open and hold said election, then any justice of the peace—or in the absence of a justice of the peace, any respectable *freeholder* may appoint an officer, judges and clerks to open and hold said election. Said officers, judges and clerks shall be sworn as now required by law, and who, after being so sworn, shall open and hold an election, open and close at the time of day, and in the manner now required by law in elections for members to the General Assembly.

SEC. 2. *Be it further enacted,* That at said election the following Declaration shall be submitted to a vote of the qualified voters of the State of Tennessee, for their ratification or rejection: DECLARATION OF INDEPENDENCE AND ORDINANCE DISSOLVING THE FEDERAL RELATIONS BETWEEN THE STATE OF TENNESSEE AND THE UNITED STATES OF AMERICA.

First. We the people of the State of Tennessee, waiving any expression of opinion as to the abstract doctrine of secession, but asserting the right as a free, and independent people, "to alter, reform or abolish, our form of government in such a manner as we think proper," do ordain and declare that all the laws and ordinances, by which the State of Tennessee became a member of the Federal Union of the United States of America, are hereby abrogated and annulled, and that all obligations on our part be withdrawn therefrom; and we do hereby resume all the rights, functions, and powers, which by any of said laws or ordinances were conveyed to the Government of the United States, and absolve ourselves from all the obligations, restraints, and duties incurred thereto; and do hereby henceforth become a free, sovereign and independent State.

Second. We furthermore declare and ordain that Article 10, sections 1 and 2 of the Constitution of the State of Tennessee, which requires members of the General Assembly, and all officers, civil and military, to take an oath to support the Constitution of the United States be, and the same are hereby abrogated and annulled; and all parts of the Constitution of the State of Tennessee, making citizenship of the United States a qualification for office, and recognizing the Constitution of the United States as the supreme law of this State, are in like manner abrogated and annulled.

Third. We furthermore ordain and declare, that all rights acquired and vested under the Constitution of the United States, or under any act of Congress passed in pursuance thereof, or under any laws of this State, and not incompatible with this ordinance, shall remain in force, and have the same effect as if this ordinance had not been passed.

SEC. 3. *Be it further enacted,* That said election shall be by ballot; that those voting for the Declaration and Ordinance shall have written or printed on their ballots, "Separation," and those voting against it shall have written or printed on their ballots, "No Separation;" that the clerks holding said election shall keep regular scrolls of the voters as now required by law in the election of members to the General Assembly; that the clerks and judges shall certify the same, with the number of votes for "Separation," and the number of votes for "No Separation." The officer holding the election shall return the same to the sheriff of the county, at the county seat, on the Monday next after the election. The sheriff shall immediately make out, certify, and send to the Governor the number of votes polled, and the number of votes for "Separation," and the number "No Separation," and file one of the original scrolls with the Clerk of the County Court; that upon comparing the vote by the Governor, in the office of the Secretary of State—which shall be at least by the 24th day of June, 1861, and may be sooner if the returns are all received by the Governor—if a majority of the votes polled shall be for "Separation," the Governor shall by his proclamation make it known, and declare all connection by the State of Tennessee with the Federal Union dissolved, and that Tennessee is a free, independent Government—free from all obligation to, or connection with the Federal Government. And that the Governor shall cause 'the vote by counties' to be published, the number for "Separation," and the number "No Separation," whether a majority votes for "Separation," or "No Separation."

SEC. 4. *Be it further enacted,* That in the election to be held under the provisions of this act, upon the Declaration submitted to the people, all volunteers and other persons connected with the service of this State, qualified to vote for members of the Legislature in the counties where they reside, shall be entitled to vote in any county in the State where they may be in active service, or under orders, or on parole, at the time of said election; and all other voters shall vote in the county where they reside, as now required by law in voting for members to the General Assembly.

SEC. 5. *Be it further enacted*, That at the same time, and under the rules and regulations prescribed for the election herein before ordered, the following ordinance shall be submitted to the popular vote, to-wit: AN ORDINANCE FOR THE ADOPTION OF THE CONSTITUTION OF THE PROVISIONAL GOVERNMENT OF THE CONFEDERATE STATES OF AMERICA.

We, the people of Tennessee, solemnly impressed by the perils which surround us, do hereby adopt and ratify the Constitution of the Provisional Government of the Confederate States of America, ordained and established at Montgomery, Alabama, on the 8th day of February, 1861, to be in force during the existence thereof, or until such time as we may supersede it by the adoption of the permanent Constitution.

SEC. 6. *Be it further enacted*, That those in favor of the adoption of said Provisional Constitution, and thereby securing to Tennessee equal representation in the declarations and councils of the Confederate States, shall have written or printed on their ballots the word *"Representation;"* those opposed, the words *"No Representation."*

SEC. 7. *Be it further enacted*, That in the event the people shall adopt the Constitution of the Provisional Constitution of the Confederate States, at the election herein ordered, it shall be the duty of the Governor, forthwith to issue writs of election for delegates to represent the State of Tennessee in the said Provisional Government; that the State shall be represented by as many delegates as it was entitled to members of Congress to the recent Congress of the United States of America, who shall be elected from the several Congressional Districts as now established by law, in the mode and manner now prescribed for the election of members of the Congress of the United States.

SEC. 8. *Be it further enacted,* That this act take effect from and after its passage.

W. C. WHITTHORNE,[3]
Speaker of the House of Representatives.
B. L. STOVALL,[4]
Speaker of the Senate

Passed May 6, 1861.

CHAPTER 2.
MESSAGE OF THE GOVERNOR.

Executive Department,
Nashville May 7, 1861.

Gentlemen of the Senate and House of Representatives.

By virtue of the authority of your joint resolution, adopted on the 1st day of May inst., I appointed Gustavus A. Henry,[5] of the county of Montgomery, Archibald O. W. Totten,[6] of the county of Madison, and Washington Barrow,[7] of the county of Davidson, "Commissioners on the part of Tennessee, to enter into a Military League with the authorities of the Confederate States, and with the authorities of such other slaveholding States as may wish to enter into it, having in view the protection and defence of the entire South against the war that is now being carried on against it."

The said Commissioners met the Hon. Henry W. Hilliard,[8] the accredited representative of the Confederate States, at Nashville on this day, and have agreed upon and executed a Military League between the State of Tennessee and the Confederate States of America, subject, however, to the ratification of the two Governments; one of the duplicate originals of which I herewith transmit for your ratification or rejection. For many cogent and obvious reasons, unnecessary to be rehearsed to you, I respectfully recommend the ratification of this League at the earliest practicable moment.

Very respectfully,
ISHAM G. HARRIS.

⟨⟨⟨ ⟩⟩⟩

CONVENTION BETWEEN THE STATE OF TENNESSEE AND
THE CONFEDERATE STATES OF AMERICA.

The State of Tennessee looking to a speedy admission into the
Confederacy established by the Confederate States of America, in accordance with the Constitution for the Provincial Government of said
States, enters into the following temporary Convention, Agreement
and Military League, with the Confederate States, for the purpose of
meeting pressing exigencies affecting the common rights, interests,
and safety of said States, and said Confederacy.

First. Until the said State shall become a member of said
Confederacy according to the Constitution of both powers, the whole
military force, and military operations, offensive and defensive of said
State, in the impending conflict with the United States, shall be under
the chief control and direction of the President of the Confederate
States, upon the same basis, principles and footing, as if said State
were now, and during the interval a member of said Confederacy, said
force, together with that of the Confederate States, to be employed
for the common defence.

Second. The State of Tennessee will, upon becoming a member of said Confederacy under the Permanent Constitution of
said Confederate States, if the same shall occur, turn over to said
Confederate States, all the public property acquired from the United
States, on the same terms, and in the same manner as the other States
of said Confederacy have done in like cases.

Third. Whatever expenditures of money, if any, the said State
of Tennessee shall make before she becomes a member of said
Confederacy, shall be met and provided for by the Confederate States.

This Convention entered into and agreed, in the city of Nashville,
Tennessee, on the seventh day of May, A. D., 1861, by Henry W.
Hilliard, the duly authorized commissioner, to act in the matter of
the Confederate States, and Gustavus A. Henry, Archibald O. W.
Totten, and Washington Barrow, commissioners duly authorized to act
in like manner for the State of Tennessee—the whole subject to the

approval and ratification of the proper authorities of both Governments respectively.

In testimony whereof, the parties aforesaid have herewith set their hands and seals, the day and year aforesaid, in duplicate originals.

HENRY W. HILLIARD,   [SEAL.]
    Commissioner for the Confederate States of America.
GUSTAVUS A. HENRY,   [SEAL.]
A. O. TOTTEN,   [SEAL.]
WASHINGTON BARROW,   [SEAL.]
    Commissioners on the part of Tennessee.

JOINT RESOLUTION RATIFYING THE LEAGUE.

WHEREAS, A military league, offensive and defensive, was formed on the 7th of May, 1861, by and between A. O. W. Totton {*sic*}, Gustavus A. Henry, and Washington Barrow, Commissioners on the part of the State of Tennessee, and H. W. Hilliard, Commissioner on the part of the Confederate States of America, subject to the confirmation of the two Governments;

Be it therefore resolved by the General Assembly of the State of Tennessee, That said league be in all respects ratified and confirmed and the said General Assembly hereby pledges the faith and honor of the State of Tennessee to the faithful observance of the terms and conditions of said league.

W. C. WHITTHORNE,
Speaker of the House of Representatives.
B. L. STOVALL,
Speaker of the Senate.

Adopted May 7, 1861.

Source: *Public Acts of the State of Tennessee, Passed at the Extra Session of the Thirty-Third General Assembly, April, 1861* (Nashville, Tenn.: J. O. Griffith and Co., Public Printers, Union and American Office, 1861), 15–21. See also Robert H. White, ed., *Messages of the Governors of Tennessee: 1857–1869* (Nashville: Tennessee Historical Commission, 1959), 289–93.

LEGISLATIVE ADDRESS TO
THE PEOPLE OF TENNESSEE
May 9, 1861

Recognizing that the legislative session begun on April 25 had been closed to the public and that Governor Harris and the general assembly had already taken steps to align Tennessee with the Confederate States of America, the legislature determined that an address to the voting populace would be appropriate. The resulting public letter presented the state's case to the voters that Lincoln's action left the state only two choices: "maintain a distinct and separate nationality, or to unite with the other States of the South." The Joint Select Committee on Federal Affairs, which drafted the address, made it clear that remaining a part of the United States was not an option. Calling Lincoln a "usurping tyrant and a false hearted hypocrite," the legislators maintained war had been declared on the slave states when the president sent an unarmed resupply ship to Fort Sumter. (President Lincoln specifically notified South Carolina's governor that the suppy effort would be for provisions only.) Nevertheless, the general assembly described the mission as a "hostile fleet" setting sail upon a "mission of death." The address, like Governor Harris's April 25 speech, attempted to present the South as a victim of President Lincoln's plans to "murder Southern freemen and to desecrate Southern soil."

Filled with hyperbole, the address dismissed the fact that Confederate batteries had attacked Fort Sumter, arguing that President Lincoln had provoked the South by attempting to resupply the federal installation. While it made several references to the refusal of Congress to assist the president in his "mad experiment of holding sovereign States together by means of the bayonet," it failed to mention that Congress had been functionally adjourned since March 4.[9] "Our proud State," the message proclaimed, "will never seek to be represented in the counsels of its enemies and where wild fanaticism holds its infernal orgies over

the mutilated and mouldering corpse of a once noble Republic."
The legislators concluded their message by proclaiming that the
state had "taken her position and has proudly determined to throw
her banners to the breeze, and will give her strength to the sacred
cause of freedom for the WHITE MAN OF THE SOUTH."

Mr. Payne[10] from the Joint Select Committee to prepare an Address
to the people of Tennessee, submitted the following Address:

LEGISLATIVE ADDRESS TO THE PEOPLE OF TENNESSEE

Fellow-Citizens: The extraordinary legislation forced upon the
General Assembly, by the necessities of the times, makes it not inappropriate that your Representatives should present some of the reasons
which have influenced their action.

The Joint Select Committee, under the direction and with the
approval of the Assembly, beg leave to submit the following statement
to the calm judgment and consideration of their constituents:

The present session was called by the Executive authority to dispose of more important questions than ever had engaged the attention
of a Tennessee Legislature; the members of the two Houses could but
feel most sensibly the responsibilities of their positions, well knowing
that their action would not only affect the present, but the future destinies of the State. They had no interest to subserve apart from those
of their constituents, and whatever may be the result of their labors,
whether for good or evil, it will fall alike upon themselves and those
whom they represent.

The election of a sectional President by an unreasoning appeal to
numerical superiority, precipitated a crisis in the Government which
many wise men anticipated and patriots would have gladly adjourned
to another and far distant period. Several of the slaveholding States,
upon the happening of this event, commenced preparations for leaving
a Union which in their judgments, promised to become an instrument
of destruction to the constitutional rights of the South. The excitement
consequent upon the action of those States produced a necessity for
the last extra session of this body, and the proposition for calling a

Convention was submitted to the people. It was by them determined that no Convention should be held, thus giving the assurance of a fixed purpose to abide by the Union so long as a hope of safety or protection remained to them. A Peace Congress was called for, and anxious to give every evidence of a sincere desire to settle existing difficulties, prudent and discrete men were sent to confer with delegates from other States.[11] The Congress resulted in a failure, as did the faithful efforts of Southern men in the Congress of the United States. To every proposition a deaf ear was turned by the party in power. These ominous failures to come to an adjustment, while they weakened, did not dispel altogether the hope of a peaceable solution of existing troubles. It was believed that the masses of the Northern people would do justice to the demands of the South, if not prevented by the arts of their politicians. Subsequent acts prove that the masses are, if possible, more bitter in their hostility to the South than their leaders.

The inaugural of the newly-elected President, however doubtful in its terms, was charitably construed into a message of peace. It was considered absurd to suppose that any President of a free country would ever venture upon the mad experiment of holding sovereign States together by means of the bayonet. No one not blinded by fanaticism, can fail to recognize the fact that a government based upon the popular will can only be maintained in its integrity by appealing to that powerful and controlling influence. Force, when attempted, changes the whole character of the Government; making it a military despotism, and those that submit become the abject slaves of power. The people of Tennessee have fully understood this important fact, and hence their anxiety to stay the hand of coercion. They well know that the subjugation of the seceded States involved their own destruction, and that, however plausible the pretext, an enforcement of the laws against an unwilling people had been the exercise of tyrants in every age of the world. That the people of the South were, many of them, deceived in the pretended peace policy of Lincoln, is not a matter of surprise or astonishment. The duplicity and double-dealing of this miserable tyrant, finds no parallel save in the corrupt governments of the dark ages, and would disgrace the diplomatic policy of a barbarian chieftain. A few facts will suffice to make good our assertions. To Southern Senators that approached him, he verbally construed his own inaugural into a peace document.

He caused it to be given out that he would abandon Fort Sumter, when at the very time he was privately preparing a powerful armament for its relief.

Under false pretenses, he introduced an officer into Fort Sumter, who took advantage of the privilege to concert a plan of relief with the commandant of that fortress.

Congress refused to vote a dollar for the prosecution of hostilities against the people of the South; but he and his agents got the appropriation by falsehood, pretending that it was needed to pay off the Government debts, and instead of so using it, fails to pay even the maimed and wounded soldier his pension, or the hard-working census-taker his salary, but scatters it among a brutal soldiery, whom he has hired to murder Southern freemen and to desecrate Southern soil.

Congress refused to pass a coercion bill, yet this contemptible usurper proclaims war against the South in defiance of the Constitution, in violation of his oath and his oft-repeated and positive pledges to the contrary.

Congress would not authorize the call for a single soldier, yet, in the face of the laws and the Constitution, this petty tyrant calls for armies of immense magnitude to march against peaceful and unoffending citizens.

He assured Tennessee members of Congress that his policy would be peaceful; his Premier, W. H. Seward, announced such to be the purpose of his Cabinet on every occasion; and yet, after lulling the people to repose, he impudently called upon the Governor of Tennessee for troops to follow his standard in a war of subjugation against their own native section.

The Mississippi river is declared to be free by the Constitution of Tennessee, and yet this vile usurper stations troops at Cairo to obstruct the navigation of this great highway and its tributaries, and these miserable instruments are now engaged in making war upon the commerce of non-seceding States.

Tennessee, ever loyal to the Constitution, has been an advocate for peace, and has struggled to bring together the broken fragments of the Union, yet in the midst of her well meant efforts, a war is made upon her; every avenue of trade is closed up, and the people are suffering all the privations of a blockade. Not even provisions, demanded by the necessities of the people, are allowed to be shipped into the State, and property of private individuals is made subject to piratical and illegal seizure. Boats have been plundered of their cargoes by authority of the Government, and when called on for an explanation by the Governor of Tennessee, even the honor of a reply is refused.

The States that desired to live in the Union, and to be on terms of friendship with all, are insultingly told that neutrality is impossible, and that they must aid in this ungodly war of subjugation, or else suffer the penalties. Had Tennessee ever desired to remain neutral, the miserable and degrading privilege is denied to her by the tyrants that assume to rule in the name of the Constitution.

The Confederate States sought for peace, and sent their agents to the Federal capital to consummate that object. They were assured that peace would be made, and while resting under the belief that they were dealing with honorable men, Lincoln and his Cabinet were secretly collecting an immense armament for the relief of Fort Sumter.[12] It is a matter of no importance who fired the first gun in the attack on Fort Sumter, the war commenced when a hostile fleet set sail upon its mission of death.

Lincoln pretends in his inaugural that his only object is to protect the property of the nation, yet he organizes immense armies all along the lines of the border slave States, commissions them to seize and take the property of private citizens, holds Maryland in subjugation by the aid of her treacherous Governor and his armed hirelings, and converts the Federal capital into an entrenched camp, and subjects it to all the rigors of martial law.

We ask, if a man marked by every attribute that can disgrace a usurping tyrant and a false hearted hypocrite, should be permitted to control for a day, or an hour, the destinies of a free people? In this state of affairs the Legislature assembled at Nashville. The Governor had defiantly refused to call out a man to prosecute a war of subjugation, and had also refused to issue a writ of election for members to Congress. We were bound to recognize the fact that war had been already made upon the State, that for all practical purposes Tennessee was out of the Union, and every act of legislation has been based upon that palpable state of affairs. The Legislature endorsed and approved the action of the Executive. He could have pursued no other course without disgrace to himself and dishonor to his State. These resolutions are submitted along with this report.

Tennessee is unarmed, and the first great object was to organize the military and adopt every means of defence, within our power, menaced as our country is by armies of alarming magnitude. Our western borders exposed to attack, with life, liberty and property staked upon the issue, it is no time to think of half-way measures. The money and the blood of Tennessee will be called for in no stinted quantities, if it be necessary to protect the priceless heritage of freedom that we possess, and which we hold as a sacred trust for our children. The military bill is also submitted with this address to the judgment of our constituents. Tennessee is now politically isolated from all of her sisters. She has no voice in any of their counsels. She will not disgrace her fair escutcheon by sending delegates to a Government that has made war against her, and where they are compelled to vote and speak with the glittering bayonets of a brutal soldiery gleaming around them. Our proud State will never seek to be represented in the counsels of its enemies and where wild fanaticism holds its infernal orgies over the mutilated and mouldering corpse of a once noble Republic. In the present dangerous attitude, we felt it to be due to ourselves, to the honor and safety of the State, and to the imperious demands of our constituents, that an opportunity should be promptly furnished for cutting loose every real or supposed tie that binds the people to the Lincoln Government, and to enable them by a vote at the ballot box to form other political relations, if it were so desired. In conformity with these obligations of duty, the Legislature has prepared two instruments to be voted upon by the people, on Saturday, the 8th of June.

Upon the first proposition the people will vote for or against separation from the old Confederacy. By the second proposition you will decide for or against a political union with the Confederate States. Both are submitted along with this address. The proposition for a union adopts the provisional, and *not* the permanent Constitution of those States; this Constitution is also submitted to the people. The Legislature has done what has already been done by Virginia, and will no doubt be the policy of North Carolina, and in the company of these time honored Commonwealths, Tennessee need entertain no fears for her own safety.[13] If objections are found to the permanent Constitution, they can be removed as a condition of continued union with those States.

In submitting these two grave questions to the popular judgment, the Legislature dispensed with all intermediate agencies, preferring to go at once to the great source of all political power—*the people themselves*. The delays, embarrassments and expense of a convention are thus avoided. Nothing is left to trickery or political management. You can say whether you desire to separate from the old Government; you can also declare at the ballot box whether you desire to unite the fortunes of the State along with Virginia, North Carolina and Arkansas to the new Confederacy. By two words—"*separation*" or "*no separation*," "representation" or "no representation," you will decide the whole question and fix the future destinies of the State. A convention can do no more, though in session for weeks or months. Whatever be your decision it will be conclusive, and from it there *can be no appeal*. The Legislature has no power to put Tennessee out of the Union, nor to place it among the Confederate States; that body has the authority to order an election, which it has done, and it is to be sincerely hoped that *every voter* in Tennessee will be found at the polls on the day appointed by the Legislature.

We remark before passing from this subject, that while differences of opinion exist as to the abstract right of secession, no one denies the right of a people to *revolutionize*. The right to "change, alter or abolish," their form of government is a principle engrafted in the fundamental laws of the State. Your representatives have therefore steered clear of the mooted question of secession, and submitted a revolutionary document, which, if ratified by the popular vote, will sever the ties that bind Tennessee to her enemies and oppressors, and *that*, after all, is the object to be attained, by whatever name it may be called.

The military league which has been formed with the Southern Confederacy is also submitted with this address. It was a measure of safety imperiously demanded by the war that has been made upon our State. In accomplishing this object we have fallen back upon the lessons of our ancestors, and regarded the promptings of self-preservation in forming alliances when different parties are threatened with a common danger. Our State is *unarmed*; we must have weapons placed in the hands of our volunteers to defend the freedom of the South. The Confederate States can *aid us* in this all-important matter. We must have a common head to direct the armies of freedom. Those States furnish in their Chief Magistrate[14] a soldier who has proven his capacity to lead upon the hardest fought battle fields known to the history of American warfare. Our people must be relieved, too, from the burden of keeping up a separate and distinct military organization. By the terms of the contract, it will be seen that the expenses of the State are to be transferred to the common Confederacy that the South is forming, and will be paid from the fruitful sources of impost duties levied upon commerce when peace is established.

This league places Tennessee where she deserves to stand—in company with the old States of Virginia, North Carolina, South Carolina and Georgia, whose histories are redolent with the glories of past struggles for liberty, and whose sons are now prepared to stand upon their ancient battlefields to emulate the deeds of their ancestors. This alliance places the State, too, in close compact with the younger States of the South, with whom it is indispensably connected by a thousand ties.

It is gratifying to know the league referred to meets the approval of men entertaining heretofore all shades of opinion. Let it be remembered, that the Legislature, impelled as it was, by imperious necessity, in the formation of this alliance, is only the more confident in the correctness of its policy by the conscious belief that it has formed for the State no ignoble or degrading association. Whatever may be thought of the action of the States that have left the Union, in regard to their supposed precipitancy, all must admit that their legislative action has been marked by sound conservatism and profound statesmanship. These States have ventured upon no new or untried experiment in the formation of their Government; they have wisely refrained from making a new Constitution, but have piously adopted the one framed by the authors of independence, and under which Tennessee has always abided as a State—some alterations and changes have been made, but only such as time and experience had suggested as important improvements.[15] It may be truthfully *averred* that the *Constitution of the United States* is *now* the permanent Constitution of the Confederate States; that noble instrument has no existence in any other State or Government. It has been superseded in the North by a military despotism; it no longer shields the people of Tennessee; but this admirable framework of freedom, still regarded as the ark of political safety, and strengthened in its massive proportions, has been erected upon Southern soil, and under its broad aegis generations of freemen repose in safety.

It is painful to reflect that Tennessee has no representation in any national or confederate council; her gallant soldiers will go forth to battle for a common cause, and but for a short time, at least, her voice cannot be heard, only through the ballot box in June.

It is submitted that Tennessee has but one of two alternatives— either to attempt to maintain a distinct and separate nationality, or to unite with the other States of the South. If you decide on the former, provisions should at once be made for new departments of government. A Post Office and a Department of Foreign Affairs will be necessary, besides other arrangements peculiar to a separate nationality. We ask if the people will not be at once crushed by the burthens of taxation? The idea of a Border State Confederacy must be abandoned. The free States embraced in this plan are the first to lead off for Southern subjugation. Through their Governors they have proclaimed that there is no such thing as neutrality, and have already impudently demanded that Kentucky shall take the field against the slaveholding States. With them Tennessee can have *no Union*. Through the action of a treacherous Governor, Maryland has been manacled by the chains of the tyrant. The heart of the South is with her, and its sons stand ready to drive the invaders from her soil, and to give to her the rights that traitors and usurpers are seeking to destroy. Our noble and gallant neighbor, Kentucky, is an unarmed knight, confronted by the reckless assassin whose dagger is ready to be driven to his heart. The State of Tennessee, the whole South, will offer their sons to the gallant State, and who now stand ready to pour out their blood as a rich libation upon the alters of the dark and bloody ground. Let past differences, fellow-citizens, be forgotten in this hour of common danger, and let us work for a united South. Though our enemies are strong, and united in their unholy purposes, yet standing upon our own side, and defending our alters [*sic*] and our friends, the cause is *too sacred* to be lost. God will prosper the right; that Being who defended the fathers will not desert their children while unitedly battling for the inalienable rights of man.

When this body met, it determined to sit with closed doors. We are aware that this mode of legislation is objected to by some. It is the first time in the history of the State that the rule had been adopted, because in that history no case had occurred to call forth its exercise. The proceedings of the convention that framed the Declaration of Independence were in *secret*. The convention that framed the *Constitution of the United States*, held in secret sessions, and the Senate of the United States not unfrequently sits with closed doors. Those who have taken occasion to condemn *us*, may be purer than those who framed the Declaration of Independence, and the Constitution of the United States; but we very much doubt whether they will have a greater hold upon public confidence. But the reasons for our course are our best justification: the country was excited, and the public demands imperious. We desired to legislate uninfluenced and unretarded by the crowds that would otherwise have attended our deliberations; but still more important than this, the western portion of Tennessee was in an *exposed condition*, with *no* military defence whatever; the towns and counties bordering on the Mississippi river were liable to be assailed at any hour by the armed forces collected at Cairo, and we desired that no act of legislation on our part, should form the pretext for such an invasion, so long as it could be avoided. Our fellow-citizens of West Tennessee, and of Arkansas are laboring night and day to erect batteries on the river to prevent a descent of the enemy. A duty that we owed to them and to the cause of humanity demanded that we should not make our action known till the latest possible moment. If some desired light, while we were at work, we equally desired to save the blood and the property of Tennesseans. Our doors have now been thrown open, the Journals will be published—every *vote* is recorded, and he must be a *fault-finder* indeed who will complain after hearing the reasons that prompted our actions.

We have briefly touched the principal subjects that engaged the attention of the Legislature. Tennessee has taken her position and has proudly determined to throw her banners to the breeze, and will give her strength to the sacred cause of freedom for the WHITE MAN OF THE SOUTH.

R. G. PAYNE,
Chairman of Joint Select Committee.
EDMUND J. WOOD,
S. S. STANTON,
J. A. MINNIS,
G. GANTT,
W. W. GUY,
ROBT. B. HURT,
BENJ. J. LEA,
JOSEPH G. PICKETT.[16]

On motion of Mr. Wood, the address submitted by the Committee was adopted.

Mr. Minnis moved that ten thousand copies of the address be printed; which motion was agreed to.

Source: *Senate Journal of the Second Extra Session of the Thirty-Third General Assembly of the State of Tennessee, Which convened at Nashville on Thursday, the 25th Day of April, A. D. 1861* (Nashville: J. O. Griffith and Company, Public Printers, 1861), 83–91. See also Robert H. White, ed., *Messages of the Governors of Tennessee, 1857–1869* (Nashville: Tennessee Historical Commission, 1959), 294–300.

GOVERNOR HARRIS'S ADDRESS
TO THE GENERAL ASSEMBLY
June 18, 1861

Gentlemen of the Senate and House of Representatives:

Since your adjournment on the 9th of the last month, the people of Tennessee, acting in their sovereign capacity, and in the exercise of an inalienable right, have, in the most solemn and deliberate manner dissolved their connection with the Government of the United States, and by the adoption of the Provisional Constitution of the Confederate States of America, have made Tennessee a member of that Government.

I pause in the midst of the arduous duties which devolve upon me, to congratulate you and the country upon the near approach to unanimity, and the readiness with which the brave and patriotic people of our proud commonwealth have severed their connection with a Government endeared to them by so many recollections, and to which they had been so long attached, but which has been subverted by gross usurpations and converted into an engine of oppression, destructive of their rights, liberties and equality, and which in the mere wantonness of the boasted power, demands that these inalienable attributes of freemen shall be promptly—nay, basely surrendered or maintained at the point of the bayonet.

Those who have read and comprehended the patriotic devotion of our people to the eternal principles of justice, equality, and right, their native love of independence, and their chivalrous deeds in defence of those principles, as shown by the whole history of the State, could not have doubted as to the position that Tennessee would occupy upon the presentation of such an issue.

While it is to me a source of regret that entire unanimity was not attained at the ballot-box, in the decision of the vitally important and exciting questions referred to, I have entire confidence that now the deliberate and impartial judgment of the overwhelming majority of the people of the State having been recorded, the whole people, forgetting these differences of opinion, however earnestly and honestly entertained, will stand together as one man in maintaining the rights, honor and dignity of Tennessee, and in preserving the domestic tranquility of the community. The time for crimination and recrimination has passed; threatened by a common enemy, imperiled by the common danger, bound together by ties which cannot be severed, we are identical in interest, we must be so in action.

The State of Tennessee, co-operating with her sister States of the South, has been compelled to take up arms in defence of rights she could not surrender. To this war thus forced upon us, there can be but two sides. I cannot believe that there is any portion of our people who will espouse the cause of the enemies of Tennessee, or be indifferent spectators of the contest.

Impartial history will attest that no free people, jealous of their rights, have been more observant of their constitutional duties, or more loyal to their Government. Exacting no peculiar privileges, they have at all times been ready to acknowledge and maintain the rights of others. In times of common peril they have always stood firm and contributed their full proportion of talent, both to the Cabinet and the field, and now that we have exhausted the last remedy, have made the last appeal to the reason and justice of those who would oppose us, and have been driven to the necessity of taking our rights into our own hands and defying the power that assails them, there certainly can not be a part of our people who will not spurn the usurper and resist him to the last extremity.

In the midst of the gloom and privations necessarily incidental to a state of war, let us console ourselves with the reflection that we occupy the same relation to posterity that our fathers of the first revolution occupied to us.

They enjoyed the glorious privilege of establishing the great principle, which secured to us civil and religious liberty, and political equality; while it is our privilege and solemn duty to maintain and transmit to posterity the same great principle unimpaired.

The spirit and determination manifested by the people of the whole South, to maintain this principle against the tyranny of usurpation, gives the highest and most cheering assurance that America will still be the abiding place of self government and free institutions; and proves the truth of the long disputed theory of our fathers, that a brave and enlightened people, educated in the doctrine of individual and State equality, are capable, and of right, ought to govern themselves. In the midst of federal revolution, perfect order has been preserved in our State Government; in the moment of dissolving our former federal fabric, another, new, and of perfect and enduring proportions, is reared, leaving us at no time without the full benefit of Government, or the security of laws.

The new relations which we have assumed, in becoming a part of the Provisional Government of the Confederate States, imposes the necessity of some additional legislation. I cheerfully submit to your consideration all questions pertaining to our federal relations, for such legislation as may be necessary to us as a part of that Government.

There has been, for many years, a statute in the State defining the crime of treason, and prescribing the punishment.

I respectfully recommend that you amend that law to the extent of striking out the words "United States," and insert, in lieu of them, *Confederate States.*

Under the provisions of the act of 1852, the principal and interest of the internal improvement bonds of the State are made payable in the city of New York. It will be impossible to pay the interest accruing, at that point, during the continuance of the war.

I recommend that you so amend the law referred to as to require the payment at the Bank of Tennessee, at Nashville, or at Charleston, or New Orleans, of all sums which may become due from the State to the people of all Governments, which are on terms of peace and friendship with us, who are and were, previous to the commencement of the war, *bona fide* owners of our bonds, and that you adopt such policy towards the owners and holders of our bonds, who are citizens of the States at war with us, as is recognized and justified by the law of nations regulating their intercourse, as belligerents.

The ordeal through which the country is now passing necessarily prostrates the trade and commerce of the country, and deranges the currency to a greater or less extent. Such legislation as will tend to secure a uniform currency throughout the Confederate States is of the highest importance. I therefore submit the question to your consideration for such action as in your opinion the general welfare demands.

By the——section of the act of the 6th of May, 1861, it is made the duty of the Governor to issue bonds of the State, for the purpose of raising a fund with which to defray the expenses of the provisional army of the State. In view of the scarcity of a circulating medium, and the probable difficulty of converting any considerable amount of bonds into money in times like the present, I respectfully recommend that you so modify that act as to authorize the issuance of Treasury Notes to the extent of three-fifths of the amount authorized to be issued, in lieu of that amount of said bonds; and that the same, when issued, be made receivable by the State in payment of all taxes or government dues.

In obedience to your act of 6th May, 1861, I have caused to be organized, armed and equipped, twenty-one regiments of infantry now in the field, ten artillery companies in progress of organization, and a sufficient number of cavalry companies to compose one regiment. The organization of an engineer corps is nearly completed.

In addition to which, we have three regiments mustered into the services of the Confederate States now in Virginia, and a number of our citizens in the service of that government stationed at Pensacola. For full and accurate information as to the army organization, I refer you to reports of the proper officers, hereafter to be laid before you, if desired. It is proper to remark, in this connection, that without even a call being made upon them, a much larger number of our patriotic citizens have tendered their services to the State than I have thought proper to accept. Should the necessities of the State at any time require a larger force, I feel assured that our brave and gallant people will rush with alacrity to the field, so as to swell the force to the point of equaling any such necessity.

I commend those brave and patriotic citizen soldiers to your most favorable consideration, and recommend the adoption of such measures as will most tend to promote their health and comfort while in the field.

It is proper that I call your attention to the fact that a few days since, Return J. Meigs, Esq.,[17] resigned the office of Librarian to the State. The office is now vacant, and the duty of filling it by election devolves upon you.

I cannot, in justice to my own feelings and sense of duty, close this communication without urging upon you, and through you upon those you represent, the importance and propriety of moderation, forbearance, and conciliation in your intercourse with each other, however widely and earnestly you may have differed in your opinions and actions upon the important and exciting questions so recently settled.

Invoking a continuation of the blessings of the Supreme Ruler of the universe upon our cause, our country, and our people, I submit the matter to your hands.

ISHAM G. HARRIS

On motion of Mr. {Robert G.} Payne, five hundred copies of the message were ordered to be printed for the use of the Senate.

Source: *Senate Journal of the Second Extra Session of the Thirty-Third General Assembly of the State of Tennessee Which Convened at Nashville on Thursday, the 25th Day of April, A.D. 1861.* (Nashville: J. O. Griffith and Company, Public Printers, 1861), 103–6.

CHAPTER SEVEN

DISSENT

May, June 1861

The four hundred men who met in Knoxville on May 30 and 31, 1861, voiced their disapproval of the "hasty and inconsiderate action" of the general assembly through a report that enumerated their concerns. Placing blame for the "perilous" condition of the country on those who promoted "the ruinous and heretical doctrine of secession," the business committee's assessment charged the legislature with disregarding the will of the people by entering into a military league with the Confederacy before the June 8 referendum was held.

Following the election, the delegates reconvened in Greeneville (June 17–20) and sharpened their criticism of the general assembly through a "Declaration of Grievances." Maintaining that the results of the vote on June 8 were gained through political chicanery, voter suppression, and ballot manipulation, the East Tennessee manifesto charged that secession fever had been sustained "by deception and falsehood." No laws had been passed by Congress to oppress the people of the state, the Constitution had "done us no wrong," and the president had "made no threat against the law abiding people of Tennessee." The declaration ended by asking the consent of the legislature to form a separate state of East Tennessee. A little over a week later, the general assembly responded by declining the request stating that a fair election had taken place and that the people East Tennessee should accept the fact that they had lost.

Personal information for the delegates to the East Tennessee Convention is less available than for members of the US Congress and the Tennessee General Assembly. To the extent possible, that information has been included below.

Report of the General Committee

May 30–31, 1861
Proceedings of the East Tennessee Convention,
held at Knoxville, May 30 and 31, 1861.

FIRST DAY.

On Thursday, 30th of May, 1861, a large number of delegates representing the people of the various sections of East Tennessee assembled at Knoxville, in pursuance of the following call:

EAST TENNESSEE CONVENTION.

The undersigned, a portion of the people of East Tennessee, disapproving the hasty and inconsiderate action of our General Assembly, and sincerely desirous to do, in the midst of the troubles which surround us, what will be best for our country and for all classes of our citizens, respectfully appoint a convention to be held in Knoxville on Thursday, the 30th of May, instant; and we urge every county in East Tennessee to send delegates to this convention, that the conservative element of our whole section may be represented and that wise, prudent, and judicious counsels may prevail, looking to peace and harmony among ourselves:

F. S. HEISKELL,[1]	C. H. BAKER,
S. R. RODGERS,[2]	DR. W. RODGERS,
JOHN BAXTER,[3]	C. F. TRIGG,[4]
DAVID BURNETT,	JOHN WILLIAMS,[5]
JOHN J. CRAIG,	W. H. ROGERS,
O. P. TEMPLE,[6]	JOHN TUNNELL,
W. G. BROWNLOW,[7]	AND OTHERS.

The convention met at Temperance Hall at 12 o'clock and was called to order by Conally F. Trigg, esq., upon whose motion the following officers were chosen:

Temporary president, John Baxter, of Knox; Temporary secretary, John M. Fleming, of Knox. The deliberations of the convention were opened by the Rev. Thomas W. Humes, of Knoxville, who addressed a fervent prayer to the Throne of Grace, as follows:

{*Following the prayer, a general business committee was appointed "to prepare and report business for the convention." General Thomas D. Arnold then spoke "at considerable length in opposition to the schemes of the Governor and Legislature of Tennessee to plunge our people, against their own will, into a ruinous and unwarranted revolution."*}

The president, at the call of the convention, introduced the Hon. Andrew Johnson, who acknowledged the compliment briefly, but owing to the lateness of the hour he deferred his remarks till to-morrow morning at 9 o'clock. And thereupon, on motion of Colonel {J. G.} Spears, of Bledsoe, the convention adjourned till 8 o'clock to-morrow morning.

SECOND DAY, FRIDAY.

The convention met pursuant to adjournment, the honorable president presiding. The roll of delegates was called by the secretary, and revised and corrected by the convention. Governor Johnson commenced his speech, but pending his remarks the committee, through their chairman, Colonel Trigg, submitted their report. After a running debate, participated in by Messrs. {John} Baxter, {O. P.} Temple, {C. F.} Trigg and {John M.} Fleming of Knox, {J. G.} Spears of Bledsoe, {William} Heiskell of Monroe, and others, the report of the committee was amended and finally adopted as follows:

In the enumeration of the rights of the citizens, which have been declared under the solemn sanction of the people of Tennessee, there are none which should be more warmly cherished or more highly estimated than that which declares that "the citizens have a right in a peaceable manner to assemble together for their common good," and at no time since the organization of our Government has there been an occasion which called so loudly for the exercise of that inestimable right as that upon which we are now assembled. Our country is at this moment in a most deplorable condition. The Constitution of the United States has been openly condemned and set at defiance, while that of our own State has shared no better fate, and by the sworn representatives of the people has been utterly disregarded. Constitutions, which in other days were wont to control and give direction to our public councils and to those in authority by the fiat of the people, have been wholly supplanted, and fanaticism, passion, and prejudice have assumed an arbitrary sway. Law and order seem to have yielded their beneficent offices for the safety of the country and the welfare of the people, and in their stead revolution, in spite of its attendant horrors, has raised its hideous head. The condition of the country is most perilous, the present crisis most fearful. In this calamitous state of affairs, when the liberties of the people are so imperiled and their most valued rights endangered, it behooves them in their primary meeting, and in all their other accustomed modes, to meet together, consult calmly as to their safety, and with firmness to give expression to their opinions and convictions of right. We, therefore, the delegates here assembled, representing and reflecting, as we verily believe, the opinions and wishes of a very large majority of the people of East Tennessee, do resolve and declare:

1. That the evils which now afflict our beloved country, in our opinion, are the legitimate offspring of the ruinous and heretical doctrine of secession; that the people of East Tennessee have ever been, and we believe still are, opposed to it by a very large majority.

2. That while the country is now upon the very threshold of a most ruinous and desolating civil war, it may with truth be said, and we protest before God, that the people (so far as we can see) have done nothing to produce it.

3. That the people of Tennessee, when the question was submitted to them in February last, decided by an overwhelming majority that the relations of the State toward the Federal Government should not be changed; thereby expressing their preference for the Union and Constitution under which they had lived prosperously and happily, and ignoring in the most emphatic manner the idea that they had been

oppressed by the General Government in any of its acts—legislative, executive, or judicial.

4. That in view of so decided an expression of the will of the people in whom "all power is inherent and on whose authority all free governments are founded," and in the honest conviction that nothing has transpired since that time which should change that deliberate judgment of the people, wc have contemplated with peculiar emotions the pertinacity with which those in authority have labored to override the judgment of the people and to bring about the very result which the people themselves had so overwhelmingly condemned.

5. That the Legislative Assembly is but the creature of the constitution of the State and has no power to pass any law or to exercise any act of sovereignty, except such as may be authorized by that instrument; and believing as we do that in their recent legislation the General Assembly have disregarded the rights of the people and transcended their legitimate powers, we feel constrained and we invoke the people throughout the State as they value their liberties to visit that hasty, inconsiderate, and unconstitutional legislation with a decided rebuke by voting on the 8th day of next month against both the act of secession and of union with the Confederate States.

6. That the Legislature of the State, without having first obtained the consent of the people, had no authority to enter into a military league with the Confederate States against the General Government, and by so doing to put the State of Tennessee in hostile array against the Government of which it then was and still is a member. Such legislation in advance of the expressed will of the people to change their governmental relations was an act of usurpation and should be visited with the severest condemnation of the people.

7. That the forming of such military league and thus practically assuming the attitude of an enemy toward the General Government (this, too, in the absence of any hostile demonstration against this State) has afforded the pretext for raising, arming, and equipping a large military force, the expense of which must be enormous and will have to be paid by the people; and to do this the taxes, already onerous

enough, will necessarily have to be very greatly increased and probably to an extent beyond the ability of the people to pay.

8. That the General Assembly, by passing a law authorizing the volunteers to vote wherever they may be on the day of election, whether in or out of the State, and in offering to the Confederate States the capital of Tennessee, together with other acts, have exercised powers and stretched their authority to an extent not within their constitutional limits and not justified by the usages of the country.

9. "That government being instituted for the common benefit, the doctrine of non-resistance against arbitrary power and oppression is absurd, slavish, and destructive of the good and happiness of mankind."[8]

10. That the position which the people of our sister State of Kentucky have assumed in this momentous crisis commands our highest admiration. Their interests are our interests. Their policy is the true policy, as we believe, of Tennessee and all the border States; and in the spirit of freemen, with an anxious desire to avoid the waste of the blood and the treasure of our State, we appeal to the people of Tennessee while it is yet in their power to come up in the majesty of their strength and restore Tennessee to her true position.

11. We shall await with the utmost anxiety the decision of the people of Tennessee on the 8th day of next month, and sincerely trust that wiser counsels will pervade the great fountain of freedom (the people) than seems to have actuated their constituted agents.

12. For the promotion of the peace and harmony of the people of East Tennessee it is deemed expedient that this convention should again assemble: Therefore.

Resolved, That when this convention adjourns it adjourns to meet again at such time and place as the president, or vice-president in his absence, may determine and publish.

The entire report, on motion of Colonel {William} Heiskell, of Monroe, was unanimously adopted.

Source: *The War of the Rebellion: A Compilation of the Official Records of the Union and Confederate Armies* (Washington: Government Printing Office, 1898), Series 1, vol. 52, part 1, 148–55.

Declaration of Grievances

June 17–20, 1861

Proceedings of the East Tennessee Convention,
held at Greeneville on the 17th day of June, 1861, and succeeding days.

SECOND SESSION.

FIRST DAY.

GREENEVILLE, TENN., *June 17, 1861.*

The convention met this day in pursuance of the following call:

EAST TENNESSEE CONVENTION

Pursuant to a resolution adopted on the 31st day of May, by which the convention adjourned to meet at such time and place as the president, or vice-president in his absence, may determine and publish, I hereby notify and request the members of the convention to meet in Greeneville on Monday, 17th day of June, 1861.

THOMAS A. R. NELSON,[9]

President.

{*Here the roll call of the counties was taken and over the subsequent two days established general orders of business.*}

FOURTH DAY.

MORNING SESSION.

THURSDAY, June 20, 1861.

Convention met at the usual hour and was opened with prayer by Rev. Mr. Milburn, of Greene. Mr. {H. P.} Murphy, of Johnson, offered a resolution restricting debate, which after amendment was adopted, as follows:

Resolved, That no member of this convention except the chairman of the committee whose report may be under consideration, shall be permitted to speak longer that fifteen minutes on any one proposition, unless allowed to proceed by the convention.

Mr. {C. F.} Trigg, from the business committee, again submitted their report. After much discussion, the declaration of grievances and resolutions were finally adopted as follows, without division:

DECLARATION OF GRIEVANCES.

We, the people of East Tennessee, again assembled in a convocation of our delegates, make the following declaration in addition to that heretofore promulgated by us at Knoxville on the 30th and 31st days of May last:

So far as we can learn the election held in this State on the 8th day of the present month was free, with but few exceptions, in no part of the State other than East Tennessee. In the larger parts of Middle and West Tennessee no speeches or discussions in favor of the Union were permitted. Union papers were not allowed to circulate. Measures were taken in some parts of West Tennessee, in defiance of the constitution and laws, which allow folded tickets to have the ballot numbered in such manner as to mark and expose the Union votes. A disunion paper, the Nashville Gazette, in urging the people to vote an open ticket, declared that "a thief takes a pocketbook or effects an entrance into forbidden places by stealthy means—a story in voting usually adopts pretty much the same course of procedure." Disunionists in many places had charge of the polls, and Union men, when voting, were denounced as Lincolnites and abolitionists. The unanimity of the votes in many large counties where but a few weeks ago the Union sentiment was so strong proves beyond doubt that Union men were overawed by the tyranny of the military power, and the still greater tyranny of a corrupt and subsidized press. In the city of Memphis, where 5,613 votes were cast, but five freemen had the courage to vote for the Union, and these were stigmatized in the public press as "ignorant traitors who opposed the popular edict." Our earnest appeal to our brethren in the other divisions of the State was published there only to a small extent, and the members and names of those who composed our convention, as well as the counties they represented, were suppressed and the effort made to impress the minds of the people that East Tennessee was favorable to secession. The Memphis Appeal (a prominent disunion paper) published a false account of our proceedings under the head, "The traitors in council," and styled us, who represented every county but two in East Tennessee, "the little batch of disaffected traitors who hover around the noxious atmosphere of Andrew Johnson's home." Our meeting was telegraphed to the New Orleans Delta, and it was falsely said that we had passed a resolution recommending submission if 70,000 votes were not cast against secession. The dispatch added that "the Southern rights men are determined to hold possession of the State, though they should be in a minority." Volunteers were allowed to vote in and out of the State, in flagrant violation of the constitution. From the moment the election was over and before any detailed statement of the vote in the different counties had been published, and before it was possible to ascertain the result, it was exultingly proclaimed that separation had been carried by from 50,000 to 70,000 votes.

This was to prepare the public mind to enable "the secessionists to hold possession of the State though they should be in a minority." The final result is to be announced by the disunion Governor, whose existence depends upon the success of secession, and no provision is made by law for an examination of the vote by disinterested persons, or even for contesting the election. For these and other causes we do not regard the result of the election as expressive of the will of a majority of the freemen of Tennessee. Had the election everywhere been conducted as it was in East Tennessee, we would entertain a different opinion. Here no effort was made to suppress secession papers or prevent secession speeches or votes, although an overwhelming majority of the people were against secession. Here no effort has been made to prevent the formation of military companies or obstruct the transportation of armies or to prosecute those who violated the laws of the United States and of Tennessee against treason. The Union men of East Tennessee, anxious to be neutral in the contest, were content to enjoy their own opinions and to allow the utmost latitude of opinion and action to those who differed from them. Had the same toleration prevailed in other parts of the State we have no doubt that a majority of our people would have voted to remain in the Union. But if this view is erroneous we have the same, and as we think a much better, right to remain in the Government of the United States that the other divisions of Tennessee have to secede from it. We prefer to remain attached to the Government of our fathers. The Constitution of the United States has done us no wrong; the Congress of the United States has passed no law to oppress us; the President of the United States has made no threat against the law abiding people of Tennessee. Under the Government of the United States we have enjoyed as a nation more of civil and religious freedom than any other people under the whole heaven. We believe there is no cause for rebellion or secession on the part of the people of Tennessee. None was assigned by the Legislature in their miscalled declaration of independence. No adequate cause can be assigned. The select committee of that body asserted a gross and inexcusable falsehood in their address to the people of Tennessee when they declared that the Government of the United States had made war upon them. The secession cause has thus far been sustained by deception and falsehood; by falsehoods as to the action of Congress; by false dispatches as to battles that were never fought and victories that were never won; by false accounts as to the purposes of the President; by false representations as to the views of Union men, and by false pretenses as to the facility with which the secession troops would take possession of the Capitol and capture the highest officers of the Government. The cause of secession or rebellion has no charms for us, and its progress has been marked by the most alarming and dangerous attacks upon the public liberty. In other States as well as our own its whole course threatens to annihilate the last vestige of freedom. While peace and prosperity have blessed us in the Government of the United States, the following may be enumerated as some of the fruits of secession:

It was urged forward by members of Congress who were sworn to support the Constitution of the United States and were themselves supported by the Government. It was effected without consultation with all the States interested in the slavery question and without exhausting peaceable remedies. It has plunged the country into civil war, paralyzed our commerce, interfered with the whole trade and business of our country, lessened the value of our property, destroyed many of the pursuits of life, and bids fair to involve the whole nation in irretrievable bankruptcy and ruin. It has changed the entire relations of States, and adopted constitutions without submitting them to a vote of the people; and where such a vote has been authorized, it has been upon the condition prescribed by Senator {James Murray} Mason of

Virginia, that those who voted the Union ticket "must leave the State." It has advocated a constitutional monarchy, a king and a dictator, and is, through the Richmond press, at this moment recommending to the convention in Virginia a restriction of the right of suffrage, and "in severing connection with the Yankees to abolish every vestige of resemblance to the institutions of that detested race." It has formed military leagues, passed military bills and opened the door for oppressive taxation without consulting the people, and then, in mockery of a free election, has required them by their votes to sanction its usurpations under the penalties of moral proscription or at the point of the bayonet. It has offered a premium for crime in directing the discharge of volunteers from criminal prosecutions and in recommending the judges not to hold their courts. It has stained our statute book with the repudiation of Northern debts, and has greatly violated the Constitution by attempting, through its unlawful extension, to destroy the right of suffrage. It has called upon the people in the State of Georgia, and may soon require the people of Tennessee, to contribute all their surplus cotton, corn, wheat, bacon, beef, &c., to the support of pretended governments alike destitute of money and credit. It has attempted to destroy the accountability of public servants to the people by secret legislation, and has set the obligation of an oath at defiance. It has passed laws declaring it treason to say or do anything in favor of the Government of the United States or against the Confederate States, and such a law is now before, and we apprehend will soon be passed by, the Legislature of Tennessee. It has attempted to destroy, and we fear soon will utterly prostrate the freedom of speech and of the press. It has involved the Southern States in a war whose success is hopeless, and which must ultimately lead to the ruin of the people. Its bigoted, overbearing, and intolerant spirit has already subjected the people of East Tennessee to many petty grievances; our people have been insulted; our flags have been fired upon and torn down; our houses have been rudely entered; our families subjected to insult; our peaceable meetings interrupted; our women and children shot at by a merciless soldiery; our towns pillaged; our citizens robbed, and some of them assassinated and murdered. No effort has been spared to deter the Union men of East Tennessee from the expression of their free thoughts. The penalties of treason have been threatened against them, and murder and assassination have been openly encouraged by leading secession journals. As secession has been thus overbearing and intolerant while in the minority in East Tennessee, nothing better can be expected of the pretended majority than wild, unconstitutional, and oppressive legislation; an utter contempt and disregard of law; a determination to force every Union man in the State to swear to the support of a constitution he abhors, to yield his money and property to aid a cause he detests, and to become the object of scorn and derision as well as the victim of intolerable and relentless oppression.

In view of these considerations and of the fact that the people of East Tennessee have declared their fidelity in the Union by a majority of about 20,000 votes, therefore we do resolve and declare:

First. That we do earnestly desire the restoration of peace to our whole country, and most especially that our own section of the State of Tennessee should not be involved in civil war.

Second. That the action of our State Legislature in passing the so called "declaration of independence" and in forming the "military league" with the Confederate States, and in adopting other acts looking to a separation of the State of Tennessee from the Government of the United States, is unconstitutional and illegal, and therefore not binding upon us as loyal citizens.

Third. That in order to avert a conflict with our brethren in other parts of the State, and desiring that every constitutional means shall be resorted to for the preservation of peace, we do therefore constitute and appoint O. P. Temple,[10] of Knox; John Netherland,[11] of Hawkins, and James P. McDowell, of Greene, commissioners, whose duty it shall be to prepare a memorial and cause the same to be presented to the General Assembly of Tennessee, now in session, asking its consent that the counties composing East Tennessee, and such counties in Middle Tennessee as desire to co-operate with them, may form and erect a separate State.

Fourth. Desiring in good faith that the General Assembly will grant this our reasonable request, and still claiming the right to determine our own destiny, we do further resolve that an election be held in all the counties of East Tennessee, and in such other counties in Middle Tennessee adjacent thereto as may desire to cooperate with us, for the choice of delegates to represent them in a general convention to be held in the town of Kingston at such time as the president of this convention, or in the case of his absence or inability, any one of the vice-presidents, or in like case with them, the secretary of this convention may designate; and the officer so designating the day for the assembling of said convention shall also fix the time for holding the election herein provided for and give reasonable notice thereof.

Fifth. In order to carry out the foregoing resolution, the sheriffs of the different counties are hereby requested to open and hold said election, or cause the same to be so held, in the usual manner and at the usual places of voting, as prescribed by law; and in the event the sheriff of any county should fail or refuse to open and hold said election, or cause the same to be done, the coroner of such county is requested to do so; and should such coroner fail or refuse, then any constable of such county is hereby authorized to open and hold said election or cause the same to be done. And if in any county none of the above named officers will hold said election, then any justice of the peace or freeholder in such county is authorized to hold the same or cause it to be done. The officer or other person holding said election shall certify the result to the president of this convention, or to such officer as may have directed the same to be holden, at as early a day thereafter as practicable; and the officer to whom said returns may be made shall open and compare the polls and issue certificates to the delegates elected.

Sixth. That in said convention the several counties shall be represented as follows: The county of Knox shall elect three delegates; the counties of Washington, Greene, and Jefferson two delegates each, and the remaining counties shall each elect one delegate.

Convention adjourned to 2 p. m.

Source: *The War of the Rebellion: A Compilation of the Official Records of the Union and Confederate Armies* (Washington: Government Printing Office, 1898), Series 1, vol. 52, part 1, 168–76.

EAST TENNESSEE MEMORIAL

KNOXVILLE, TENN., *June 20, 1861.*

To the GENERAL ASSEMBLY OF THE STATE OF TENNESSEE:

The undersigned memorialists, in behalf of the people of East Tennessee beg leave respectfully to show that at a convention of delegates holden at Greeneville on the 17th, 18th, 19th, and 20th days of June instant, in which was represented every country of East Tennessee, except the county of Rhea, it was

Resolved, First. "That we do earnestly desire the restoration of peace to our whole country, and most especially that our own section of the State of Tennessee shall not be involved in civil war."

Second. "That the action of the State Legislature in passing the so-called 'declaration of independence' and in forming the 'military league' with the Confederate States and in adopting other acts looking to a separation of Tennessee from the Government of the United States, is unconstitutional and illegal, and therefore not binding upon us as loyal citizens."

Third. *And it was further resolved,* "That in order to avert a conflict with our brethren in other parts of the State and desiring that every constitutional means shall be resorted to for the preservation of peace, we do therefore constitute and appoint O. P. Temple of Knox; John Netherland, of Hawkins, and James P. McDowell, of Greene, commissioners, whose duty it shall be to prepare a memorial and cause the same to be presented to the General Assembly of Tennessee, now in session, asking its consent that the counties composing East Tennessee and such other counties in Middle Tennessee as desire to co-operate with them, may form and erect a separate State."

The idea of a separate political existence is not a recent one, but it is not deemed necessary here to re-state the geographical, social, economical, and industrial reasons which have often been urged in support of it. The reason which operated upon the convention and seemed to them conclusive was the action of the two sections respectively at the election held on the 8th instant to determine the future national relations of the State. In that election the people of East Tennessee, by a majority of nearly 20,000 votes, decided to adhere to the Federal Union, established prior to the American Revolution, and to which Tennessee was admitted in the year 1796; while the rest of the State is reported to have decided by a majority approaching even more nearly to unanimity to leave the Federal Union and to join the body politic recently formed under the name of the Confederate States of America. The same diversity of sentiment was exhibited, but less distinctly, at the election on the 9th of February last, when the people of East Tennessee decided by a heavy majority against holding a convention to discuss and determine our Federal relations, overcoming by nearly 14,000 the majority in the rest of the State in favor of such a convention. This hopeless and irreconcilable difference of opinion and purpose leaves no alternative but a separation of the two sections of the State, for it is not to be presumed that either would for a moment think of subjugating the other, or of coercing it into a political condition repugnant alike to its interest and to its honor. Certainly the people of East Tennessee entertain no such purpose toward the rest of the State; and the avowals of their western brethren in connection with their recent political action have been too numerous and explicit to leave us in any doubt as to their views. It remains, therefore, that measures be adopted to effect a separation amicably, honorably, and magnanimously, by a settlement of boundaries so as to divide East Tennessee and any contiguous counties or districts which may desire to adhere to her from the rest of the State, and by a fair, just, and equitable division of the public property and the common liabilities. It has occurred to the undersigned as the best method of accomplishing this most desirable end that your body should take immediate action in the premises by giving a formal assent to the proposed separation, pursuant to the provisions of Section 3, Article 4, of the Constitution of the United States,[12] and by convoking a convention representing the sovereign power of the people of the respective divisions of Tennessee, with the plenary authority to so amend the constitution of the State as to carry into effect the change contemplated. With a view to such action, or to action leading to the same result, the undersigned ask permission to confer with your body, either in general session or through a committee appointed for this purpose, so as to consider and determine the details more satisfactorily than could otherwise be done.

Awaiting a response to this memorial, the undersigned beg to add assurances of every endeavor on their part not only to preserve the peaceful relations heretofore subsisting between the people in the two portions of the State, but to remove as far as possible all causes of disturbance in the future, so that each may be left free to follow its chosen path of prosperity and honor, unembarrassed by any collision with the other.

O. P. TEMPLE.

JOHN NETHERLAND.

JAS. P. MCDOWELL.

Source: *The War of the Rebellion: A Compilation of the Official Records of the Union and Confederate Armies* (Washington: Government Printing Office, 1898), Series 1, vol. 52, part 1, 178–79.

Response of the General Assembly to the Greeneville Convention Memorial
June 29, 1861

The following message was received from the Senate:

MR. SPEAKER:

The Senate has concurred in the request of the House of Representatives for a convention of the two Houses at half past 11 o'clock A.M. to-day, for the purpose of acting upon the appointment made by the Governor in the Staff of the Provisional Army of Tennessee.

Mr. Gantt from the Joint Committee on the memorial of the Commissioners appointed by the Greeneville Convention, submitted the following report; which was read, and ordered to be transmitted.

The Committee to which was referred the memorial O. P. Temple, John Netherland and James P. McDowell, on behalf of themselves and certain citizens of East Tennessee composing the Greeneville Convention, respectfully submit the following report:

The Committee are not satisfied that the citizens, seeking by their memorial to have East Tennessee erected into a new State, represent the sentiment of the people of East Tennessee. They are not aware that the important subject of the memorial has been canvassed in the State except in the Greeneville Convention. That convention, as they are informed, was composed of delegates to the Knoxville Convention, which met on the 30th of May last. These delegates were consequently chosen before the vote on the 8th of June, and without reference to the particular result of that vote. There is nothing whatever to show that they were selected with the view to the formation of East Tennessee into a new State, or that the wish of the counties which they assume to represent on that question was ascertained. Nor, indeed, does it appear that said delegates were chosen upon a full expression of public opinion. The grounds upon which the memorialists mainly rest the application is the vote of the 8th of June, which, as the memorial assumes, exhibits an irreconcilable diversity of sentiment between East Tennessee and Middle and West Tennessee. The vote occurred, as already stated, subsequent to the appointment of delegates who composed the Greeneville Convention, and hence could not have an element in the sentiment which appointed them.

In addition to this, as the question affects the whole State, we remark, that nothing whatever of the sentiment of West and Middle Tennessee is known on the grave question presented in the memorial. In many portions of the State it is not even yet known that memorialists desire to create a new State out of East Tennessee. The fact is communicated to the General Assembly in session, and with no opportunity whatever of comparing views with their constituents on so important a question. Besides, without a full expression of sentiment to the contrary, the Committee would be inclined to the opinion that our brethren of East Tennessee would acquiesce in the result of the vote on the 8th of June. Every presumption is in favor of acquiescence. They are our fellow citizens, identified with us by the closest ties of kinship and interest. We have been long accustomed to regard them as brothers. In the many contests in the State, at the ballot box, the will of a majority has been uniformly acquiesced in by the minority. Many are the instances in which East Tennessee had a large majority in favor of the prevailing policy. Such was the case in February last. Whilst in numerous instances, its favorite policy has been lost. Yet the people of the entire State have inevitably acquiesced. We are not prepared to believe that a contrary result will follow now.

If, however, there exists in the breasts of a majority of the citizens of East Tennessee a desire to form themselves into a separate State, and we are mistaken in our conclusions, we submit that the question can be better disposed of by our successors, who will assemble in a few months fresh from the people. In the meantime, over the entire State the question can be discussed, and a full expression of sentiment elicited. This will enable members to act in accordance with the known wishes of their constituents.

If the memorial did not preclude us from doing so, by asking the appointment of Commissioners to confer with Messrs. Temple, Netherland and McDowell, on the single question of erecting East Tennessee into a new State, we would recommend the appointment of Commissioners to confer with these gentlemen on the subject of the grievances complained of by the citizens composing the Greeneville Convention. The careful reading of the memorial, however, we regret to say, forbids us from so doing.

We decline to discuss the policy proposed by the memorial, as well as other questions raised by it.

We earnestly hope that all causes of irritation between citizens of the different portions of the State may soon be removed, and that we may, as heretofore, continue brethren in feeling, alike zealous to maintain the honor and promote the prosperity and general welfare of the whole State. In conclusion, under the circumstances, in our judgment, the General Assembly should at this time take no action on the subject of the memorial.

Respectfully submitted,

STOKES[13] *Chairman Senate Committee.*

GANTT,[14] *Chairman House Committee.*

The report was received and the Committee discharged.

Source: *House Journal of the Second Extra Session of the Thirty-Third General Assembly of the State of Tennessee, which convened at Nashville on Thursday, the 25th day of April, A. D. 1861* (Nashville: J. O. Griffith and Company, Public Printers, 1861), 192–93.

Appendix 1.

ELECTION RETURNS FROM THE JUNE 8, 1861, REFERENDUM[1]

EAST TENNESSEE

COUNTY	*For Separation*	*For Representation*	*No Separation*	*No Representation*
Bradley	507	505	1,382	1,380
Carter	86	86	1,343	1,343
Cocke	518	517	1,185	1,185
Hamilton	854	837	1,260	1,771
Jefferson	603	597	1,987	1,990
Johnson	111	111	787	786
Knox	1,226	1,214	3,196	3,201
Marion	414	413	600	601
Monroe	1,096	1,089	774	775
Polk	738	731	317	319
Roane	453	436	1,586	1,580
Rhea	360	336	202	217
Sevier	60	60	1,528	1,528
Sullivan	1,586	1,576	627	637
Washington	1,022	1,016	1,445	1,444

MIDDLE TENNESSEE

	For Separation	*For Representation*	*No Separation*	*No Representation*
Bedford	1,595	1,544	727	737
Cannon	1,149	1,145	127	118
Coffee	1,276	1,268	26	28
Davidson	5,635	5,572	402	441
DeKalb	833	823	642	655
Dickson	1,141	1,133	72	75
Giles	2,458	2,464	11	5
Grundy	528	528	9	9

Humphreys	1,042	1,042	0	0
Hickman	1,400	1,400	3	3
Jackson	1,483	1,482	714	710
Lawrence	1,124	1,122	75	64
Lewis	223	216	14	17
Lincoln	2,912	2,892	0	9
Macon	447	446	697	697
Marshall	1,642	1,638	101	104
Maury	2,731	2,693	58	78
Montgomery	2,631	2,630	33	29
Overton	1,442	1,442	284	285
Robertson	3,839	3,835	11	12
Rutherford	2,392	2,377	73	93
Stewart	1,839	1,839	99	73
Sumner	6,465	6,441	69	82
Warren	1,419	1,400	12	15
Wilson	2,329	2,298	353	361
White	1,370	1,367	121	121
Williamson	1,945	1,918	28	35

WEST TENNESSEE

	For Separation	For Representation	No Separation	No Representation
Benton	798	796	228	226
Carroll	967	952	1,349	1,351
Dyer	811	779	116	133
Fayette	1,364	1,364	23	23
Gibson	1,999	1,954	286	219
Hardeman	1,526	1,508	29	50
Haywood	930	924	139	143
Henry	1,746	1,734	317	317
Madison	2,754	2,751	20	21
McNairy	1,318	1,305	586	591
Shelby	7137	7,137	5	5

Appendix 2.

Tennessee Congressional Delegation: Thirty-Sixth Congress, 1859–1861

UNITED STATES SENATE

	Party	*County*
Andrew Johnson (1808–1875)	Democrat	Greene
Alfred Osborn Nicholson (1808–1876)	Democrat	Davidson

UNITED STATES HOUSE OF REPRESENTATIVES

	Party	*Dist.*	*County*
Thomas Ames Rogers Nelson (1812–1873)	Opposition	1st	Washington
Horace Maynard (1814–1882)	Opposition	2nd	Knox
Reese Bowen Brabson (1817–1863)	Opposition	3rd	Hamilton
William Brickly Stokes (1814–1897)	Opposition	4th	DeKalb
Robert Hopkins Hatton (1826–1862)	Opposition	5th	Wilson
James Houston Thomas (1808–1876)	Democrat	6th	Maury
John Vines Wright (1828–1908)	Democrat	7th	McNairy
James Minor Quarles (1823–1901)	Opposition	8th	Montgomery
Emerson Etheridge (1819–1902)	Opposition	9th	Weakley
William Tecumsah Avery (1819–1880)	Democrat	10th	Shelby

TIME LINE FOR SECESSION WINTER

1860

November 6	Abraham Lincoln elected president of the United States
December 3	2nd Session of the Thirty-Sixth Congress convenes
December 17	South Carolina convenes secession convention
December 18	Senator John J. Crittenden introduces compromise amendment
December 20	South Carolina secedes

1861

January 3	Florida convenes secession convention
January 7	Mississippi convenes secession convention
January 7	Alabama convenes secession convention
January 7	Tennessee General Assembly convenes
January 9	Mississippi secedes
January 9	South Carolina fires on the government supply ship *Star of the West*
January 10	Florida secedes
January 11	Alabama secedes
January 16	Georgia convenes secession convention
January 19	Georgia secedes
January 23	Louisiana convenes secession convention
January 26	Louisiana secedes
January 28	Texas convenes secession convention
February 4	Secessionist convention convenes in Montgomery, Alabama
February 4	Washington Peace Convention convenes
February 8	Provisional Confederate States of America established
February 9	Tennessee voters reject secession, 80% to 20%
February 9	Jefferson Davis elected provisional president of the CSA

February 13	Virginia convenes secession convention
February 18	Jefferson Davis inaugurated president of the CSA
February 23	Texas secedes
February 27	Washington Peace Convention concludes
February 28	Missouri convenes secession convention
March 4	US Senate approves Thomas Corwin's compromise amendment
March 4	US Senate votes down Washington Peace Convention amendment
March 4	Abraham Lincoln inaugurated president of the United States
March 4	Arkansas convenes secession convention
March 6	Confederate Congress authorizes the raising of 100,000 troops
March 11	Permanent Confederate Constitution created in Montgomery, Alabama
March 19	Missouri votes against secession
March 26	Permanent Confederate Constitution officially adopted
April 12	Bombardment of Fort Sumter begins
April 15	Lincoln calls for 75,000 troops
April 25	Governor Harris recommends separation from the United States
May 6	Arkansas secedes
May 6	Tennessee General Assembly approves ordinance of secession
May 6	Tennessee General Assembly authorizes raising of 55,000 troops
May 7	Tennessee General Assembly ratifies Military League with the CSA
May 16	Tennessee admitted to the CSA
May 20	North Carolina convenes secession convention

May 20	North Carolina secedes
May 23	Virginia votes to secede
June 8	Tennessee secedes; popular vote approves ordinance of secession, 68% to 32%

Notes

INTRODUCTION

1. John C. Waugh, *On the Brink of Civil War: The Compromise of 1850 and How it Changed the Course of American History* (Wilmington, Delaware: SR Books, 2003); and Michael F. Holt, *The Fate of the Country: Politicians, Slavery Extension, and the Coming of the Civil War* (New York: Hill and Wang, 2004).

2. Paul Finkelman, *Dred Scott v. Sandford: A Brief History with Documents* (Boston: Bedford/St. Martins, 1997); Don E. Fehrenbacher, *The Dred Scott Case: Its Significance in American Law and Politics* (New York: Oxford University Press, 1978); and Mark A. Graber, *Dred Scott and the Problem of Constitutional Evil* (New York: Cambridge University Press, 2006).

3. Joseph C. G. Kennedy, *Preliminary Report on The Eighth Census, 1860* (Washington: Government Printing Office, 1862), 137.

4. A recent dissection of the 1860 election can be found in Michael F. Holt, *The Election of 1860: "A Campaign Fraught with Consequences"* (Lawrence: University Press of Kansas, 2017). Given the political heat produced by the Republicans' opposition to the extension of slavery into the territories, it is interesting that under the terms of the Compromise of 1850, the New Mexico Territorial Legislature had approved in 1859 a lengthy slave code that protected slavery throughout the territory.

5. *Congressional Globe*, 36th Cong., 2nd Sess., December 19, 1860, 134–43.

6. Ibid., December 24, 1860, 185–89.

7. Robert H. White, *Messages of the Governors of Tennessee, 1857–1869*, vol. 5 (Nashville: Tennessee Historical Commission, 1959), 255–69.

8. The New York press and courts changed "Lemon" to "Lemmon." See Marie Tyler-McGraw and Dwight T. Pitcaithley, "The Lemmon Slave Case: Courtroom Drama, Constitutional Crisis, and the Southern Quest to Nationalize Slavery" *Common-Place* 14, no. 1 (Fall 2013), http://commonplace.online/article/lemmon-slave-case/.

9. White, *Messages of the Governors of Tennessee*, 255–69; Sam Davis Elliott, *Isham G. Harris of Tennessee: Confederate Governor and United States Senator* (Baton Rouge: Louisiana State University Press, 2010), 60–63.

10. Called by Virginia and attended by delegates from twenty-one states, the Washington Peace Conference met for three weeks in February 1861 seeking a solution to the secession crisis. See Mark Tooley, *The Peace That Almost Was: The Forgotten Story of the 1861 Washington Peace Conference and the Final Attempt to Avert the Civil War* (Nashville: Nelson Books, 2015); Lucius E. Chittenden, ed., *A Report of the Debates and Proceedings of the Secret Sessions of the Conference Convention, for Proposing Amendments to the Constitution of the United States, Held at Washington, D. C., in February, A. D. 1861* (New York: D. Appleton & Company, 1864).

11. See Dwight T. Pitcaithley, *The U.S. Constitution and Secession: A Documentary Anthology of Slavery and White Supremacy* (Lawrence: University Press of Kansas, 2018), 42–48, 161–275.

12. Tennessee Representative Thomas A. R. Nelson reintroduced Crittenden's amendment in the U. S. House of Representatives on December 27. See Nelson's amendment of that date in chapter 5.

13. *American National Biography*, vol. 12 (New York: Oxford University Press, 1999), 40.

14. *Congressional Globe*, 36th Cong., 2nd Sess., December 13, 1860, 83.

15. Ibid., December 12, 1860, 79.

16. Pitcaithley, *U.S. Constitution and Secession*, 42–48, 161–275. See also Daniel W. Crofts, *Lincoln and the Politics of Slavery: The Other Thirteenth Amendment and the Struggle to Save the Union* (Chapel Hill: University of North Carolina Press, 2016).

17. *Public Acts of the State of Tennessee, Passed at the Extra Session of the Thirty-Third General Assembly, for the Year 1861* (Nashville: E. G. Eastman & Co., Public Printers, Union and American Office, 1861), 15–17.

18. Jonathan M. Atkins, *Parties, Politics, and the Sectional Conflict in Tennessee, 1832–1861* (Knoxville: University of Tennessee Press, 1997), 241; White, *Messages of the Governors of Tennessee*, 271–72.

19. *House Journal of the Extra Session of the Thirty-Third General Assembly of the State of Tennessee, Which Convened at Nashville, on the First Monday in January, A. D. 1861* (Nashville: J. O. Griffith and Company, Public Printers, 1861), 25–26.

20. "Bedford County," *The Tennessee Encyclopedia of History and Culture*, http://tennesseeencyclopedia.net.

21. *House Journal of the Extra Session of the Thirty-Third General Assembly*, 47.

22. Ibid., 28.

23. *Senate Journal of the Extra Session of the Thirty-Third General Assembly of the State of Tennessee, Which Convened at Nashville, on the First Monday in January, A. D. 1861* (Nashville: J. O. Griffith and Company, Public Printers, 1861), 53.

24. *Congressional Globe*, 36th Cong., 2nd Sess., House of Representatives, Report No. 31, 3–4.

25. Ibid., January 7, 1861, 279.

26. *House Journal of the Extra Session of the Thirty-Third General Assembly*, 45.

27. Ibid., 43–44.

28. *Congressional Globe*, 36th Cong., 2nd Sess., March 2, 1861, 1350–1351.

29. E. Merton Coulter, *The Confederate States of America 1861–1865* (Baton Rouge: Louisiana State University Press, 1950), 34, 151; William W. Freehling, *The Road to Disunion: Volume II, Secessionists Triumphant 1854–1861* (New York: Oxford University Press, 2007), 476–78.

30. *Public Acts of the State of Tennessee*, 49–52.

31. Ibid.

32. Chittenden, *A Report of the Debates and Proceedings of the Secret Sessions of the Conference Convention*, 54, 453–56.

33. Freehling, *The Road to Disunion*, 323–24; James Alex Baggett, *The Scalawags: Southern Dissenters in the Civil War and Reconstruction* (Baton Rouge: Louisiana State University Press, 2003), 32–33.

34. All nine speeches are included in chapter 4.

35. *Congressional Globe*, 36th Cong., 2nd Sess., January 23, 1861, Appendix, 111–16.

36. Ibid., January 31, 1861, Appendix, 121–24.

37. Ibid., February 8, 1861, Appendix, 170–74.

38. *Congressional Globe*, 36th Cong., 2nd Sess., January 17, 1861, 435–38.

39. Ibid., January 17, 1861, 437.

40. Richard Carwardine, *Lincoln: A Life of Purpose and Power* (New York: Vintage Books, 2003), 149–52.

41. Eric Foner, *The Fiery Trial: Abraham Lincoln and American Slavery* (New York: W. W. Norton & Company, 2010), 157–61.

42. Jack B. Scroggs, "Arkansas in the Secession Crisis," *The Arkansas Historical Quarterly* 12, no. 3 (Autumn 1953), 179–224.

43. *Journal and Proceedings of the Missouri State Convention, Held at Jefferson City and St. Louis, March, 1861* (St. Louis: George Knapp & Co., Printers and Binders, 1861), 216. See also George H. Reese, ed., *Proceedings of the Virginia State Convention of 1861: February 13–May 1, In Four Volumes* (Richmond: Virginia State Library, 1965).

44. William C. Davis, *"A Government of Our Own": The Making of the Confederacy* (Baton Rouge: Louisiana State University Press, 1994), 260.

45. Ibid., 305–13.

46. Roy P. Basler, ed., *The Collected Works of Abraham Lincoln*, vol. IV (New Brunswick: Rutgers University Press, 1953), 331–32.

47. Elliott, *Isham G. Harris of Tennessee*, 68.

48. Atkins, *Parties, Politics, and the Sectional Conflict in Tennessee*, 244.

49. *Senate Journal of the Second Extra Session of the Thirty-Third General Assembly of the State of Tennessee, Which Convened at Nashville on Thursday, the 25th Day of April, A. D. 1861* (Nashville: J. O. Griffith and Company, Public Printers, 1861), 5–13.

50. *The War of the Rebellion: A Compilation of the Official Records of the Union and Confederate Armies*, Series I, vol. LII, part II (Washington: Government Printing Office, 1898), 70, 76–78, 82–84.

51. Henry W. Hilliard, *Politics and Pen Pictures At Home and Abroad* (New York: G. P. Putnam's Sons, 1892), 325–28. See also David I. Durham, *A Southern Moderate in Radical Times: Henry Washington Hiliard, 1808–1892* (Baton Rouge: Louisiana State University Press, 2008), 140–41; Davis, *"A Government of Our Own,"* 334, 346, 353.

52. *Senate Journal of the Second Extra Session of the Thirty-Third General Assembly*, 35. See also White, *Messages of the Governors of Tennessee*, 288–89.

53. *Public Acts of the State of Tennessee*, 15–18.

54. Ibid., 19–21. For a contemporary East Tennessee analysis of the league, see Oliver P. Temple, *East Tennessee and the Civil War* (Cincinnati: Robert Clarke Company, 1899), 210–12.

55. James Walter Fertig, *The Secession and Reconstruction of Tennessee* (Chicago: University of Chicago Press, 1898), 25.

56. *The Statutes at Large of the Provisional Government of the Confederate States of America, From the Institution of the Government, February 8, 1861, To Its Termination, February 18, 1862, Inclusive. Arranged in Chronological*

Order. *Together With The Constitution for the Provisional Government, and the Permanent Constitution of the Confederate States, and the Treaties Concluded by the Confederate States with Indian Tribes* (Richmond: R. M. Smith, Printer to Congress, 1864), 119. A similar eagerness to expand the Confederate States of America resulted in Virginia being admitted on May 7, several weeks before its scheduled ratification vote on May 23. Ibid., 104.

57. Lincoln carefully deconstructed this "sophism," as he termed it, in his July 4, 1861, message to Congress. *Congressional Globe*, 37th Cong., 1st Sess, Appendix, 2.

58. For an insightful analysis of this issue see Sam Elliott, "Tennessee's Declaration of Independence: Armed Revolt and the Constitutional Right of Revolution," *Tennessee Bar Journal* 44 (December 2008), 25–29, 36.

59. *Senate Journal of the Second Extra Session of the Thirty-Third General Assembly*, 83–91.

60. White, *Messages of the Governors of Tennessee*, 301.

61. Charles F. Bryan, Jr., "A Gathering of Tories: The East Tennessee Convention of 1861," *Tennessee Historical Quarterly* 39, no. 1 (Spring 1980), 27–36.

62. *War of the Rebellion*, Series 1, vol. LII, part I, 148–55.

63. Atkins, *Parties, Politics, and the Sectional Conflict in Tennessee*, 248. The official election returns no longer exist and newspaper figures varied slightly. See also Daniel W. Crofts, *Reluctant Confederates: Upper South Unionists in the Secession Crisis* (Chapel Hill: University of North Carolina Press, 1989), 341–52; W. Todd Groce, *Mountain Rebels: East Tennessee Confederates and the Civil War, 1860–1870* (Knoxville: University of Tennessee Press, 1999), 36–45; White, *Messages of the Governors of Tennessee*, 302–3.

64. White, *Messages of the Governors of Tennessee*, 302. See also Fertig, *Secession and Reconstruction of Tennessee*, 26–28; Bryan, "A Gathering of Tories," 38–39.

65. Quoted in Steve Humphrey, ed., *"That D——d Brownlow," Being a Saucy & Malicious Description of Fighting Parson WILLIAM GANNAWAY BROWNLOW, Knoxville Editor and Stalwart Unionist, Who Rose from a Confederate Jail to become One of the Most Famous Personages in the Nation,*

Denounced by his Enemies as Vicious and Harsh, Praised by his Friends as Compassionate and Gentle (Boone, North Carolina: Appalachian Consortium Press, 1978), 210–11.

66. Bryan, "A Gathering of Tories," 39–40.

67. *War of the Rebellion*, Series 1, vol. LII, part I, 173–76.

68. *House Journal of the Second Extra Session of the Thirty-Third General Assembly of the State of Tennessee, Which Convened at Nashville on Thursday, the 25th Day of April, A. D. 1861* (Nashville: J. O. Griffith and Company, Public Printers, 1861), 192–93. See also Bryan, "A Gathering of Tories," 44–45; Atkins, *Parties, Politics, and the Sectional Conflict in Tennessee*, 252–53.

69. Bryan, "A Gathering of Tories," 45–47; Fertig, *Secession and Reconstruction of Tennessee*, 30.

70. Dwight T. Pitcaithley, "Revisiting Secession: Reassessing the Evidence," *North & South*, Series II, vol. 1, no. 3 (January 2020), 48–57. For an analysis of the connections between secession and white supremacy, see Ulrich B. Phillips, "The Central Theme of Southern History," *American Historical Review*, 34, no. 1 (October 1928), 30–43.

71. For an explication of Lincoln's journey toward emancipation, see William W. Freehling, *Becoming Lincoln* (Charlottesville: University of Virginia Press, 2018).

72. Elliott, *Isham G. Harris of Tennessee*, 177–78; Humphrey, *"That D——d Brownlow,"* 281–84; *Acts of the State of Tennessee, Passed at the First Session of the Thirty-Fourth General Assembly, for the Year 1865* (Nashville: S.C. Mercer, Printer to the State, 1865), 134. While Tennessee was among the first of the former states of the Confederacy to ratify the Thirteenth and Fourteenth Amendments, it became the last of all the states to ratify the Fifteenth Amendment—waiting until 1997 to do so. See Eric Foner, *The Second Founding: How the Civil War and Reconstruction Remade the Constitution* (New York: W. W. Norton & Company, 2019), 108.

73. *Senate Journal of the First Session of the General Assembly of the State of Tennessee, 1865, Which Convened at Nashville, Monday, April 3* (Nashville: S. C. Mercer, Printer to the State, 1865), 18–22.

74. *Republican Banner and Nashville Whig*, May 10, 1861.

75. Ibid.; Joseph Howard Parks, *John Bell of Tennessee* (Baton Rouge: Louisiana State University Press, 1950), 395–401.

76. Derek William Frisby, *"Homemade Yankees": West Tennessee Unionism in the Civil War Era* (PhD diss., University of Alabama-Tuscaloosa, 2004), 45–74.

77. William L. Barney, *Rebels in the Making: The Secession Crisis and the Birth of the Confederacy* (New York: Oxford University Press, 2020), 300.

78. Stephen V. Ash, *Middle Tennessee Society Transformed, 1860–1870: War and Peace in the Upper South* (Baton Rouge: Louisiana State University Press, 1988), 73.

79. Temple, *East Tennessee and the Civil War*, 244.

80. Annette Gordon-Reed, *Andrew Johnson* (New York: Henry Holt and Company, 2011), 66. See also Crofts, *Reluctant Confederates*, 329.

81. Quoted in Crofts, *Reluctant Confederates*, 351.

CHAPTER ONE: SENATORS ANDREW JOHNSON AND ALFRED OSBORN POPE NICHOLSON

1. From Patrick Henry's famous 1756 speech before Virginia's House of Burgesses protesting King George's Stamp Act.

2. James Monroe, president of the United States from 1817 to 1825 announced this policy which became known as the Monroe Doctrine.

3. *Congressional Globe*, 36th Cong., 1st Sess., February 2 and May 24, 1860, 658, 2322.

4. Joseph Addison (1672–1719), English playwright, poet, essayist, and politician. His play, *Cato, a Tragedy*, dealt with themes of individual liberty versus governmental tyranny, and logic versus emotion.

5. *Congressional Globe*, 36th Cong., 2nd Sess., December 17, 1861, 99–104.

6. From the 1856 Republican platform.

7. Joshua Reed Giddings (1795–1864) served as a representative from Ohio from 1837 until 1859 as a Whig, Free-Soil candidate, Opposition Party candidate, and as a Republican.

8. Millard Fillmore (1800–1874) became president upon the death of Zachary Taylor and served from July 9, 1850, until March 4, 1853. He was nominated as the presidential candidate by the American Party in 1856 coming in a distant third behind James Buchanan (Democrat) and John C. Fremont (Republican).

9. The 1860 Republican platform contained the following plank: "That the maintenance of the principles promulgated in the Declaration of Independence and embodied in the Federal Constitution, 'That all men are created equal; that they are endowed by their Creator with certain inalienable rights; that among these are life, liberty and the pursuit of happiness; that to secure these rights, governments are instituted among men, deriving their just powers from the consent of the governed,' is essential to the preservation of our Republican institutions; and that the Federal Constitution, the Rights of the States, and the Union of the States must and shall be preserved."

CHAPTER TWO: GOVERNOR ISHAM G. HARRIS

1. For Governor Harris's role during the war, see Sam Davis Elliott, "'A Fighting Governor': Isham G. Harris and the Army of Tennessee," in *Border Wars: The Civil War in Tennessee and Kentucky*, eds. Kent T. Dollar, Larry H. Whiteaker, and W. Calvin Dickinson (Kent: Kent State University Press, 2015), 256–70.

2. As a result of the 1860 election for the Thirty-Seventh Congress (1861–1863), the Democratic Party would have held majorities in both the House of Representatives and the Senate had the South not seceded.

3. A reference to the Missouri Compromise during the presidency of James Monroe. The Democratic-Republican Party (led by President Monroe) held overwhelming majorities in both houses throughout the Sixteenth Congress (1819–1821).

4. Between 1845 and 1850, Texas included that portion of New Mexico east of the Rio Grande, the Oklahoma panhandle, a small corner of Kansas, and a swath of Colorado and Wyoming to the 42nd parallel. As a condition of statehood, Texas had the option of dividing itself into as many as five states providing that any north of 36°30' would be free.

5. As a result of the Compromise of 1850, Texas was admitted with its current boundaries. The remainder, claimed by the earlier Republic of Texas, Congress divided between the territories of New Mexico and Utah.

6. Throughout the Thirty-First Congress (1849–1851), pro-slavery Democrats controlled both houses of Congress, and dominated the statehood vote

for California: 150–56 in the House and 48–3 in the Senate. Between 1850 and 1860, California elected only Democrats to the United States Congress with the sole exception of George Washington Wright (1816–1885) who served as an Independent in the House of Representatives from September 1850 until March 1851.

7. Although strongly supported by President Buchanan, the proslavery Lecompton Constitution had been soundly rejected by the settlers of Kansas on January 4, 1858.

8. On March 11, 1850, during Senate debates over the disposition of the Mexican Cession, William H. Seward (a Whig at the time) delivered his controversial "Higher Law" speech. Speaking in opposition to the compromise which allowed the possibility of slavery in the newly acquired territory, Seward claimed, "There is a higher law than the Constitution, which regulates our authority over the domain, and devotes it to the same noble purposes. The territory is a part, no inconsiderable part, of the common heritage of mankind, bestowed upon them by the Creator of the universe." Seward's notion that God's law was higher than that of the Constitution became part of Democratic grievances against Lincoln and the Republican Party.

9. For an examination of Northern personal liberty laws, see Thomas D. Morris, *Free Men All: The Personal Liberty Laws of the North, 1780–1861* (Baltimore: Johns Hopkins University Press, 1974).

10. James Montgomery (1814–1871) was the recognized leader of the free state faction in Kansas and led a raid on Fort Scott in December 1858.

CHAPTER THREE: TENNESSEE GENERAL ASSEMBLY

1. See Senator Johnson's December 19, 1860, speech in chapter 1.

2. The 1856 Republican platform contained a plank that read: "That the Constitution confers upon Congress sovereign powers over the Territories of the United States for their government; and that in the exercise of this power, it is both the right and the imperative duty of Congress to prohibit in the Territories those twin relics of barbarism—Polygamy, and Slavery."

3. A reference to William Henry Seward's speech titled "On the Irrepressible Conflict," delivered in Rochester, New York, October 25, 1858.

1. The "sage of Quincy" John Quincy Adams (1767–1848) died twelve years before Lincoln's nomination, not eighteen. On February 25, 1839, Representative Adams proposed three amendments to the Constitution that would have abolished slavery throughout the nation. No subsequent amendment proposing the abolition of slavery would be introduced in Congress until late 1863. See *Congressional Globe*, 25th Cong., 3rd Sess., 205.

2. From Lincoln's "House Divided" speech (June 16, 1858) accepting the Republican Party's nomination to challenge the Senate seat held by Stephen Arnold Douglas.

3. Committee of the Whole on the State of the Union. The Committee of the Whole consists of all members of the House of Representatives.

4. A reference to the several thousand German soldiers who fought for the British during the American Revolution. Many who were captured decided to settle in the colonies rather than return to Europe.

5. Nathanael Greene (1742–1786) was a major general of the Continental Army during the American Revolutionary War. After the British surrender at Yorktown, he relocated to Georgia where he managed several plantations awarded him during the war, including Mulberry Grove outside Savannah.

6. As in a small chest or box for holding jewels.

7. In medieval Europe, *villein in gross* referred to peasants who occupied social space between a free peasant and a slave.

8. Presbyterian Church minister Benjamin Morgan Palmer (1818–1902), from his Thanksgiving Day sermon of November 29, 1860, titled "The South: Her Peril and Her Duty." The complete text for his sermon can be found in Jon L. Wakelyn, *Southern Pamphlets on Secession, November 1860–April 1861* (Chapel Hill: University of North Carolina Press, 1996), 63–77.

9. Representative John Singleton Millson (1808–1874).

10. Kentucky representative Henry Cornelius Burnett (1825–1866) from Trigg County; later expelled from Congress for support of the Confederacy and served as a senator in the First and Second Confederate Congresses elected by the provisional government of Kentucky.

11. The 1860 census revealed that Tennessee had reported 29 fugitive slaves for that year; .0105% of the state's 275,719 slaves. Joseph C. G. Kennedy, *Preliminary Report on The Eighth Census, 1860*, 37th Cong., 2nd Sess., House Ex. Doc. 116, 137.

12. By January 23, there had been thirteen proposed amendments to the Constitution containing such a prohibition. Etheridge possibly knew that the Tennessee General Assembly had approved, just the day before, an amendment containing this clause. It was Republican senator William H. Seward's language that Congress ultimately accepted in the Corwin Amendment on March 4, 1861, prohibiting Congress from interfering with slavery in the states.

13. A reference to Richard Mentor Johnson (1780–1850), who represented Kentucky in the US House of Representatives and Senate and served as Martin Van Buren's vice president (1837–1841). Unconventional for his time, Johnson lived openly with his former slave, Julia Chinn (a mulatto, or more specifically, an octoroon), considered her his common-law wife, and acknowledged their two daughters as his children. Because of his unorthodox domestic relations, southern Democrats refused to support his renomination for vice president in 1840.

14. Article 3, Section 1 of the 1796 constitution reads: "Every freeman [i.e. free man] of the age of twenty one years and upwards possessing a freehold in the County wherein he may vote and being an inhabitant of this State, and every freeman [i.e. free man] being an inhabitant of any one County in the State six months immediately preceeding [i.e. preceding] the day of election shall be entitled to vote for members of the General Assembly for the County in which he shall reside." The 1835 constitution amended this section to read, in part, "Every free white man of the age of twenty-one years, being a citizen of the United States, and a citizen of the county wherein he may offer his vote . . ."

15. Republican representative Thomas Corwin (1794–1865) chaired the House Committee of Thirty-Three.

16. South Carolina's secession convention deliberated four days before voting to secede, Florida's eight days, Alabama's five days, and Mississippi's deliberated a mere three days before choosing disunion.

17. Virginia representative Shelton Farrar Leake (1812–1884). On December 12,

1860, Leake had been the first to introduce a constitutional amendment preventing Congress from interfering with slavery in the states.

18. In 1859, the New Mexico Territorial Legislature approved a lengthy bill establishing and protecting slavery throughout the territory. In 1860, there were approximately two dozen slaves in New Mexico, most brought in by military personnel. The legislature repealed the law on December 10, 1861.

19. John J. Crittenden (1786–1863).

20. William Shakespeare, *Hamlet*, act 3, scene 1.

21. Ibid., act 3, scene 1.

22. Henry Clay (1777–1852), Kentucky statesman influential in crafting the Missouri Compromise (1820) and the Compromise of 1850.

23. On September 11, 1851, Edward Gorsuch, a Maryland slave owner, was killed in Christiana, Pennsylvania, by a group of armed black men while attempting to capture several of his fugitive slaves. James H. Kennedy of Hagerstown, Maryland, was likewise killed in Carlisle, Pennsylvania, in 1847 attempting to recover a dozen or so of his slaves.

24. See chapter 2, Governor Isham Harris's address to the general assembly on January 7, 1861.

25. Freeman Harlow Morse (1807-1891) was a Republican from Maine. After participating as a delegate to the Washington Peace Conference, he served as United States consul and general consul to England from 1861 until 1870.

26. The Tennessee Supreme Court uses the Latin translation of this phrase as its motto; it appears on the seal of the court and is inlaid into the floor of the lobby of the court's building in Nashville.

27. Independent Democrat Andrew Jackson Hamilton (1815–1875) was the Texas representative on the House Committee of Thirty-Three. Lincoln appointed him military governor of Texas in 1862, a designation changed by Andrew Johnson in 1865 to provisional governor.

28. 36th Cong., 2nd Sess., *The Report of the Committee of Thirty-Three*, January 29, 1861, H.R. 31.

29. From William Lowndes Yancey (1814–1863), letter dated June 15, 1858, to his friend James S. Slaughter. A prominent secessionist from Alabama, Yancey led a Confederate diplomatic delegation to England and France in 1861 and later served three terms in the Confederate Senate.

30. Job 39:25.

31. South Carolina governor William Henry Gist (1807–1874).

32. George Gordon (Lord) Byron (1788–1824), *The Siege of Corinth*, 1816.

33. Matthew 5:25.

34. See speech by Emerson Etheridge, January 23, 1861, in chapter 4.

35. Millard Fillmore (1800–1874). President of the United States from July 1850 to March 1853.

36. See speech by Thomas Amos Rogers Nelson, January 25, 1861, in chapter 4.

37. See full text of the general assembly's proposed amendment in chapter 5.

38. Alabama senator Clement Claiborne Clay Jr. (1816–1882). His speech of January 21, 1861, can be found in the *Congressional Globe*, 36th Cong., 2nd Sess., 486.

39. Andrew Jackson Hamilton (1815–1875), Independent Democrat. Hamilton spoke immediately before Stokes; see *Congressional Globe*, 36th Cong., 2nd Sess., February 1, 1861, Appendix, 174–78.

40. *Congressional Globe*, 36th Cong., 1st Sess., January 7, 1860, 364–68.

41. Dispatched by President Buchanan to provide reinforcements and supplies to US troops at Fort Sumter, the *Star of the West* was repulsed by artillery fire from South Carolina shore batteries on January 9, 1861.

42. Abolitionists William Lloyd Garrison (1805–1879) and Wendell Phillips (1811–1884).

43. Representative John Henninger Reagan (1818–1905); later postmaster general of the Confederacy and acting secretary of the Treasury.

44. In the Thirty-Fifth Congress (1857–1859) Democrats controlled the House by a margin of 132 to 90, and the Senate 41 to 20.

45. Opposition Party representative John Adams Gilmer (1805–1868). See *Congressional Globe*, 36th Cong., 2nd Sess., January 26, 1861, 580–83.

46. Democratic representative Sherrard Clemens (1820–1881).

47. Ohio Republican representative John Armor Bingham (1815–1900).

48. Louisiana American Party representative John Edward Bouligny (1824–1864).

49. Sir Walter Scott, "The Lady of the Lake," canto 6.

50. Ruth 1:16.

51. American Party representative James Morrison Harris (1817–1898).

52. Republican Roscoe Conkling (1829–1888).

53. See Abraham Lincoln's "House Divided" speech, June 16, 1858, accepting the Republican Party's nomination to run against Democratic senator Stephen A. Douglas.

54. William Henry Seward (1801–1872); speech titled "On the Irrepressible Conflict," delivered in Rochester, New York, October 25, 1858. Seward, a leading Republican opposing the extension of slavery into the territories, became Lincoln's secretary of state.

55. Henry John Temple, 3rd Viscount Palmerston (1784–1865), prime minister of the United Kingdom, 1859–1865.

56. Èdouard Thouvenel (1818–1866), French minister of foreign affairs, 1860–1862.

57. This quote, attributed to Lincoln, cannot be documented.

58. The James Buchanan administration.

59. Democratic senator Stephen A. Douglas (1813–1861).

60. Republican Charles Francis Adams (1807–1886). On December 28, 1860, Adams had proposed an amendment to the Constitution that would have protected slavery in the states where it already existed.

61. Democrat George Hunt Pendleton (1825–1889). During the Civil War, Pendleton favored peace with the Confederacy and was nominated to the 1864 Democratic ticket as George B. McClellan's vice presidential running mate. Pendleton was the son-in-law of Francis Scott Key (1779–1843), who is best known for writing the lyrics to "The Star-Spangled Banner."

62. Oppositionist Thomas Amos Rogers Nelson (1812–1873).

63. Unionist John Jordan Crittenden (1786–1863).

64. John Bell (1796–1869), who at different times aligned himself with the Jacksonian, Anti-Jacksonian, Whig, Opposition, and American Parties. He was a candidate for president in 1860 on the Constitutional Union ticket.

65. Job 30:1. The land of Uz is a location mentioned in the book of Job.

66. In the presidential election of 1844, James G. Birney of Michigan ran on the Liberty Party ticket against James Knox Polk (Democrat) and Henry Clay (Whig). Birney came in a distant third, but votes for the third-party candidate allowed Polk to defeat Clay (the "statesman of the West") by a slim margin. In the election of 1860, Tennessean John Bell received no electoral votes in the North.

67. A derogatory term used to describe northerners who favored the southern position in political disputes.

68. A reference to the Kansas-Nebraska Act that overturned the 1820 Missouri Compromise and allowed settlers to decide for themselves the fate of slavery in the two territories.

69. Crittenden's original proposition delivered to the Senate on December 18, 1860, contained the phrase "now held, or hereafter acquired."

70. Daniel O'Connell (1775–1874) was an Irish attorney and politician.

71. On February 4, 1861, 131 delegates from twenty-one states convened in Washington at the request of Virginia's general assembly. The Washington Peace Conference concluded its deliberations on February 27 having produced a constitutional amendment only slightly different from Senator Crittenden's. Tennessee's 12 representatives constituted the largest delegation from any state.

72. Opposition Party representative Emerson Etheridge (1819–1902).

73. See Charles M. Cummings, "Robert Hopkins Hatton: Reluctant Rebel," *Tennessee Historical Quarterly* 23, no. 2 (June 1964), 169–81.

74. Robert Penn Warren, *The Legacy of the Civil War* (Lincoln: University of Nebraska Press, 1998), viii. Quote is from the introduction by Howard Jones.

75. Republican representative Charles Baldwin Sedgwick (1815–1883). See *Congressional Globe*, 36th Cong., 2nd Sess., February 7, 1861, 795–98.

76. Ohio Republican representative John Sherman (1823–1900), younger brother of William Tecumseh Sherman (1820–1900). Sherman's address opposing slavery and secession was delivered on January 18, 1861; see *Congressional Globe*, 36th Cong., 2nd Sess., 450–56.

77. Republican representative Charles Francis Adams (1807–1886), son of John Quincy Adams and grandson of John Adams. He was appointed minister to England by President Lincoln.

78. Republican Benjamin Franklin Junkin (1822–1908).

79. A reference to the US Supreme Court's decision in *Dred Scott v. Sandford*, March 6, 1857.

80. Francis Marion (1732–1795), Revolutionary War officer also known as "The Swamp Fox"; Thomas Sumter (1734–1832), brigadier general in the South Carolina militia during the Revolution. Fort Sumter in Charleston Harbor is named for Thomas Sumter.

81. Proverbs 3:16.

82. William Waters Boyce (1818–1890); representative from South Carolina (1853–1860), appointed as a delegate to the Confederate Provisional Congress, elected as a member of the First and Second Confederate Congress.

83. President Andrew Jackson's "Message to the Senate and House Regarding South Carolina's Nullification Ordinance," January 16, 1833.

84. Most likely Leonidas W. Spratt, editor of the *Charleston Standard*, an advocate for the reopening of the African slave trade, and South Carolina's secession commissioner to Florida. See Charles B. Dew, *Apostles of Disunion: Southern Secession Commissioners and the Causes of the Civil War* (Charlottesville: University Press of Virginia, 2001), 42–45.

85. South Carolina governor William Henry Gist (1807–1874); Mississippi governor John James Pettus (1813–1867).

86. South Carolina's "Declaration of Immediate Causes Which Induce and Justify the Secession of South Carolina from the Federal Union" (adopted December 24, 1860), did not mention protective tariffs as a reason for disunion.

87. On February 4, Virginia voters insisted that any secession ordinance be approved by a state-wide referendum; Tennessee voters rejected secession by an 80 to 20 percent margin on February 9; on February 18, Missouri overwhelmingly elected Unionist delegates to its secession convention.

88. Oliver Goldsmith (1730–1774), "The Deserted Village."

CHAPTER FIVE: PROPOSED CONSTITUTIONAL AMENDMENTS

1. William H. Barksdale (1835–1868) represented Smith, Sumner, and Macon Counties as a Democrat.

2. Washington Curran Whitthorne (1825–1891) represented Maury, Lewis, Hickman, and Dickson Counties as a Democrat.

3. Tazewell W. Newman (1827–1867) represented Franklin and Lincoln Counties as a Democrat.

CHAPTER SIX: SEPARATION

1. See Harris's January 7 speech in chapter 2.

2. Declaration of Independence, July 4, 1776. Harris's verison differs slightly from the original, most significantly in his use of the phrase "the right of the people to alter and abolish it." The original reads, "the right of the people to alter or to abolish it."

3. Washington Curran Whitthorne (1825–1891) represented Williamson, Maury, and Lewis Counties as a Democrat.

4. Burton Lewis Stovall (1812–1879) represented Henry, Obion, and Weakley Counties as a Democrat.

5. Gustavus Adolphus Henry (1804–1880) graduated from Transylvania University in Lexington, Kentucky, in 1825 and began practicing law in Hopkinsville, Tennessee. He later represented Montgomery County as a state representative in the 29th General Assembly (1851–1853), and served as one of Tennessee's two senators in the Confederate Congress.

6. Archibald O. W. Totten (1809–1867) served as a justice on the Tennessee Supreme Court from 1850 until 1855. He had been a member of Tennessee's delegation to the Washington Peace Conference, February 1861.

7. George Washington Barrow (1807–1866) was representing Davidson County in the Tennessee Senate as a Whig when selected by Governor Harris. He had practiced law in Nashville, edited several newspapers, and served as *charge d'affaires* for the United States in Lisbon, Portugal, from 1841 to 1844 during the presidency of John Tyler. Barrow was elected to Congress as a Whig in 1847 where he served one term. During the war, he served in the Confederate State Senate until February 1862; following Nashville's surrender, Military Governor Andrew Johnson arrested Barrow for treason. Barrow refused to take the Oath of Allegiance and was eventually exchanged in March 1863.

8. Henry Washington Hilliard (1808–1892) graduated from South Carolina College (now the University of South Carolina) in 1828 and taught at the University of Alabama at Tuscaloosa (1831–1834) before commencing his law practice in Montgomery, Alabama. He was elected as a Whig to the Twenty-Ninth, Thirtieth, and Thirty-First Congresses (1845–1851). During the war he served as a brigadier general in the Confederate Army.

9. The House of Representatives had adjourned on March 4, the Senate on March 28.

10. Senator Robert Garnett Payne (1813–1861) represented Fayette and Shelby Counties as a Democrat.

11. Called by Virginia, the Washington Peace Conference met from February 4 until February 27.

12. The ship Lincoln dispatched for the relief of Fort Sumter carried food and medicine, but no arms. See Foner, *The Fiery Trial*, 161.

13. On April 17, 1861, Virginia's secession convention voted for secession (62 percent to 38 percent) and then scheduled a ratification vote of the people for May 23; that vote affirmed the action of the convention 86 percent to 14 percent. North Carolina specifically voted against allowing the voters to second-guess the convention and then seceded with a unanimous vote on May 20.

14. Confederate president Jefferson Davis (1808–1889) graduated from the United States Military Academy in 1828, and commanded the First Regiment of Mississippi Riflemen during the War with Mexico (1846–1847).

15. Recognizing that time was of the essence, the Confederate Congress adopted the Constitution of the United States in its entirety and then modified it. Two of the most significant changes were limiting the president to a single term of six years and nationalizing the institution of slavery. It was officially ratified by the requisite number of states on March 26, 1861. See Charles Robert Lee, Jr., *The Confederate Constitutions* (Chapel Hill: University of North Carolina Press, 1963), 141–50.

16. Senator Robert Garnett Payne (1813–1861), Democrat, represented Fayette and Shelby Counties; Senator Edmund J. Wood (1838–1894), Democrat, represented Cannon, Coffee, Grundy, Van Buren, and Warren Counties; Senator Sidney Smith Stanton (1833–1864), Oppositionist, represented Jackson, Macon, and White Counties; Senator John A. Minnis (1813–1886), Democrat, represented Hamilton, Bledsoe, Bradley, Marion, and Rhea Counties; Representative George R. Gantt (1824–1897), Democrat, represented Maury County; Representative William Wallace Guy (1832–1879), Democrat, represented Hardeman County; Representative Robert Bailey Hurt (1821–1881), Whig, represented Madison County; Representative

Benjamin J. Lea (1833–1894), Democrat, represented Haywood County; Representative Joseph G. Pickett (1826–?), Oppositionist, represented Smith County.

17. Return Jonathan Meigs III (1801–1891) became Tennessee's first state librarian in 1856. He held strong Unionist sentiments and, upon the secession of Tennessee, moved to New York City and later Washington, DC. Lincoln appointed him clerk of the Supreme Court of the District of Columbia.

CHAPTER SEVEN: Dissent

1. Frederick Steidinger Heiskell (1786–1882) represented Knox County. A printer and newspaper publisher by trade, Heiskell owned the plantation Fruit Hill west of Knoxville in 1861.

2. Samuel R. Rodgers (1798–1866) represented Knox County.

3. John Baxter represented Knox County.

4. Connally F. Trigg (1810–1880) represented Knox County.

5. John Williams II (1818–1881) represented Knox County and served as assistant vice-president to the Convention.

6. Oliver P. Temple (1820–1907) represented Knox County and in 1899 published *East Tennessee and the Civil War*.

7. William Gannaway Brownlow (1805–1877) edited the *Knoxville Whig* and used it to proclaim his staunch Unionist views. After the war he served as Tennessee's governor (1865–1869) and US Senator (1869–1875).

8. Article I, Section II of Tennessee's 1835 constitution.

9. Thomas Amos Rogers Nelson (1812–1873) practiced law in Washington County, Tennessee. Served in the US House of Representatives from 1859 to 1861 (Thirty-Sixth Congress) as a member of the Opposition Party, and was elected to the Thirty-Seventh Congress as a Unionist.

10. Oliver Perry Temple (1820–1907) was an attorney in Knoxville in partnership with Connally F. Trigg.

11. John Netherland (1808–1887) practiced law in Franklin, Williamson County, and Kingsport, Sullivan County, before settling in Rogersville, Hawkins County. Netherland had been the Opposition Party's candidate for governor in 1859.

12. The cited section is Article IV, Section 3, which states: "New States may be admitted by Congress into this Union, but no new State shall be formed or erected within the Jurisdiction of any other State; nor any State be formed by the Junction of two or more States, or Parts of States, without the Consent of the Legislatures of the States concerned as well as that of Congress."

13. Jordan Stokes (1817–1886) was a member of the Opposition Party representing Wilson and DeKalb Counties. Born in North Carolina, he practiced law in Lebanon.

14. George R. Gantt (1824–1897) represented Maury County as a Democrat. He practiced law in Columbia. During the war he served as a lieutenant colonel, 9th Battalion, Tennessee Cavalry, Confederate States Army, until wounded on July 1863 and discharged.

APPENDIX I

1. Results reported in the *Nashville Patriot*, June 15, 1861.

Bibliography

PRIMARY SOURCES

Chittenden, Lucius E. *A Report of the Debates and Proceedings in the Secret Sessions of the Conference Convention, for Proposing Amendments to the Constitution of the United States, Held at Washington, D.C., in February, A.D. 1861.* New York: D. Appleton & Company, 1864.

House Journal of the Extra Session of the Thirty-Third General Assembly of the State of Tennessee, which Convened at Nashville, on the First Monday in January, A.D. 1861. Nashville: J. O. Griffith and Company, Public Printers, 1861.

House Journal of the Second Extra Session of the Thirty-Third General Assembly of the State of Tennessee, which convened at Nashville on Thursday, the 25th day of April, A. D. 1861. Nashville: J. O. Griffith and Company, Public Printers, 1861.

Proceedings of the E. T. Convention, Held at Knoxville, May 30th and 31st, 1861, and at Greenville, on the 17th day of June, 1861, and following days. Knoxville: Printed at H. Barry's Book and Job Office, 1861.

Public Acts of the State of Tennessee, Passed at the Extra Session of the Thirty-Third General Assembly, April, 1861. Nashville, Tenn.: J. O. Griffith and Co., Public Printers, Union and American Office, 1861.

Senate Journal of the Extra Session of the Thirty-Third General Assembly of the State of Tennessee, Which Convened at Nashville, on the First Monday in January, A. D. 1861. Nashville: J. O. Griffith and Company, Public Printers, 1861.

Senate Journal of the Second Extra Session of the Thirty-Third General Assembly of the State of Tennessee, Which convened at Nashville on Thursday, the 25th Day of April, A. D. 1861. Nashville: J. O. Griffith and Company, Public Printers, 1861.

United States, *The War of the Rebellion: A Compilation of the Official Records of the Union and Confederate Armies.* 128 vols. Washington: Government Printing Office, 1881–1901.

United States Congress. *Congressional Globe*, 36th Cong., 2nd Sess., December 1860–March 1861. http://memory.loc.gov/ammem/amlaw /lwcglink.html#anchor36.

Wakelyn, Jon L., ed. *Southern Pamphlets on Secession, November 1860–April 1861*. Chapel Hill: University of North Carolina Press, 1996.

White, Robert H. *Messages of the Governors of Tennessee, 1857–1869*. Nashville: Tennessee Historical Commission, 1959.

SUGGESTIONS FOR FURTHER READING

Ash, Stephen V. *Middle Tennessee Society Transformed 1860–1870*. Baton Rouge: Louisiana State University Press, 1988.

———. *Secessionists and Other Scoundrels: Selections from Parson Brownlow's Book*. Baton Rouge: Louisiana State University Press, 1999.

Atkins, Jonathan M. *Parties, Politics, and the Sectional Conflict in Tennessee, 1832–1861*. Knoxville: University of Tennessee Press, 1997.

Ayers, Edward L. *What Caused the Civil War?: Reflections on the South and Southern History*. New York: W. W. Norton & Company, 2005.

Baggett, James Alex. *The Scalawags: Southern Dissenters in the Civil War and Reconstruction*. Baton Rouge: Louisiana State University Press, 2003.

Barney, William L. *Rebels in the Making: The Secession Crisis and the Birth of the Confederacy*. New York: Oxford University Press, 2020.

Bestor, Arthur. "The American Civil War as a Constitutional Crisis." *American Historical Review*, vol. 69, no. 2 (January 1964), 327–52.

———. "State Sovereignty and Slavery: A Reinterpretation of Proslavery Constitutional Doctrine, 1846–1860." *Journal of the Illinois State Historical Society*, vol. 54, no. 2 (Summer 1961), 117–80.

Bowman, Davis Bowman. *At the Precipice: Americans North and South During the Secession Crisis*. Chapel Hill: University of North Carolina Press, 2010.

Bryan, Charles F., Jr. "A Gathering of Tories: The East Tennessee Convention of 1861." *Tennessee Historical Quarterly*, vol. 39, no. 1 (Spring 1980), 27–48.

Cook, Robert J.; Barney, William, L.; and Varon, Elizabeth, R. *Secession Winter: When the Union Fell Apart*. Baltimore: Johns Hopkins University Press, 2013.

Crofts, Daniel W. *Lincoln & the Politics of Slavery: The Other Thirteenth Amendment and the Struggle to Save the Union*. Chapel Hill: University of North Carolina Press, 2016.

———. *Reluctant Confederates: Upper South Unionists in the Secession Crisis*. Chapel Hill: University of North Carolina Press, 1989.

Dew, Charles B. *Apostles of Disunion: Southern Secession Commissioners and the Causes of the Civil War*. Charlottesville: University Press of Virginia, 2001.

Durham, David I. *A Southern Moderate in Radical Times: Henry Washington Hilliard, 1808–1892*. Baton Rouge: Louisiana State University Press, 2008.

Elliott, Sam Davis. *Isham G. Harris of Tennessee: Confederate Governor and United States Senator*. Baton Rouge: Louisiana State University Press, 2010.

Fehrenbacher, Don E. *The Slaveholding Republic: An Account of the United States Government's Relations to Slavery*. New York: Oxford University Press, 2001.

Fertig, James Walter. *The Secession and Reconstruction of Tennessee*. Chicago: University of Chicago Press, 1898.

Foner, Eric. *The Fiery Trial: Abraham Lincoln and American Slavery*. New York: W. W. Norton & Company, 2010.

Freehling, William W. *Becoming Lincoln*. Charlottesville: University of Virginia Press, 2018.

———. *The Road to Disunion: Secessionists Triumphant*. Vol. II. New York: Oxford University Press, 2007.

Gordon-Reed, Annette. *Andrew Johnson*. New York: Henry Holt and Company, 2011.

Humphrey, Steve, ed. *"That D——d Brownlow," Being a Saucy & Malicious Description of Fighting Parson WILLIAM GANNAWAY BROWNLOW, Knoxville Editor and Stalwart Unionist, Who Rose from a Confederate Jail to become One of the Most Famous Personages in the Nation, Denounced by his Enemies as Vicious and Harsh, Praised by his Friends as Compassionate and Gentle.* Boone, North Carolina: Appalachian Consortium Press, 1978.

Lee, Charles Robert, Jr. *The Confederate Constitutions.* Chapel Hill: University of North Carolina Press, 1963.

Lufkin, Charles L. "Secession and Coercion in Tennessee, the Spring of 1861." *Tennessee Historical Quarterly*, vol. 50, no. 2 (Summer 1991), 98–109.

McBride, Robert M., and Dan M. Robinson, eds. *Biographical Directory of the Tennessee General Assembly*, vol. I. Nashville: Tennessee State Library and Archives and the Tennessee Historical Commission, 1975.

Morris, Thomas D. *Free Men All: The Personal Liberty Laws of the North, 1780–1861.* Baltimore: Johns Hopkins University Press, 1974.

Pitcaithley, Dwight T. *The U.S. Constitution and Secession: A Documentary Anthology of Slavery and White Supremacy.* Lawrence: University Press of Kansas, 2018.

Robinson, Michael D. *A Union Indivisible: Secession and the Politics of Slavery in the Border South.* Chapel Hill: University of North Carolina Press, 2017.

Temple, Oliver P. *East Tennessee and the Civil War.* Cincinnati: Robert Clarke Company, 1899.

Warren, Robert Penn. *The Legacy of the Civil War.* Lincoln: University of Nebraska Press, 1998. (First published in 1961.)

Questions for Discussion

1. Between Lincoln's election in November 1860, and his inauguration on March 4, 1861, what had changed in the federal/state relationship that pushed seven states to secede?

2. Considering the Senate speeches by Andrew Johnson and Alfred O. P. Nicholson, which one seems more persuasive? Why?

3. In his January 7, 1861, speech to the general assembly, Governor Harris seemed confident that agitation over slavery and the implied threat of racial equality were at the core of the sectional crisis. What evidence is there that might have cast doubt on his perspective? Is there any reason to doubt his analysis?

4. In that same speech, what infractions of law or the Constitution does Governor Harris charge the federal government with having committed?

5. Considering the documents found in chapter 3, if you were an interested citizen, which of the resolutions proposed in the general assembly in response to Lincoln's election would you support? Why?

6. As you read the speeches of Tennessee's delegation to the United States House of Representatives, did you find some more reasonable than others? Why? If you were a Tennessee voter during Secession Winter, would you align yourself with the Democratic or Opposition Party? Why?

7. The nine proposals to amend the United States Constitution (found in chapter 5) were all suggested as solutions to the political problems facing the country. Should we presume that the amendments accurately reflect the concerns of their proposers? Why? Why not?

8. The general assembly's "plan of adjustment" passed on January 22, 1861, contained an article specifically recognizing slaves as property in the slave states and "all places within the exclusive jurisdiction of Congress." If the amendment had been ratified, how would it have affected slavery in the non-slave states? Considering the comity clause of the Constitution (Article IV, Section 1), would the Supreme Court have been able to prevent slaves from being imported into northern states? How might the phrase "whilst temporarily sojourning" be interpreted? Could Chief Justice Roger B. Taney have used this amendment to declare the nationalization of slavery?

9. Compare Lincoln's April 15 call for troops to Governor Harris's and the general assembly's characterization of it on April 25 and May 9. Did Lincoln pose the threat represented in the latter two documents? How should Lincoln have responded to the Confederate attack on Fort Sumter?

10. Do you believe the general assembly's creation and ratification of the military league with the Confederate States of America on May 7 was warranted? Why? Why not?

11. Over Secession Winter, Tennessee's elected officials consistently made a distinction between the right of constitutional secession and the right of revolution. Why might these distinctions be important?

12. What message was the general assembly sending when it ended its "Address to the People of Tennessee" with the phrase, "the sacred cause of freedom for the WHITE MAN OF THE SOUTH"?

13. Would you agree that the East Tennessee Convention's "Declaration of Grievances" listed legitimate concerns? Why? Why not?

14. Can a connection be made between the hyperbole evident in many of these documents and political discourse used today? Is there a lesson in those connections?

Index

abolition/abolitionists/abolition-
ism, 15–16, 25, 27, 41–42, 73, 93,
102, 120, 129, 177, 179–80, 183,
185, 205, 211, 245, 254, 287, 318n1
Adams, Charles Francis, 9, 130, 185,
196, 322n60, 323n77
Adams, John, 171
Adams, John Quincy, 101, 318n1,
323n77
American Revolution, 39, 76, 92,
107, 111, 168, 171, 276, 295,
318nn4–5, 323n80; right of
revolution, 21, 152, 166, 211,
313n58
Anderson, Robert, 18
Arnold, Thomas D., 283
Articles of Confederation, 36
Ash, Stephen V., 29
Atkins, Jonathan M., 19, 31
Avery, William T., 15–16, 26, 97,
138, 303

Baker, C. H., 282–83
Barney, William L., 29
Barrow, George W., 20, 261–63,
325n7
Baxter, John, 282–83, 327n3
Beaty, Joseph J., 11, 26, 85
Bell, John, 3–4, 28–29, 86, 144,
156–57, 186, 322n64, 322n66
Bingham, John A., 173–74
Birney, James G., 186,
322n66

Black Republicans, 11–12, 19, 87, 95,
137, 231
Bouligny, John E., 174, 321n48
Boyce, William W., 203, 324n82
Brabson, Reese, 97, 206, 303
Brazil, 102
Breckinridge, John C., 3–4, 6, 28,
45, 157
Brown, John, 14, 70, 114, 118, 120,
130, 132, 154, 200, 209
Brownlow, William G., 22–23, 25,
282, 327n7
Buchanan, James, 2, 6–7, 116, 121,
154–55, 182, 315n8, 317n7,
321n41, 322n58
Burnett, David, 282
Burnett, Henry C., 115, 318n10

Calhoun, John C., 45
Canada, 115–16, 160, 199–200
Chase, Salmon P., 145
Clay, Henry, 39, 129, 138, 320n22,
322n66
Clemens, Sherrard, 168, 321n46
coercion by the federal government, 13, 16–18, 26, 30, 37–38,
77, 94, 109–10, 159, 181, 191,
266–67
Committee of Thirty-Three, 121,
150, 168, 173, 177–78, 194, 196–
97, 200, 207, 223, 320n28
Compromise of 1850, 1, 309n4,
316n5, 320n22

335

Fort Pickens, 97
Fort Scott, 317n10
Fort Sumter, 1, 18, 22, 27, 30, 245,
        264, 267–68, 321n41, 323n80,
        326n12
Fort Taylor, 97
Fourteenth Amendment. *See* US
        Constitution
France, 40–41, 67. 103, 181, 206, 222,
        320n29
Franklin, Benjamin, 171
Frisby, Derek, 29
Fugitive Slave Act of 1793, 69, 122
Fugitive Slave Act of 1850, 7, 15, 27,
        50, 68, 87, 89–91, 114, 116–17,
        122, 126, 145, 153, 162, 210, 221,
        227
fugitive slaves, 3, 8, 11–12, 50, 63, 69,
        86–87, 99, 106, 115–17, 173, 193,
        198, 222–23, 227, 319n11, 320n23

Gantt, George, 12, 274, 296, 299,
        328n14, 326n16; proposed
        amendment, 230–34
Garrison, William L., 154, 205,
        321n42
Giddings, Joshua Reed, 53, 315n7
Gilmer, John A., 162–63, 321n45
Gist, William, H., 135, 212, 321n31,
        324n85
Gordon-Reed, Annette, 30
Gorsuch, Edward, 130, 320n23
Great Britain/England, 40–41, 63,
        169, 171, 180–81, 200, 320n25,
        320n29, 323n77

Greene, Nathanael, 107, 318n5
Guy, William W., 274, 326n6

Hamilton, Andrew J., 150, 152,
        320n27, 321n39
Hamlin, Hannibal, 11, 45, 87, 94
Harris, Isham G., 5–8, 11–13, 18–20,
        22–23, 25–28, 63, 245–46, 248,
        261, 264, 275–76; proposed
        amendment, 73–74
Harris, James M. 178, 321n51
Hatton, Robert, 16, 97, 193, 303
Hebb, George V., 82
Heiskell, Frederick S., 282, 327n1
Heiskell, William, 283, 286
Henry, Gustavus A., 20, 261–63,
        325n5
Heriges, John, 78
Hilliard, Henry W., 19–21, 245,
        261–63, 325n8
Hindman, Thomas C., 9
Humes, Thomas W., 283
Hurt, Robert B., 274

Jackson, Andrew, 35, 39, 45, 119, 138,
        145–46, 152
Jay, John, 171
Jefferson, Thomas, 35, 39, 152, 175,
        198
Johnson, Andrew, 5, 8, 11–13, 15,
        22, 25, 31, 35, 88, 126, 283, 287,
        303, 320n27, 325n7; proposed
        amendment, 223–24
Jones, William E. B., 26, 91
Junkin, Benjamin F., 197, 323n78

Thomas, James H., 16, 26. 97–98, 303

Thompson, James L., 11, 26, 81, 94

Thouvenel, Èdouard, 181, 322n56

Toombs, Robert, 9

Totten, Archibald O. W., 20, 261–63, 325n6

transit with slaves, 7, 14, 73, 143–44, 199, 221, 233, 236–37, 239

Treaty of Guadalupe Hidalgo, 168

Trigg, Connally F., 22, 282–83, 287

Tunnell, John, 282

US Constitution, 4–5, 7, 14, 23, 27, 36–39, 42–43, 46–47, 55, 65, 82, 108, 214, 250, 258, 273, 295, 326n15, 328n12; Fifteenth Amendment, 314n72; Fourteenth Amendment, 314n72; slavery in, 5–6, 9, 16, 55, 58–59, 63, 65, 68–70, 72–73, 86, 170–71, 231; Thirteenth Amendment, 25, 314n72; violation of, 23, 38, 43, 56, 58, 75, 87, 95, 115, 129, 147, 153, 289, 291

US flag, 13, 113, 125, 139, 147–49, 152, 175, 216–19

Utah Territory, 2, 169, 316n5

Vallandigham, Clement, 124

Wade, Benjamin Franklin, 47–48

Warren, Robert P., 194

Washburn, Cadwallader C., 107

Washington, George, 38–39, 138, 152, 175, 198

Washington Peace Conference, 8, 14, 18, 31, 266, 305–6, 310n10, 320n25, 323n71, 325n6, 326n11

Webster, Daniel, 39

Whiskey Rebellion, 37–38

White, Robert H., 22–23

white supremacy, 25–26, 30, 310n11, 314n70

Whitthorne, W. C., 263

Wigfall, Louis T., 43

Williams, John, 282, 327n5

Wisener, William H., 10, 84

Wood, Edmund J., 274, 326n16

Wright, John V., 16, 97, 303

Yancey, William L., 134, 320n29